D1551560

marianne hirsch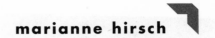

# *F*AMILY FRAMES

photography

narrative

and

postmemory

**HARVARD UNIVERSITY PRESS**

CAMBRIDGE, MASSACHUSETTS, AND LONDON, ENGLAND

Second printing, 2002

Designed by Marianne Perlak

*Library of Congress Cataloging-in-Publication Data*

Hirsch, Marianne.
    Family frames : photography, narrative, and postmemory /
Marianne Hirsch.
        p.  cm.
    Includes bibliographical references and index.
    ISBN 0-674-29265-0 (cl)
    ISBN 0-674-29266-9 (pb)
    1. Photography of families.   2. Photographic criticism.
3. Family—Folklore.   I. Title.
TR681.F28H573   1997
770'.1—dc21                                           96-49295

*for leo*

# contents

When my book *The Mother/Daughter Plot* was published I decided to send a copy to my cousin Brigitte who lives in Vienna. Although we talk and see each other only rarely, I wanted her to have an insight into the work that had preoccupied me during the preceding years. She called almost immediately, exclaiming over the picture that was on the cover on the book, a picture of my grandmother and aunt—her great-aunt and cousin: "So that's who that woman is! I have boxes full of pictures of her, and when I last went through them we all had to laugh about her strange hats and get-ups."

I was both thrilled about the prospect of having access to family pictures I had not known about, and somewhat taken aback that my grandmother, many decades after posing for her pictures in what must have been her most elegant outfits, should have been laughed at so unthinkingly and irreverently. Brigitte's parents had died young, she inherited many unknown photographs. I asked if I could go through her collection on my next visit to Austria, or if she would send me the ones of the woman with the strange hats. I was eager to save my grandmother from further ridicule, however benign, to reinscribe her into the albums where she would be known, recognized, respected. But, when my cousin looked for the old photos, she could no longer find them. Her husband had cleaned house and they were gone.

Where are those photos now? Did they end up in some flea market, depersonalized signifiers of a distant place and a bygone era? Or were they simply thrown away? Why should their fate matter? I do, after all, have other pictures of my grandmother, pictures which might well be identical to the ones that disappeared in Vienna a few years ago. But in lives shaped by exile, emigration and relocation, such as my family's, where relatives are dispersed and relationships shattered, photographs provide perhaps even more than usual some illusion of continuity over time and space. The

missing pictures of my grandmother have stayed with me as pointed signifiers of loss. I've tried to imagine them and the stories they might have
told about a time before either I or my mother was born.

In some strange way, I have written this book in response to the disappearance of those photographs. I needed to explain why images that to my
cousin were anonymous, meaningless, and even funny, because she could
not identify them, to me would have been integral pieces of a life story, full
of meaning and resonance. Family pictures depend on such a narrative act
of adoption that transforms rectangular pieces of cardboard into telling
details connecting lives and stories across continents and generations. This
book is an attempt to trace the process of that transformation, the process
of reading family photographs.

I was fortunate to be able to write this book in a number of stimulating
and supportive institutional environments, surrounded by colleagues and
friends who were always ready to respond to my questions, thoughts, and
drafts. I am deeply grateful to the National Humanities Center for a year's
fellowship in 1992–93 that provided the space and time to immerse myself
into a new project in an engaging intellectual community, both at the Center
and in the Duke/University of North Carolina/North Carolina State University area. The discussion groups on Autobiographical Criticism and on
Cultural Memory have left profound traces in this work. I am particularly
indebted to the concrete and sustained support of Temma Kaplan, Steve
Caton, Kate Bartlett, Susan Porter-Benson, Alex Zwerdling, and Kent Mul-
likin, as well as Alice Kaplan, Linda Orr, Naomi Schor, Miriam Cooke,
Elaine Orr, Judith Ferster, and Kate Daniels.

A number of invitations to speak and write have stimulated my thinking
about these chapters, some of which have benefited from being read and
edited as articles. I am particularly grateful to Kathleen Woodward, Renee
Hoogland and Pamela Pattinama, Judith Kegan Gardiner, Angelika Bammer,
Mieke Bal and Inge Boer, Susan Suleiman, and Lori Saint-Martin, for their
revisions and suggestions. Audiences at Dartmouth, the University of Amsterdam, the University of Wisconsin at Milwaukee, the University of Michi-
gan, Middlebury, Harvard, Brown, Duke, Haverford, Johns Hopkins, the
University of North Carolina, and North Carolina State University have
furthered my thinking with their questions.

I would also like to thank my students and colleagues at Dartmouth
College for their continued support and stimulation, for the challenging
arguments, and the help they have given me throughout the years of this
project. Many have read chapters of this book and have generously given

of their time to discuss my work with me. I thank them for forging an intellectual community where work and friendship are shared. In this light I would especially like to acknowledge Carol Bardenstein, Susan Brison, Gerd Gemünden, Mary Jean Green, Lynn Higgins, Irene Kacandes, Larry Kritzman, Ivy Schweitzer, Brenda Silver, Silvia Spitta, Virginia Swain, Diana Taylor, Roxana Verona, Susanne Zantop, and Melissa Zeiger. The Dartmouth Faculty Research Fund and the Parents Chair provided generous financial support that made it possible to do research in a variety of locations in the United States and abroad and to include the images in this book.

There is no more beautiful, peaceful, and productive place in which to revise a book than the Rockefeller Center's Bellagio Study and Conference Center. I appreciate the chance to spend a residency there in the fall of 1995 and the lively intellectual community that was shaped and reshaped during that month.

The discussions at the Humanities Institute on Cultural Memory and the Present held at Dartmouth College during the spring of 1996 were influential at the final stages of revision, and I thank its organizers, Jonathan Crewe and Leo Spitzer, as well as all its participants for their encouragement and for the stimulating exchange that will enable me to continue work on photography and memory.

I am especially grateful to a number of artists who have corresponded and talked about their work with me: Camille Billops and James Hatch, Lorie Novak, Vance Gellert, Sally Mann, Shimon Attie, Christian Boltanski, and Valerie Walkerdine. Timothy Rub and the staff of the Hood Museum of Art worked with me on the exhibition "The Familial Gaze" in the spring of 1996. The discussions generated by the exhibition and the conference "Family Pictures: Shapes of Memory" confirmed my passion about this topic and I would like to thank all the participants in the conference for moving my thinking forward even at the final stages of this book.

Other colleagues have most generously read parts or all of the manuscript at various stages: Elizabeth Abel, Mieke Bal, Dick Blau, Jane Coppock, Jane Gallop, Karin Voth Harman, Anne Higonnet, Margo Kasdan, Evelyn Fox Keller, Lori Lefkowitz, Joanne Leonard, Nancy K. Miller, Marta Peixoto, Gail Reimer, Marita Sturken, Ernst Van Alphen, Nancy Vickers, Laura Wexler, and Susan Winnett. Their questions and suggestions have been invaluable. I am most grateful to Carol Peper, Gail Vernazza, and Jason Christian for all of their practical help, and to Peg Fulton, Marianne Perlak, and Camille Smith for making the editorial process so pleasant.

Not surprisingly, this book on family pictures, written in the personal voice, has engaged most intensely the participation of my family—my parents, Lotte and Carl Hirsch, my husband, Leo, and my children, Alex, Oliver, and Gabriel. Not only have they lived with my obsessions and preoccupations during the last five years, but they have been willing to be exposed in the stories and images that I include here. Although we have not always agreed, they have been helpful readers of these chapters and of the images I discuss. I appreciate, greatly, their trust and their unfailing encouragement. Many of the insights contained in these pages emerged in the sustaining daily dialogue I have the privilege of sharing with Leo Spitzer. It is in the spirit of these conversations that I dedicate this book to him.

*family frames*

# *F*AMILY FRAMES

"Is History not simply that time when we were not born? I could read my non-existence in the clothes my mother had worn before I can remember her. There is a kind of stupefaction in seeing a familiar being dressed *differently,*" writes Roland Barthes in *Camera Lucida* as he searches through family photographs from before his birth.[1] The one picture that enables him to recognize his mother shows a five-year-old girl standing with her brother in the winter garden of their family home. All the other old photographs reveal only aspects of his mother; they refuse to yield her essence and return him to the Sisyphean task of trying, again and again, to find one that captures her fundamental core. To Barthes's needy eye only the ancient winter-garden photo brings her back whole, true to herself.

In that single picture, Barthes tells us, the young child rejoins the frail old woman he nursed through her last illness: "She had become my little girl, uniting for me with that essential child she was in her first photograph" (72). There he finds his mother's assertive gentleness, her kindness. There he finds not only his mother but the qualities of their relationship, a congruence between "my mother's being and my grief at her death" (70). In reading the photograph, Barthes himself assumes again the nurturing maternal role he played when he nursed her in her illness. Yet again he becomes the parent to her as a child. Thus he bridges the gap between his five-year-old mother and his own mourning for her. The photo of his mother as a child in her parents' house standing next to her brother is read by her son after her death, a son who has become her "mother." While caring for her in her illness, Barthes feels as if he "engendered my mother." Now that she is dead, he can only look toward his own death. He can read that death in her picture. Her first picture, read by her son, is also her and his last, the picture of the mother/child.

Multiple looks circulate in the photograph's production, reading, and description: Roland's mother, facing her parents as she is being photographed, at the same "time" faces her son who finds himself in her picture. The picture of a little girl and her brother is traversed and constituted by a series of "familial looks" that both create and consolidate the familial relations among the individuals involved, fostering an unmistakable sense of mutual recognition. Identity, for Barthes and his mother, is certainly familial in the sense of the "lineage" or "stock" he discusses later while combing family pictures for hints of likeness and resemblance (104, 105). But it is also familial in this exchange of looks: that of the girl's parents, who are only implied in the picture, and whose discord, retrospectively revealed by their subsequent separation, unites the brother and sister; that of the daughter/mother who faces the viewer in her "essence"; that of the son who reads in the mother's childhood photo her life and his own death.

Our own look as readers of Barthes's description is excluded from that exchange: the picture Barthes finds and cherishes is the only photograph he discusses in detail that is not reproduced in his book. Barthes cannot *show* us the photograph because we stand outside the familial network of looks and thus cannot *see* the picture in the way that Barthes must. To us it would be just another generic family photograph from a long time ago. He cannot show it because, although it is a picture of his mother and uncle, he claims it as a very private kind of self-portrait, revealing, unexpectedly, the most intimate and unexposed aspects of himself. The picture of his mother provokes a moment of self-recognition which, in the reading process, becomes a process of self-discovery, a discovery of a self-in-relation.

Finding and reading the picture, recognizing himself in it, are acts of identity as familiality for Barthes. But even as he experiences this inclusion and recognition, he cannot heal the wound made of love and death that is central to the winter-garden photo. Neither can he overcome or negate the stupefaction he feels as he looks at the other old pictures. Photographs reflect him, draw him in, pierce and shock him, yet they continue to wound, repel and exclude him. They reveal even as they conceal. They are as opaque as they are transparent. Daniel Boudinet's monochromatic color image "Polaroid," the frontispiece of *Camera Lucida*, serves as a figure for the impenetrable façade of the domestic picture (Figure 0.1). The dark picture simply depicts a slightly transparent curtain obscuring a light source which just barely allows the viewer to see a large cushion on a bed in front of the curtain. The bed is in the foreground but the obscured light prevents the reader from seeing it clearly. How might we gain access to this domestic space? Only words could pull back the curtain, but can words reveal, can they empower us to imagine what's behind the surface of the image?

0.1

If Barthes can recognize his mother's essential being in the winter-garden picture of her, it is only possible through the description and narrative in which he articulates his response to her image. In his book, his mother's picture exists only in the words he uses to describe it and his reaction to it: the image has been transformed and translated into a "prose picture," what W. J. T. Mitchell has called an "imagetext."[2] Like Boudinet's curtain, a verbal overlay hides the image from our view even while disclosing its structure and effect: the multiplicity and mutuality of looking, the relational network that composes all family pictures and the stab of recognition that selects this one among a plurality of choices.[3] Writing the image accomplishes even more in this scene of mourning: it undoes the objectification of the still photograph and thereby takes it out of the realm of stasis, immobility, mortification—what Barthes calls "flat death"—into fluidity, movement, and thus, finally, life.[4]

But it is too simple to equate writing with life, photography with death. The winter-garden photo defines for Barthes a certain photographic reading practice, a certain relationship to photographs, even as it allows him to meditate on the phenomenology of the photographic image. It also allows us to reconsider his earlier discussion of the *punctum*—that prick and shock of recognition, that unique and very personal response to the photographic detail that attracts and repels us at the same time: "*Punctum* is also: sting, speck, cut, little hole—and also a cast of the dice. A photograph's *punctum* is that accident which pricks me (but also bruises me, is poignant to me)" (27). On the one hand, the *punctum* disturbs the flat and immobile surface of the image, embedding it in an affective relationship of viewing and thus in a narrative; on the other, it arrests and interrupts the contextual and therefore narrative reading of the photograph that Barthes calls the *studium*. "It always refers to a classical body of information . . . It is by *studium* that I am interested in so many photographs, whether I receive them as political testimony or enjoy them as good historical scenes: for it is culturally . . . that I participate in the figures, the faces, the gestures, the settings, the actions" (25, 26). These Latinate terms serve to define and circumscribe, to make safe, the relationship of love and loss, presence and absence, life and death that for him are the constitutive core of photography. In *Camera Lucida,* pictures and words come together to articulate "prose pictures," such as the absent image of the mother which exists only in prose, and "visual narratives," such as the numerous images reproduced in the book, many of which comment, however obliquely, on the family romance of the winter-garden photo. Text and image, intricately entangled in a narrative web, work in collaboration to tell a complicated story of loss and longing that Barthes's critical terminology can barely approximate.[5]

Unlike other representational forms, Barthes insists, photography holds a unique relation to the real, defined not through the discourse of artistic representation, but that of magic, alchemy, indexicality, fetishism:

I call "photographic referent" not the *optionally* real thing to which an image or a sign refers but the *necessarily* real thing which has been placed before the lens, without which there would be no photograph . . . The photograph is literally an emanation of the referent. From a real body, which was there, proceed radiations which ultimately touch me, who am here; the duration of the transmission is insignificant; the photograph of the missing being, as Sontag says, will touch me like the delayed rays of a star. A sort of umbilical cord links the body of the photographed thing to my gaze: light, though impalpable, is here a carnal medium, a skin I share with anyone who has been photographed. (76–77, 80–81)

Through the image of the umbilical cord, itself inspired by the conflation of mother/son/daughter in the winter-garden image and the almost total disregard of the brother in it, Barthes makes photography—taking the picture, developing it, printing and looking at it, reading it and writing about it—inherently familial and material, akin to the very processes of life and death. And he defines loss—the cutting of that cord, and its reparation through the photographic imagetext—as central to the experience of both family and photography. The referent is both present (implied in the photograph) and absent (it has been there but is not here now). The referent haunts the picture like a ghost: it is a revenant, a return of the lost and dead other.[6] Ultimately, the puncture of the *punctum* is not the detail of the picture but time itself: "I read at the same time *This will be* and *this has been;* I observe with horror an anterior future of which death is the stake. By giving me the absolute past of the pose (aorist), the photograph tells me death in the future. What *pricks* me is the discovery of this equivalence" (96). In pricking him, this conflation of past and future already undoes its devastating effect. The arresting anti-narrative wound of the *punctum* can combat the narrative of death, leaving time—death and life—suspended, signaling irreplaceable loss and interminable mourning.

This is the familial story we can read in Barthes's description—the mother's death and the son's mourning, his anticipation of his own death, the multiple and mutual looks through which mother and son are constituted as subjects in relation to each other. Family is structured by desire and disappointment, love and loss. Photographs, as the only material traces of an irrecoverable past, derive their power and their important cultural role from their embeddedness in the fundamental rites of family life, the rites Barthes performs in *Camera Lucida* and buttresses with his fundamental belief in photographic reference.

Throughout this book, I will return again and again to these passages in Barthes's *Camera Lucida* and to his controversial reading of photographic reference. His trajectory through his reflections on photography—from a general analysis of how photographs acquire meaning to an elegiac autobiographical narrative—touches me profoundly. As much as I remind myself that photographs are as essentially constructed as any other representational form, that every part of the image can be manipulated and even fabricated, especially with ever more sophisticated digital technologies, I return to Barthes's basic "ça a été" ("this has been") and an unassailable belief in reference and a notion of truth in the picture. Barthes goes beyond Charles Sanders Peirce's tripartite definition of the sign—symbol, icon, and index. In the Peircean system, the photograph is defined as both an icon, based on physical resemblance or similarity between the sign and the object it represents, and as an index, based on a relationship of contiguity, of cause and effect, like a trace or a footprint. Linguistic signs, in contrast, are arbitrary, and thus symbols. Barthes intensifies the indexical relationship when he speaks of the photograph as a physical, material emanation of a past reality; its speech act is constative: it authenticates the reality of the past and provides a material connection to it. Reference, for Barthes, is not content but presence. "The realists of whom I am one . . . do not take the photograph for a 'copy' of reality, but for an emanation of *past reality:* a *magic,* not an art . . . The important thing is that the photograph possesses an evidential force, and that its testimony bears not on the object but on time. From a phenomenological viewpoint, in the Photograph, the power of authentication exceeds the power of representation" (88, 89).

The picture exists because something was there, and thus, in my own family pictures, I, like Barthes, can hope to find some truth about the past, mine and my family's—however mediated. I find this "adherence of the referent," in the sense of its indexical presence, in my own thinking both burdensome and fascinating. This book is, in many ways, a reflection on the continuing power and "burden" of photographic reference, a power that shapes family pictures.[7] My resistant reading of family photographs thus turns the indexical reference emphasized by Barthes into something more telling.

Barthes's metaphor of the umbilical cord only confirms photography's connection to the family, its inscription in family life and its perpetuation of familial ideology. When George Eastman invented the "Kodak" in 1888, his intended consumers were not professional photographers but people who had seen photographs but had not thought of actually taking them any more than they might have considered painting pictures, writing novels, or composing music. With the slogan "You push the button, we do the rest," the camera entered the domain of the ordinary and the domestic. Thus photography quickly became the family's primary instrument of self-knowledge and representation—the means by which family memory would be continued and perpetuated, by which the family's story would henceforth be told.

Now, more than one hundred years later, photography's social functions are integrally tied to the ideology of the modern family.[8] The family photo both displays the cohesion of the family and is an instrument of its togetherness; it both chronicles family rituals and constitutes a prime objective of those rituals.[9] Because the photograph gives the illusion of being a simple transcription of the real, a trace touched directly by the event it records, it has the effect of naturalizing cultural practices and of disguising their stereotyped and coded characteristics. As photography immobilizes the flow of family life into a series of snapshots, it perpetuates familial myths while seeming merely to record actual moments in family history. At the end of the twentieth century, the family photograph, widely available as a medium of familial self-presentation in many cultures and subcultures, can reduce the strains of family life by sustaining an imaginary cohesion, even as it exacerbates them by creating images that real families cannot uphold.

The still picture is captured by a single camera eye whose point of view, that of the photographer, determines the viewer's position. Victor Burgin suggests that "the structure of representation—point-of-view and frame—is intimately implicated in the reproduction of ideology (the 'frame of mind' of our 'points-of-view')." But the structure of looking is reciprocal: photographer and viewer collaborate on the reproduction of ideology. Between the viewer and the recorded object, the viewer encounters, and/or projects, a screen made up of dominant mythologies and preconceptions that shapes the representation.[10] Eye and screen are the very elements of ideology: our expectations circumscribe and determine what we show and what we see. If we had different conceptions of beauty, of femininity and masculinity, of whiteness and blackness, of any of our cultural institutions, we would perceive them differently. As the filmmaker Pratibha Parmar has said: "The deeply ideological nature of imagery determines not only how other people think about us but how we think about ourselves."[11]

Increasingly, family pictures have themselves become objects of scrutiny. Contemporary writers, artists, and filmmakers, as well as contemporary cultural critics, have used family photographs in their work, going beyond their conventional and opaque surfaces to expose the complicated stories of familial relation—the passions and rivalries, the tensions, anxieties, and problems that have, for the most part, remained on the edges or outside the family album. Artists and writers have thus attempted to use the very instruments of ideology, the camera, the album, and the familial gaze, as modes of questioning, resistance, and contestation. They have interrogated not only the family itself, but its traditions of representation. They have shown that in disrupting their own documentary authority and their use as evidence—the burden of Barthes's "ça a été"—photographs can become powerful weapons of social and attitudinal change.

This work of contestation appears not so much in actual family photographs as in meta-photographic texts which place family photographs into narrative contexts, either by reproducing them or by describing them: novels and short stories, fiction and documentary films, photographic albums, installations and exhibits, autobiographies and memoirs, as well as essays and theoretical writings about photography. The composite imagetexts that are the subjects of this book both expose and resist the conventions of family photography and hegemonic familial ideologies. Thus, I discuss, in similar terms, both real images, themselves embedded in narrative contexts, and fictional images described in novels, both "visual narratives" and "prose pictures." Only in the context of this meta-photographic textuality and in this self-conscious contextuality can photographs disrupt a familiar narrative about family life and its representations, breaking the hold of a conventional and monolithic familial gaze.

I do not want to imply that what I refer to as a "hegemonic familial ideology" imposed by a "monolithic familial gaze" is a static or ahistoric structure, cross-culturally or trans-historically valid. On the contrary, the ideology of the family is as much subject to particular historical, social, and economic circumstances as the lived reality of family life. What may be constant, however, at least in the cultural moment that is the focus of this book, is the existence of a familial mythology, of an image to live up to, an image shaping the desire of the individual living in a social group. This myth or image—whatever its content may be for a specific group—dominates lived reality, even though it can exist in conflict with it and can be ruled by different interests. It survives by means of its narrative and imaginary power, a power that photographs have a particular capacity to tap. I would like to suggest that photographs locate themselves precisely in the space of contradiction between the myth of the ideal family and the lived reality of family life. Since looking operates through projection and since the photographic image is the positive development of a negative, the plenitude that constitutes the fulfillment of desire, photographs can more easily show us what we wish our family to be, and therefore what, most frequently, it is not.

Barthes's winter-garden photo is a "prose picture" embedded in a book that introduces images by both reproducing and describing them and that places texts and images into several different types of relationship: opposition, collaboration, parallelism. Mostly, images and texts both tell stories and demand a narrative reading and investment on the reader's part, a reading figured by the structure and form of the photographic album. And, as Barthes's book demonstrates, that reading tends to go back to an originary proto-narrative of mother and child, in which the child points, simply saying "ça": assuring himself of his mother's presence and of her (approving) return look.

But the perpetual present of photography complicates this moment considerably: the mother is a child and the son an aging man. I suspect that one of the things we find so powerful in Barthes's description and discussion of the winter-garden image of his mother is that it allows us to think of an aspect of familial experience that has, for the most part, remained unspoken: the ways in which the individual subject is constituted in the space of the family through looking. The winter-garden picture contains a series of intersecting and mutually confirming looks that tell the story of this nonverbal form of familial relationship. It suggests how looks position members of the family in relation to one another, in their predetermined but forever negotiated and negotiable roles and interactions: mother and son, brother and sister, daughter and parents.

Barthes's passionate desire for recognition, satisfied, curiously, by means of a picture he could not possibly recognize, raises the possibility of a distinctive form of looking that emerges in familial interaction. Barthes's look is affiliative and identificatory. His desire is to recognize not only his mother but himself, not only to recognize but to be recognized by her. It is no wonder that he keeps coming back to the luminosity, the clarity of her eyes: "Yet in these photographs of my mother there was always a place set apart, reserved and preserved: the brightness of her eyes" (66).

The familial look, then, is not the look of a subject looking at an object, but a mutual look of a subject looking at an object who is a subject looking (back) at an object. Within the family, as I look I am always also looked at, seen, scrutinized, surveyed, monitored. Familial subjectivity is constructed relationally, and in these relations I am always both self and other(ed), both speaking and looking subject and spoken and looked at object: I am subjected and objectified.

If looking entails a relationship of power, of domination and subjection, of mutuality and interconnection, how is power deployed and contested within the family's visual dynamics? It is my argument that these constitutive optical relations are often concealed and unacknowledged. We have no easy access to these nonverbal exchanges which nevertheless shape and reshape who we are. What means, what instruments do we have available to us to explore this aspect of family relation? What texts are available for our analysis? Can we read domestic images and family photographs as records of or clues to these processes? What theoretical language could help us to understand the psychological layers of familial looking?

The readings which compose *Family Frames* use the photographic imagetexts that are its subjects to forge a theoretical vocabulary that will allow us to talk about specific elements of family photography. This search for a usable idiom has to be a feature of every reading of composite cultural texts, but it is especially critical to a reading of objects as private, familiar, and virtually invisible as family pictures. What we need is a language that will allow us to see the coded and conventional nature of family pictures—to bring the conventions to the foreground and thus to contest their ideological power.

Roland Barthes enables us to think about how photographs—particularly in the narrative meta-photographic discourse in which they are embedded—might give insight into this unspoken network of looking. Walter Benjamin has gone further in claiming for the camera, with the help of the technologies of enlargement and stop motion, very particular powers of detection beyond the capacity of the human eye. By means of the camera eye, and he has both the still and the movie camera in mind, we can see some motions and processes, some minute details of behavior invisible to the human eye: "The camera introduces us to unconscious optics as does psychoanalysis to unconscious impulses."[12] Benjamin's suggestion that the camera and the photograph can expose a complicated and otherwise invisible network of looking, or an "unconscious optics" ("das Optisch-Unbewußte"), is very powerful, especially in relation to the family and the family picture. Applying the notion of "unconscious optics" to the family allows us to peruse family photographs for clues to the family's visual interactions.

In the second half of the twentieth century, however, the family itself becomes the object of intense social and cultural scrutiny and observation.[13] There is nothing about the notion of family that can be assumed or in any way taken for granted. The point of discussing "family" through the practice of photography is precisely to underline its contingency, to delineate the openness of its boundaries and the many factors, beyond biology, that underscore its definitional power. The "family" is an affiliative group, and the affiliations that create it are constructed through various relational, cultural, and institutional processes—such as "looking" and photography, for example. "Families" are shaped by individual responsiveness to the ideological pressures deployed by the familial gaze.

When we look at one another within what we think of as our families, we are also the objects of an external gaze, whether sociological, psychological, historical, or nostalgic and mythical. The dominant ideology of the family, in whatever shapes it takes within a specific social context, superposes itself as an overlay over our more located, mutual, and vulnerable individual looks, looks which always exist in relation to this "familial gaze"—the powerful gaze of familiality which imposes and perpetuates certain conventional images of the familial and which "frames" the family in both senses of the term.[14] The particular nature of the familial gaze, the image of an ideal family and of acceptable family relations, may differ culturally and evolve historically, but every culture and historical moment can identify its own "familial gaze." Its content and even its mode of operating may be variable, but what doesn't change is that this ideal image exists and can be identified, and that it has determining influence. Within a given cultural context, the camera and the family album function as the instruments of this familial gaze.

As I see it, the familial gaze situates human subjects in the ideology, the mythology, of the family as institution and projects a screen of familial myths between camera and subject. Through this screen the subject both recognizes and can attempt to contest her or his embeddedness in familiality. The looks family members exchange, on the other hand, are located in specific points; they are local and contingent; they are mutual and reversible; they are traversed by desire and defined by lack. They are the looks that pass between Roland Barthes and his mother, his perusal of her photograph and his fantasy of her return look, the luminosity of her eyes. A familial look is thus an engagement in a particular form of relationship, mutually constitutive, mediated by the familial gaze, but exceeding it through its subjective contingency.

Because of their conventional nature and the monocular lens's ideological effect, family photographs can reveal the operation of the familial gaze. If we are interested in the interaction of the familial gaze and familial looks, however, we have to go beyond the pictures themselves, as Barthes does when he opens the Boudinet curtain, when he writes about pictures, embedding them in a familial story. If we turn to photographs themselves for clues to the family's unconscious optics, we have to take the intervention of the camera into account and see how it in itself interrupts and shapes visual relations. But if we read imagetexts, the forms of familial looks and gazes can emerge more forcefully and through a variety of lenses. The family album, shaped through its own particular perspective, is the most basic of such imagetexts, and the novels, exhibits, and photography books I analyze in this book are all, in some sense, published and aestheticized family albums.

Through my readings of this series of photographic imagetexts, I focus on the construction of the individual subject in the family and on the family's construction in culture and society *in the visual field*—on the ways in which the family is inscribed within a heterogeneous system of representation.

I think of this book as an album in itself, but not one that is organized chronologically. As in an album, each chapter offers a different take, a different lens or exposure of a similar series of issues and questions, concerning the family and its modes of representation in the postmodern moment: How is the familial subject constructed through looking, and what do photographs tell us about this process? How does photography mediate family memory and thus familial ideology? Can the technologies and cultural forms that interpellate us also be used to contest that interpellation: can the camera and the image, in the words of Jo Spence, be used for its "unfixing" rather than its "fixing" qualities?[15] What are the relationships of looking and power, and how do the camera and the album intervene and mediate these relationships? How does photography insert itself into a heterogeneous tradition of familial representation, and how does it inflect and shape this tradition? How are these relationships marked by national tradition, gender, class, race, ethnic community? Are there distinctive representational traditions, divergent "familial gazes," particular memorial traditions?

I raise these questions within a very particular cultural, historical, and intellectual context in the second half of the twentieth century. The moment I address is postmodernity—the monumental shifts in individual and collective consciousness that occur in the period following World War II, the Holocaust, and the Gulag, the moment of decolonization and the Cold War, of widespread engagements in civil rights and feminist struggles. I believe that this moment has given rise to new aesthetic questions and perhaps to new aesthetic forms which I hope to explore in this book.

Art Spiegelman's *Maus* functions as a paradigmatic and generative text for my argument, allowing me to mark out the aesthetic and political parameters raised within my particular reading of postmodernity. *Maus* is a familial story, collaboratively constructed by father and son. The Spiegelman/Zylberberg families have lived through the massive devastation of the Holocaust, and thus the details of family interaction are inflected by a history that refuses to remain in the background or outside the text. Their story is told, drawn, by the son, who was born after the war but whose life was decisively determined by this familial and cultural memory. Art Spiegelman's memory is delayed, indirect, secondary—it is a postmemory of the Holocaust, mediated by the father-survivor but determinative for the son. He uses his father's oral testimony and the few personal artifacts that have endured—photographs, documents, the few remaining records of a culture almost completely annihilated.

Spiegelman's challenge is to be able to inscribe in the story his ambivalence—both his passionate interest and desire and his inevitable distance and lack of understanding—a task he meets admirably in the graphic genre he has chosen. His inclusion of family photographs demonstrates both their power and their silence: there is nothing in the pictures themselves that reveals the complicated history of loss and destruction to which they testify. The Spiegelman family photos look just like yours and mine: images of victims cannot be distinguished from pictures of perpetrators or bystanders. And yet, within Spiegelman's larger narrative, they become eloquent witnesses of an unspeakable history, in themselves stubborn survivors of cultural genocide. Inserted into his graphic text, they offer him a representational structure adequate to the task of postmemory.

In the postmodern moment, the family occupies a powerful and powerfully threatened place: structurally a last vestige of protection against war, racism, exile, and cultural displacement, it becomes particularly vulnerable to these violent ruptures, and so a measure of their devastation. But, as *Maus* also demonstrates, these external perils do not disguise the violence and destruction that occur within the family itself, the power of the father to silence the mother's voice, the power of the son to rewrite the father's words.

In *Family Frames* I trace this intersection of private and public history. I examine the idea of "family" in contemporary discourse and its power to negotiate and mediate some of the traumatic shifts that have shaped postmodern mentalities, and to serve as an alibi for their violence. I am not alone in seeing the family in the postmodern moment as fractured and subject to conflicting historical and ideological scripts. Photographs offer a prism through which to study the postmodern space of cultural memory composed of leftovers, debris, single items that are left to be collected and assembled in many ways, to tell a variety of stories, from a variety of often competing perspectives.

As Jo Spence and Patricia Holland have suggested: "Family photography can operate at this junction between personal memory and social history, between public myth and personal unconscious. Our memory is never fully 'ours,' nor are the pictures ever unmediated representations of our past. Looking at them we both construct a fantastic past and set out on a detective trail to find other versions of a 'real' one."[16] Photographs mediate familial memory and postmemory, but in the face of the monumental losses figured by the Holocaust, they carry an emotional weight that is often difficult to sustain. In returning to the Holocaust as a frame for these chapters, I attempt to give the emotional power of family photography its full due. This is not to assert that the Holocaust occupies a unique place in the discourses of postmodernity, but merely to choose the place that is personally most devastating and thus potentially most telling for me.

Photographs as well as fictional texts, moreover, represent most forcefully, as Linda Hutcheon has pointed out, the paradoxes inherent in postmodernity: "They are equally omnipresent in both high art and mass culture and their very ubiquity has tended to grant their representations both a certain transparency and a definite complexity."[17] Reading snapshots and photo albums, art photographs and gallery installations, verbal descriptions of actual and of invented photographic images in the same terms and with equal attention is in itself a postmodern critical gesture. The textual analysis of family pictures, in particular, can illustrate the aspects of postmodernity I find most troubling and most exciting: the incorporation of the aesthetic in the practice of everyday life; the plural, decentered, and transactional or relational dimensions of subjectivity; the need to demonstrate, again and again, the cultural and constructed character of what appears transparent and natural; and, most important, the rigorous critique of power and domination that recognizes its own complicity in the very structures it critiques.

We live in a culture increasingly shaped by photographic images. But these technologies develop more rapidly than our ability to theorize about their effect. How can we explore the moral dimensions of the instruments shaping our personal and cultural memory? What forms of moral and theoretical engagement does family photography promote? What theories might help us read family pictures and, conversely, what theoretical constructions might we derive from an encounter with photographs? The etymological roots of *theoria* define it as an act of viewing, contemplation, consideration, insight, in other words, in terms of visuality. By reverting to roots we can perhaps overturn the prevalent conception of theory as a master discourse. We can redefine both its discursive nature and its will to mastery. "If we understand theory in its etymological background (which is, after all, visual)," Mieke

Bal suggests in *Reading Rembrandt,* ". . . [it] ceases to be a dominating discourse and becomes rather a willingness to step into the visual, and to make discourse a partner, rather than dominant opponent, of visuality" (288).[18] To step into the visual is not to engage in theory as systematic explanation of a set of facts, but to practice theory, to make theory just as the photographer materially makes an image. I will suggest that theory as a form of reflection and contemplation emphasizes mutual implication over domination, affiliation over separation, interconnection over distance, tentativeness over certainty.

For me, this practice defines the different registers in which I write this book—theoretical, critical, and autobiographical. I offer them all as different forms of narrative, as a set of stories—narrative snapshots—about family photography. I need these stories to account for the powerful appeal of those cultural forms which perpetuate hegemonic codes and conventions and, at the same time, to make space for critique, revision, and redefinition. In relation to the visual, such a composite practice can, perhaps, enable us to imagine how we might replace the regime of the *gaze* with the field of the *look.* Focusing that look on the family—on the family picture—might help us to loosen the family's own structures of hierarchy and power in favor of a form of self-reflection that makes the practice of theory what Hal Foster has called a "counterpractice of interference."[19] Such is my aim in *Family Frames.*

# 1

# *M*OURNING AND POSTMEMORY

All photographs are *memento mori.*
SUSAN SONTAG

All such things of the war, I tried to put out from my mind once
for all . . . until you rebuild me all this from your questions.
ART SPIEGELMAN

In order to represent himself completely, the son must represent
his mother, his other, without omitting a word.
NANCY K. MILLER

## *family pictures*

When my parents and I immigrated to the United States in the early 1960s,
we rented our first apartment in Providence, Rhode Island, from the
Jakubowiczs, a Polish- and Yiddish-speaking family of Auschwitz survivors.
Although we shared their hard-earned duplex for four years, I felt I never
came to know this tired elderly couple nor their pale and other-worldly
daughter Chana, who was only ten, though her parents were in their late
fifties. We might have been neighbors in distant Eastern Europe—Poland
and Rumania did not seem so far apart from the vantage point of Providence—and were neighbors on Summit Avenue, but worlds separated us.
They were orthodox Jews and kept kosher; they would not even drink a
glass of water in our house. We were eager to furnish our first American
apartment with the latest in what we considered modern and cosmopoli-
tan—Danish walnut furniture and Rya rugs—while their flat, with its hap-
hazard mixture of second-hand furniture and Sears formica, topped with
doilies and fringes, had a distinctly old-world look about it.

I was simultaneously fascinated and repulsed by the numbers tattooed on
their pale arms, and could not stop asking my mother for details of their sur-

vival in Auschwitz, the loss of their spouses and children, how they met each other after the liberation, how they decided to marry, to have Chana, to start a new life all on the traces of such inconceivable pain and loss.

I well remember going to their apartment and staring at the few framed photos on a small, round, doily-covered living room table. These were pictures of Mr. and Mrs. Jakubowicz's first families—Mrs. Jakubowicz, her first husband and three sons, Mr. Jakubowicz, his first wife and three daughters. I can't remember these photos visually—in my memory they have acquired a generic status of old-looking studio family portraits. Perhaps one was a wedding photo, others might have depicted the parents and children. I just don't know any more. But there was something discomforting about them which made me both want to keep staring at them and to look away. What I most remember is how unrecognizable Mr. and Mrs. Jakubowicz seemed in the photos, and how hard I thought it must be for Chana to live in the shadow of these legendary "siblings" whom she had already outlived in age, whom, because she had never known them, she could not mourn, whom her parents could never stop mourning. I thought that their ghostly presence might explain Chana's pallor, her hushed speech, her decidedly unchildlike behavior. I spent a lot of time wondering how these photos had survived. Had the Jakubowiczs left them with Polish neighbors or friends? Had they perhaps mailed them to family abroad? Had they been able to keep them through their time in Auschwitz, and, if so, how?

I had forgotten the Jakubowiczs and their photos until I saw another photo that seemed to me, as much as those, to be hovering between life and death—a photo of Frieda Wolfinger, my husband Leo's aunt, a survivor of the Riga ghetto and concentration camp. Rose, my mother-in-law, who had survived the war as a refugee in Bolivia, had this picture in her collection, and later we found another copy among the photos of another aunt, Käthe, who had survived the war in England. In one of his most vivid childhood memories, Leo recalls the moment—in 1945—when this photo arrived in a letter announcing Frieda's survival and detailing the death of the rest of her family. I can picture the family sitting around their kitchen table in La Paz, reading Frieda's letter, crying and studying the picture which had crossed the ocean as proof of life and continuity. I can picture Käthe receiving the identical picture in England, and I can imagine her relief to see Frieda, at least, alive. How many copies of the picture did Frieda have printed, I wonder, and to how many relatives did she send it? And how could those relatives just get up from their kitchen tables, how could they integrate into their lives Frieda's image and the knowledge it brought?

I am fascinated with this multiple dissemination of the same image, by the weight of its message in relation to its own unassuming character. There is nothing *in the picture* that indicates its connection to the Holocaust: Frieda does not look emaciated or deathlike. On the contrary, she looks very much alive and "normal." She is firmly situated in an ordinary domestic setting—seated on a bench in front of a pretty house surrounded by flowering trees, she is holding a newspaper and smiling, a bit sadly it seems to me, at the camera. Alone, she seems to be asking something of the onlooker, beckoning to be recognized, to be helped perhaps, although, at the same time, she wears a distinctly self-sufficient expression. Her posture articulates some of these contradictions: her body is twisted in on itself, uncomfortable at the edge of the seat. For me, this picture has become an emblem of the survivor who is at once set apart from the normalcy of postwar life and who eagerly waits to rejoin it: in the picture, Frieda remains outside the garden fence, seems to inhabit neither house nor garden. She is the survivor who announces that she has literally "sur-vived," lived too long, outlived her intended destruction. She is the survivor who has a story to tell, but who has neither the time to do so in the instant of the photograph nor the audience to receive it.

## holocaust photographs

As much as the pictures in the Jakubowicz living room represented death for me, so Frieda's picture says "I am alive," or perhaps, "I have survived,"—a message so simple and, at the same time, so overlaid with meaning that it seems to beg for a narrative and for a listener, for a survivor's tale. Theorists of photography have often pointed out this simultaneous presence of death and life in the photograph: "Photographs state the innocence, the vulnerability of lives heading toward their own destruction and this link between photography and death haunts all photos of people," says Susan Sontag in *On Photography*.[1] Roland Barthes, in *Camera Lucida*, agrees but points out the reverse as well when he connects photography to life: "The photograph is literally an emanation of the referent . . . light, though impalpable, is here a carnal medium, a skin I share with anyone who has been photographed" (80–81). But it is precisely the indexical nature of the photo, its status as relic, or trace, or fetish—its "direct" connection with the material presence of the photographed person—that at once intensifies its status as harbinger of death and, at the same time and concomitantly, its capacity to signify life. With the image of the umbilical cord, Barthes connects photography not just to life but to life-giving, to maternity. Life is the presence of the object before the camera and the "carnal medium" of light which produces its image; death is the "having-been-there" of the object—the radical break, the finality introduced by the past tense. For Barthes, it is the mother's death and the son's desire to bring her back. The "ça a été" of the photograph creates the scene of mourning shared by those who are left to look at the picture. More than memory is at stake here: Barthes insists that "the photograph does not call up the past" (82); photography, he implies, does not facilitate the work of mourning. Going further, Marguerite Duras writes that "photographs promote forgetting . . . It's a confirmation of death."[2] And Barthes agrees: "not only is the Photograph never, in essence, a memory . . . but it actually blocks memory, quickly becomes a counter-memory" (91). Photography's relation to loss and death is not to mediate the process of individual and collective memory but to bring the past back in the form of a ghostly revenant, emphasizing, at the same time, its immutable and irreversible pastness and irretrievability.

Sontag elaborates on what she calls the photograph's "posthumous irony," describing Roman Vishniac's pictures of the vanished world of Eastern European Jewish life, which are particularly affecting, she argues, because as we look at them we know how soon these people are going to die (70). We also know, I would add, that they will *all* die (have all died), that their world will be (has been) destroyed, and that the future's (our) only access to it will be (is) through those pictures and through the stories they have left behind. The Holocaust photograph is uniquely able to bring out this particular capacity of photographs to hover between life and death, to capture only that which no longer exists, to suggest both the desire and the necessity and, at the same time, the difficulty, the impossibility, of mourning.

In the broad category of "Holocaust photograph," I include the Jakubowiczs' family portraits, Frieda's picture, Roman Vishniac's pictures of Jewish shtetl life, as well as the many pictures of atrocities from the concentration and extermination camps. I include those pictures which are connected for us to total death and to public mourning—pictures of horror and also ordinary snapshots and portraits, family pictures connected to the Holocaust by their context and not by their content. I recognize, of course, that there are differences between the picture of Frieda and the documentary images of mass graves, especially in the work of reading that they require. Confronted with the latter image, we respond with horror, even before reading the caption or knowing its context. The context, then, increases the horror as we add to the bodies, or the hair, or the shoes depicted, all those others we know about but which are not in the picture. Confronted with the former image—the portrait or family picture—we need to know its context, but then, I would argue, we respond with a similar sense of disbelief.

These two photographs are complementary: it is precisely the displacement of the bodies depicted in the pictures of horror from their domestic settings, along with their disfigurement, that brings home the enormity of Holocaust destruction. And it is precisely the utter conventionality of the domestic family picture that makes it impossible for us to comprehend how the person in the picture was, or could have been, annihilated. In both cases, the viewer fills in what the picture leaves out: the horror of looking is not necessarily *in* the image but in the story the viewer provides to fill in what has been omitted. For each image we provide the other complementary one. "There was no stone that marked their passage," says Helen Epstein about her deceased relatives. "All that was left were the fading photographs that my father kept in a yellow envelope underneath his desk. Those photographs were not the usual kind of snapshots displayed in albums and shown to strangers. They were documents, evidence of our part in a history so powerful that whenever I tried to read about it in the books my father gave me or see it in the films he took me to, I could not take it in."[3] This statement defines the process of reading the Holocaust photograph: looking at the family pictures, placing them in context through reading and seeing films, being unable to understand or to name that context—note how Epstein repeats the indeterminate "it." Epstein's inability "to take *it* in" is perhaps the distinguishing feature of the Holocaust photograph.

I started thinking about the connection between the Jakubowiczs' family pictures and the photograph Frieda sent to her relatives—pictures I saw twenty-five years apart—when I read *Maus II*, the second volume of Art Spiegelman's controversial cartoon representation of his father Vladek's survival in Auschwitz. Volume I of *Maus* contained one photograph of Art Spiegelman and his mother which, emerging among the drawings of mice and cats, I had found particularly moving. But *Maus II* complicates the levels of representation and mediation of its predecessor. The photo on the first page, of Artie's dead brother Richieu, and the one near the end, of the survivor Vladek Spiegelman in a starched camp uniform, came to focus for me the oscillation between life and death that defines the photograph. These photographs connect the two levels of Spiegelman's text, the past and the present, the story of the father and the story of the son, because these family photographs are documents both of memory (the survivor's) and of "postmemory" (that of the child of survivors). As such, the photographs included in the text of *Maus,* and, through them, *Maus* itself, become sites of remembrance, what Pierre Nora has termed *lieux de mémoire.* "Created by a play of memory and history," *lieux de mémoire* are "mixed, hybrid, mutant, bound intimately with life and death, with time and eternity, enveloped in a Möbius strip of the collective and the individual, the sacred and the profane, the immutable and the mobile." Invested with "a symbolic aura," *lieux de mémoire* can function to "block the work of forgetting."[4] Although I find Nora's reified distinction between history and memory and his organistic distinctions between life and death troubling, his notion of "lieux de mémoire" does usefully describe the status with which Holocaust photographs are often invested. The spatiality of memory mapped onto its temporality, its visual combined with its verbal dimension, makes memory, as W. J. T. Mitchell suggests, in itself an "imagetext, a double-coded system of mental storage and retrieval."[5] Images and narratives thus constitute its instruments and its very medium, extending well into subsequent generations. Photographs, ghostly revenants, are very particular instruments of remembrance, since they are perched at the edge between memory and postmemory, and also, though differently, between memory and forgetting.

I propose the term "postmemory" with some hesitation, conscious that the prefix "post" could imply that we are beyond memory and therefore perhaps, as Nora fears, purely in history. In my reading, postmemory is distinguished from memory by generational distance and from history by deep personal connection. Postmemory is a powerful and very particular form of memory precisely because its connection to its object or source is mediated not through recollection but through an imaginative investment and creation. This is not to say that memory itself is unmediated, but that it is more directly connected to the past. Postmemory characterizes the experience of those who grow up dominated by narratives that preceded their birth, whose own belated stories are evacuated by the stories of the previous generation shaped by traumatic events that can be neither understood nor recreated. I have developed this notion in relation to children of Holocaust survivors, but I believe it may usefully describe other second-generation memories of cultural or collective traumatic events and experiences.[6]

I prefer the term "postmemory" to "absent memory," or "hole of memory," also derived in Nadine Fresco's illuminating work with children of survivors.[7] Postmemory—often obsessive and relentless—need not be absent or evacuated: it is as full and as empty, certainly as constructed, as memory itself. My notion of postmemory is certainly connected to Henri Raczymow's "mémoire trouée," his "memory shot through with holes," defining also the indirect and fragmentary nature of second-generation memory.[8] Photographs in their enduring "umbilical" connection to life are precisely the medium connecting first- and second-generation remembrance, memory and postmemory. They are the leftovers, the fragmentary sources and building blocks, shot through with holes, of the work of postmemory. They affirm the past's existence and, in their flat two-dimensionality, they signal its unbridgeable distance.

Like all pictures, the photos in *Maus* represent what no longer is. But they also represent what has been and, in this case, what has been violently destroyed. And they represent the life that was no longer to be and that, against all odds, nevertheless continues to be. If anything throws this contradictory and ultimately unassimilable dimension of photography— perched between life and death—into full relief, it has to be the possibility, the reality, of survival in the face of the complete annihilation that is the Holocaust. Holocaust photographs, as much as their subjects, are themselves stubborn survivors of the intended destruction of an entire culture, its people as well as all their records, documents, and cultural artifacts.[9]

The photographs in *Maus* are indeed defined by their inclusion in Spiegelman's very particular imagetext, his provocative generic choice of an animal fable comic book to represent his father's story of survival and his own life as a child of survivors. If Holocaust representation has been determined by Theodor Adorno's suggestion in his 1949 essay "After Auschwitz," that "after Auschwitz you could no longer write poems," then what can we say of Spiegelman's comics and of the photographs embedded in them?

Despite his own careful reconsideration and restatement, Adorno's radical suspicion has haunted writing for the last fifty years.[10] One of its consequences has been the effort to distinguish between the documentary and the aesthetic. Most theoretical writing about Holocaust representation, whether historical or literary, by necessity debates questions such as truth and fact, reference and representation, realism and modernism, history and fiction, ethics and politics—questions that may seem dated in theoretical thought, but that revisionist histories have brought to the fore with great urgency. Peter Haidu summarized this preoccupation: "Our grasp of the Event must inevitably be mediated by representations, with their baggage of indeterminacy. But this is a context in which theory is forced to reckon with reference—as unsatisfactory as contemporary accounts of reference may be—as a necessary function of language and all forms of representation."[11] The consequent validation of the documentary makes the archival photograph—

along with the spoken survivor testimony—an especially powerful medium, due to its incontrovertible connection to reference. Julia Kristeva has even argued that film is the "supreme art of the apocalyptic" and that the profusion of visual images in which we have been immersed since the Holocaust, in their extraordinary power to evoke its horror, have silenced us verbally, impairing the symbolic instruments that might have enabled us to process the apocalyptic events of our century: "For these monstrous and painful spectacles disturb our mechanisms of perception and representation. Our symbolic modes are emptied, petrified, nearly annihilated, as if they were overwhelmed or destroyed by an all too powerful force . . . That new apocalyptic rhetoric has been realized in two extremes, which seem to be opposites but which often complement each other: the profusion of images and the withholding of the word."[12] John E. Frohmayer, former chairman of the National Endowment of the Arts, goes farther than Kristeva in endowing all documentary visual representation with awesome power. He has claimed, for example, that Holocaust photographs are so upsetting that their public display needs to be strictly controlled: "Likewise, a photograph, for example of Holocaust victims might be inappropriate for display in the entrance of a museum where all would have to confront it, whether they chose to or not, but would be appropriate in a show which was properly labeled and hung so that only those who chose to confront the photographs would be required to do so."[13] To Frohmayer, documentary images are a form of evidence. They affirm the "having-been-there" of the victim and the victimizer, of the horror. They remove doubt, they can be held up as proof to the revisionists. In contrast, the aesthetic is said to introduce agency, control, structure and, therefore, distance from the real, a distance which might leave space for doubt. Art Spiegelman seems to confirm such a distinction when, contrary to his earlier ambition to write the "Great American Comic Book Novel," he subsequently insisted that *Maus* be classified as nonfiction.[14]

But some have questioned this distinction between the documentary and the aesthetic, highlighting the aestheticizing tendencies present in *all* visual representation and therefore presumably its diminished power truly to represent horror. Christina von Braun, for example, decries the way in which the image—the image in general—can "transform horror into the aesthetic," suggesting that "film and the photograph have inserted themselves like a protective barrier between us and the real," becoming what she has aptly termed a "photo morgana."[15] The immobilizing quality of the still photograph—its deathlike fixing of one moment in time—clearly contributes to this perceived incapacity of the photo to maintain its initial power. After looking repeatedly at any image, the viewer builds up sufficient psychological resistance to become desensitized, just in order to survive the horror of looking. In Von Braun's reading, this would be as true of a picture of atrocities as of the family picture of a child who later died in the gas chambers. For her, the photograph—in itself—can no more evoke horror than it can promote memory or facilitate the work of mourning. In contrast, Spiegelman's text maintains the photographs' visual power through their sparse use and through their placement.[16]

By placing three photographs into his graphic narrative, Art Spiegelman raises not only the question of how, forty years after Adorno's dictum, the Holocaust can be represented, but also the question of how different media—comics, photographs, narrative, testimony—can interact to produce a more permeable and multiple text that may recast the problematics of Holocaust representation and definitively eradicate any clear-cut distinction between documentary and aesthetic. In moving us from documentary photographs—perhaps the most referential representational medium—to cartoon drawings of mice and cats, Spiegelman lays bare the levels of mediation that underlie *all* visual representational forms. But confronting these visual media with his father's spoken testimony adds yet another axis to the oppositions between documentary and aesthetic, on the one hand, testimony and fiction, on the other. Considering these two axes in relation to each other may enable us to come back to the Holocaust photo—and, through it, to photography more generally—and to look at its particular articulation of life and death, representation and mourning.

## a survivor's tale

*Maus*, the title Spiegelman has chosen for his "survivor's tale," illustrates well the interplay between the visual and aural codes that structure his text. *Maus* sounds like the English word "mouse," but its German spelling echoes visually the recurring Nazi command "Juden raus" ("Jews out"—come out or get out) as well as the first three letters of "Auschwitz"—a word that in itself has become a trope of the Holocaust. Spiegelman reinforces this association when, in the second volume, he refers to the camp as "Mauschwitz" and boldly entitles the first chapter "From Mauschwitz to the Catskills and Beyond." Similarly, the subtitle of Volume I plays with the visual and aural dimensions of the word "tale"—when we see it we know it means "story," but when we hear it after hearing "mouse" we may think that it is spelled t-a-i-l. Furthermore, on the cover and title imprint, the author includes his own name without capitals, thereby making himself a visual construct able to bring out the tensions between aesthetic and documentary, figural and mimetic: "art," on the one hand, and "Spiegelman" or "mirrorman," on the other. Spiegelman's audacious visual/verbal punning not only lays bare the self-consciousness of his textual production—a self-reflexivity that disarmingly pervades his text—it also defines from the beginning the two primary elements of his representational choices, the visual and the aural. These work together in the text in complex interaction.

On one level, *Maus* tells the story of Spiegelman's father, Vladek, from the 1930s in Poland to his liberation from Auschwitz in 1945; on another level, *Maus* recounts the story of father and son in 1980s Queens and the Catskills, the story of the father's testimony and the son's attempt to transmit that testimony in the comics genre which has become his profession, and the story of Art Spiegelman's own life dominated by memories which are not his own. When Art visits Vladek at his home, in his workshop, or on his vacations, as they sit, or walk, or work, or argue, Vladek talks into a tape recorder and Art asks him questions, follows up on details, demands more minute descriptions. The testimony is contained in Vladek's voice, but we receive both more and less than that voice: we receive Art's graphic interpretation of Vladek's narrative. This is a "survivor's tale"—a testimony—mediated by the survivor's child through his idiosyncratic representational and aesthetic choices.[17] These choices are based on an almost obsessive desire for accuracy and, at the same time, clearly abandon (or refigure) that desire by setting the story in an animal fable. On the one hand, then, the tape recorder captures Vladek's story *as he tells it,* and the text gives us the impression that Art has transcribed the testimony verbatim, getting the accent, the rhythm, the intonation just right. On the other hand, he has not provided the visual counterpart of the tape recorder—the camera. Instead, he has drawn the Jews as mice, the Poles as pigs, the Germans as cats, the French as frogs, the Americans as dogs, the gypsies as ladybugs. While in the visual realm Spiegelman chooses multiple mediations, in the aural, by contrast, he seems to seek absolute unmediated authenticity. But the three family photos that are reproduced in the text complicate considerably this apparent disjunction between the visual and aural dimensions of Spiegelman's imagetext.[18]

At first glance, Spiegelman's animal fable is a literalization of Hitler's line which serves as its epigram: "The Jews are undoubtedly a race, but they are not human." If indeed, Jews are not human, Spiegelman seems to ask, what are they, and, more important, what are the Germans? In response, he draws schematic mice and cat heads resting on human-looking bodies. But these are mice and cats who perceive themselves as human, who in all respects except one—their heads—are human. When Anja Spiegelman discovers a rat in the basement where she is hiding she is terrified, and Art is amused when he finds a framed photo of a pet cat on the desk of his survivor psychiatrist. On the one hand, Spiegelman would like to make it clear throughout his books that his representational choices are just that—choices—and that identities are assumed rather than given. When Vladek gets out of hiding to walk through Sosnowiec, he wears a pig mask, trying to pass for Polish. Some children call him a Jew but the adults believe the mask and apologize. Art has trouble deciding how to draw his French wife—should she be a frog because she is French, or a mouse because she converted to Judaism? On the other hand, however, Spiegelman seems to come close to duplicating the Nazis' racist refusal of the possibility of assimilation or cultural integration when he represents different nationalities as different animal species. But in the second volume these oppositions blur as Art often represents himself not as a mouse but as a human wearing a mouse mask. Eventually, as he starts to draw and gets into his father's story, the mouse head becomes his own head. If Jews are mice and Germans are cats, then, they seem to be so not immutably but only *in relation to each other* and in relation to the Holocaust and its memory. They are human except for the predator/victim relationships between them. Yet Art and Françoise's Vermont friends are dogs, even in the 1980s. Obviously, Spiegelman's reflections on "race," ethnicity, and nationality, as essential (natural) or as socially and ideologically constructed, contain a number of contradictions and incongruities, and during the years of the two books' production, they have evolved. That evolution can be traced by the differences between his original self-portrait and the one he adopted upon the publication of *Maus II* (Figures 1.1 and 1.2). In *Maus I,* the cartoonist is a hybrid creature, with a schematically drawn man's body and a mouse's head, a lonely artist at his drawing table, with his back to the viewer. In the second, the artist is a more fully drawn cartoon man wearing over his own head a large mouse mask which he anxiously holds in his hands as, facing out, he contemplates his work. No longer isolated, he is surrounded both by the world of his imagination (a Nazi guard is shooting outside his window) and that of his craft (a picture of *Raw* and the cover of *Maus* are on the wall). For him to enter his book has become more problematic and overlaid, the access to his mouse identity more mediated. Spiegelman's animal fable is both more and

1.1

Art Spiegelman is co-founder/editor of *Raw*, the acclaimed magazine of avant-garde comics and graphics. His work has been published in the *New York Times*, *Playboy*, and the *Village Voice*, among other periodicals, and his drawings have been exhibited at the Museum of Modern Art in New York and in galleries here and abroad. Honors he has received for *Maus* include a special Pulitzer Prize and a Guggenheim fellowship. He lives in New York City with his wife, Francoise Mouly, and their children, Nadja and Dashiell.

1.2

less than an analysis of national and ethnic relations: it is his aesthetic strategy, his affirmation of identity as construction.

At the same time, readers and viewers raised on "Mickey Mouse," "Tom and Jerry," and, Spiegelman's favorite, *Mad Magazine*, quickly accept the convention of the animal fable and learn to discern subtle facial and bodily expressions among the characters of *Maus* even though the figures' faces rarely vary. Even the breaks in illusion that multiply in *Maus II* do not interfere. We appreciate Art's self-consciousness, his questions about the validity of his enterprise and his capacity to carry it out, and we sympathize with his discomfort at the success of *Maus*. Art, drawn as a mouse, or wearing his mouse mask, is a figure to whom we have become accustomed. Even the incongruity, the uneasy fit, between the characters' heads and their bodies, the book's confusions about the nature of racial and ethnic differ-ence, the monumental and pervasive dissonance between the past and pre-sent levels of the narrative (Vladek describing his deportation while riding his exercise bicycle in Queens, for example) all ultimately come to be normalized, even erased, in the reading process.

The truly shocking and disturbing breaks in the visual narrative—the points that fail to blend in—are the section called "Prisoner on the Hell Planet" in *Maus* in which an actual photograph appears, and the two photos in *Maus II*. These three moments protrude from the narrative like unassimi-lated and unassimilable memories. The "Prisoner" section stands out pow-erfully not only because of the picture of mother and son but also because of its different drawing style and the black-bordered pages which disturb the otherwise uniformly white edging of the closed book. In *Maus II*, Spiegelman sets off the two photos through contrast. They emerge through their difference not only from the narrative itself but also from several pages where "photographs"—schematic representations of framed mice—are shown and discussed by Vladek: "Anja's parents, the grandparents, her big sister Tosha, little Bibi and our Richieu . . . All what is left, it's the photos" (Figure 1.3; *Maus II*, 113–116). They emerge also in contrast to the lack of photos. Vladek, deploring the absent photos of his own side of the family, sadly stands in for them, filling up an entire page with his own body: "It's nothing left, not even a snapshot" (Figure 1.4; *Maus II*, 116). When we get to the actual photographs of Richieu and Vladek they break out of the framework of Spiegelman's book as much as the black pages of the "Pris-oner" section did, and thus they bring into relief a tension that is present on every level of the text.

"Breaking the framework" is a term Shoshana Felman uses in her book *Testimony*, where she recounts that, in a course on the literature of testi-mony, the screening of videotaped interviews with Holocaust survivors broke "the very framework of the class" just as all the writers of testimony ended up breaking through the framework of the books they had initially set out to write.[19] Felman sees what she calls this "dissonance" as essential to her pedagogical experience in the age of testimony. Breaking through the framework is a form of dissonance: visual *and* verbal images are used to

1.3

1.4

describe an incongruity necessary to any writing or teaching about the Holocaust. How are we to read the radical breaks in the representational continuity of *Maus*? How do Spiegelman's family pictures mediate his narrative of loss? What alternate story—in the margins of the central narrative of *Maus*—is told by the family pictures?

## breaking the frame

Taken together, the three photographs in *Maus I* and *II* reassemble a family violently fractured and destroyed by the Shoah: they include, at different times, in different places, and in different guises, all the Spiegelmans—Art and his mother, Art's brother Richieu, and the father, Vladek. Sparsely distributed over the space of the two volumes, these three pictures tell their own narrative of loss, mourning and desire, one that inflects obliquely, that both supports and undercuts the story of *Maus*.[20]

But these three images are not equal. The first, the picture of mother and son (Figure 1.5), has a unique generative power in the son's text, a power that comes from the "double dying" and the double survival in which it is embedded.[21] The photograph clarifies the importance of the mother's suicide twenty-three years after her liberation from Auschwitz in the story the father and son construct, reinforcing the work of memory and postmemory that generates their text.

The photograph of Artie and his mother, labeled "Trojan Lake, N.Y. 1958" (*Maus*, 100) introduces "The Prisoner on the Hell Planet," the account

1.5

of Anja Spiegelman's suicide. In the picture, the family is obviously vaca-tioning—the 10-year-old Art is squatting in a field, smiling at the camera, and Anja is standing above him, wearing a bathing suit, one hand on his head, staring into space. Presumably the picture is taken by the invisible father, a conventional division of labor in 1950s family pictures. But the very next frame announces the destruction of this interconnected family group: "In 1968, when I was 20, my mother killed herself. She left no note." Poignantly, Spiegelman juxtaposes the archival photograph with the message of death which, through the presence of the photo's "having-been-there," is strengthened, made even more unbearable. This echoes an earlier moment in the text when Art, holding his mother's photograph, tries to engage his father in the project of testimony: "Start with Mom" (*Maus*, 12).

The drawings in the "Hell Planet" section are completely different from the rest of the volume: drawings of humans rather than mice and cats, they express grief, pain and mourning in much more direct, melodramatic, ex-pressionist fashion—tears running down faces, skulls, Vladek lying on top of the casket screaming "Anna." Art, dressed in the striped concentration camp uniform that has come down to him through his parents' stories, metaphorically equates his own confinement in his guilt and mourning with their imprisonment in the concentration camp. "Hell Planet" is both Ausch-witz and Art's own psyche. "Left alone with [his] thoughts," Art con-nects "MENOPAUSAL DEPRESSION, HITLER DID IT, MOMMY, [and] BITCH" (*Maus*, 103)—memory is unbearable and, in his representational choices, Spiegelman tries to convey just how unbearable it is. "Hell Planet" demonstrates how immediately present their war memories have remained for Art and his parents in their subsequent life, and how unassimilated. But the grieving Art does not actually *remember* the concentration camp whose uniform he wears—mediated through his parents' memories, his is a post-memory. Art remains imprisoned in his camp uniform and in the black-bor-dered spaces of his psyche. Drawing *Maus*, it is implied, represents his attempt both to get deeper into his postmemory and to find a way out. In "Hell Planet" the two chronological levels of *Maus* merge, and in this convergence between past and present, destruction and survival, primary and secondary trauma—incarnated by Anja's suicide—lies the root of Art's (perhaps temporary) insanity. But in this merging, this segment merely exacerbates what occurs at every level of *Maus*; Art's stay at the mental institution in "Hell Planet" is a more pronounced version of the insanity he lives through every day of his postmemory.

The other characters attest to the power of "Hell Planet"—Mala, Vladek's second wife, insists it is unlike other comics because it is "so personal" but "very accurate . . . objective" too. Vladek says he only read it because it contained Anja's picture and he says that he cried when he read it because it brought back memories of his wife (*Maus*, 104). Vladek keeps his wife's memory alive through the pictures of her he has all over his desk, which, as his second wife complains, is "like a shrine." The photo of mother and son sets the stage for the personal, as well as the objective, realistic, and accurate—it legitimizes "Hell Planet" as a document of life and death, of death in life. In the photo, mother and son are connected by her hand, which touches the top of his head; but the photo itself is, in Barthes's terms, a carnal medium, connecting all those who look at it (Art, Mala, and Vladek, as well as the reader of *Maus*) with the living Anja who stood in front of the camera in 1958, touching her son. In each case, hands become the media of interconnection: Anja places her hand on Art's head, a hand (presumably Art's) is holding the photo at an angle at the top of the page, and Art's hand is holding the pages of "Hell Planet" as they are represented in *Maus*. The reader's access to Anja and her story is multiply mediated by Art's hands and hers—his drawing hand which stands in stark contrast to her arm where the photograph does not reveal what, in another text, Spiegelman says she was always intent on hiding: her tattooed Auschwitz number.[22]

Anja left no note—all that remains is her picture—her hand on Art's head, their visible bodily attachment, and his memories of her transformed into drawings. It is a picture modulated by other memories, such as the one in "Hell Planet" of Anja asking Artie, in the only speech of hers he remembers directly (the others are all reported by his father) whether he still loves her. He turns away, refuses to look at her, "resentful of the way she tightened the umbilical cord," and says "sure, Ma." In guilty recollection all Art can say is "Agh!" (*Maus*, 103).

But *Maus* is dominated by this absence of Anja's voice, the destruction of her diaries, her missing note. Anja is recollected by others; she remains a visual and not an aural presence. She speaks in sentences imagined by her son or recollected by her husband. In their memory she is mystified, objectified, shaped to the needs and desires of the one who remembers—whether it be Vladek or Art. Her actual voice could have been in the text, but it isn't: "These notebooks, and other really nice things of mother," Vladek explains to Art, ". . . One time I had a very bad day . . . and all of these things I destroyed." "You what?" Art exclaims. And Vladek replies: "After Anja died I had to make an order with everything . . . these papers had too many memories, so I burned them" (*Maus*, 158–159). Vladek did not read the papers Anja left behind, he only knows that she said: "I wish my son, when he grows up, he will be interested by this" (*Maus*, 159). Her legacy was destroyed and *Maus* itself can be seen as an attempt to reconstruct it, an attempt by father and son to provide the missing perspective of the mother. Much of the *Maus* text rests on her absence and the destruction of her papers, deriving from her silence its momentum and much of its energy. Through her picture and her missing voice Anja haunts the story told in both volumes, a ghostly presence shaping familial interaction—the personal and the collective story of death and survival.

"Prisoner on the Hell Planet" was initially published in an underground journal, and in *Maus* Art says he never intended for his father to see it. "Prisoner" is Art's own recollection, but *Maus* is the collaborative narrative of father and son: one provides most of the verbal narrative, the other the visual; one gives testimony while the other receives and transmits it. In the process of testimony they establish their own uneasy bonding. In his analysis of the process of testimony, the psychoanalyst Dori Laub says: "For lack of a better term, I will propose that there is a need for a tremendous libidinal investment in those interview situations: there is so much destruction recounted, so much death, so much loss, so much hopelessness, that there has to be an abundance of holding and of emotional investment in the encounter, to keep alive the witnessing narration" (*Testimony*, 71). Art and Vladek share one monumental loss, Anja's, and on that basis, they build the "libidinal investment" demanded by the "witnessing narration" they undertake.[23] The absence of the mother, the masculine collaboration between father and son, are crucial to the power of *Maus*, and the mother-son photograph, a record of a "double dying," reinforces this gendered narration.

Anja's role in their familial construction makes Art and Vladek's collaboration a process of masculine, Orphic creation, in the terms of Klaus Theweleit's *Buch der Könige*.[24] Art and Vladek do indeed sing an Orphic song—a song about the internal workings of a Hades which few have survived, and about which even fewer have been able to speak. In Theweleit's terms, Orphic creation—the birth of human art forms, social institutions, and technological inventions—results from just such a descent into and a reemergence from Hades: a masculine process facilitated by the encounter with the beautiful dead woman who may not herself come out or sing her own song. Orphic creation is thus an artificial "birth" produced by men: by male couples who can bypass the generativity of women, whose bonding depends on the tragic absence of women. In this process women are relegated to the role of "media," of intermediaries; they are not the primary creators or witnesses. In *Maus* father and son together attempt to reconstruct the missing story of the mother. They do not go to Mala, Vladek's second wife, for assistance, even though she too is a survivor. Mala, in fact, is also disturbingly absent as a voice and even as a listener. When she tries once to tell parts of her own story of survival, Art interrupts her to go to check on his father. Her role is only to care for the aging Vladek and to put up with his litany of complaints. Moreover, Mala brings us face to face with the limitations of the book's fairy-tale mode, with its polarization of mice and cats, good guys and bad: her name "Mala" emphasizes her position as foil to the idealized deceased Anja and sets her up, at least symbolically, as the evil stepmother. And Art leaves her in that role even when he seems to consult with her about Vladek. Françoise, Art's French wife, is at best a sounding board, an enabling presence, for the confused cartoonist. In his acknowledgments Spiegelman thanks both women for their roles as "media": Mala was his translator from Polish and Françoise his editor. Art's hostile comments about dating Jewish women complete the banishment of female voices from his narrative and show that his story, in Orphic fashion, depends on female absence and death. Art and Vladek perform the collaboration of the creative male couple: the difficulties that structure their relationship only serve to strengthen the ties which bind them to each other and to the labor they have undertaken.

In the Orpheus story, Orpheus may not turn around to *look* at Eurydice's face. In "Hell Planet," Spiegelman draws Anja and even hands us her photograph—Anja's face and body, connected to the body of her son, are there for everyone to see. Seeing her photograph is a "memento mori"—a sign of the "having been," of Anja's one-time presence and of her subsequent, perpetual, and devastating absence. The photograph thus becomes the visual equivalent of the Orphic song which, through the intermediary of a cultural artifact—*Maus*—can bring Eurydice out of Hades, even as it actually needs to leave her behind. Thus the photograph, the product of both the aesthetic and the documentary/technological, signals this dual presence and absence, in Barthes's terms, this "anterior future of which death is the stake." It figures the son's desire for his mother, for her bodily presence, for the touch of her hand, and for her look of recognition.

This is no simple Orphic or Oedipal conflict echoing classical mythic patterns. Familial conflict based on gender and generation is there, but is refocused by those violent historical forces that have rewritten family plots in the twentieth century. Psychoanalytic and mythic paradigms need to be qualified by the extreme historical circumstances in which they take shape.

FOR    RICHIEU

AND    FOR    NADJA                1.6

Thus father and son transcend their roles when they become witness and listener; son and mother become historian and the object of historical quest. Brothers are divided by war and Holocaust, inhabitants of different worlds and of different families. The photographs included in *Maus,* reassembling a nuclear family violently fractured by circumstance, point both to the power of the familial mythos in the face of external threat and to the powerlessness of the family as institution to act in any way as a protection. Just as these photographs are embedded, however uneasily, in the squares of Spiegelman's graphics, so the familial gaze of *Maus* is shaped by these overwhelming historical circumstances, encircling and refocusing the exchange of familial looks.

While "Prisoner on the Hell Planet" is the work of memory, *Maus* itself is the creation of postmemory. In fact, that is the status of the two photographs in *Maus II.* The second volume carries two dedications: "For Richieu and for Nadja" (Figure 1.6). Richieu is the brother Art never knew because he died during the war, before Art's birth; Nadja is Spiegelman's daughter. The volume is dedicated to two children, one dead, the other alive, one who is the object of postmemory, the other who will herself carry on her father's postmemory. Whose picture, in fact, illustrates the dedication page? I have assumed that it is Richieu's: a serious child about three years old, hair parted, wearing knit overalls. But upon reflection the picture is quite indeterminate. Could it be Nadja? Could it be a childhood image of Vladek, I wonder, noting the resemblance between the two pictures which frame *Maus II*? Or could it be Art himself? A few pages into *Maus II,* Art alludes to a photograph of his "ghost-brother," wondering if they would have gotten along: "He was mainly a large blurry photograph hanging in my parents' bedroom." Françoise is surprised: "I thought that was a picture of you, though it didn't look like you" (*Maus II,* 15). Based on appearance alone, the picture could be Art or Vladek or Nadja or Richieu, and Spiegelman does not specify. But in terms of function, the picture in the bedroom and the one on the dedication page clearly have to be Richieu: "That's the point. They didn't need photos of me in their room, I was alive! The photo never threw tantrums or got in any kind of trouble . . . It was an ideal kid, and I was a pain in the ass. I couldn't compete" (*Maus II,* 15). This photograph signifies death and loss, even while, as a kind of "fetish object," it disavows loss. The parents keep it in their bedroom to live with; Art competes with it; and we take it as the ultimately unassimilable fact that it was a child who died unnaturally, before he had the chance to live. The child who could not survive to live his own life—especially in his equivalence with Art and Nadja—becomes the emblem of the incomprehensibility of Holocaust destruction. In her book *Children with a Star,* Debórah Dwork provides a chilling statistic: in Nazi-occupied Europe, only 11 percent of Jewish children survived the war years.[25] Richieu was poisoned by the aunt who hid him so that he might be saved; she poisoned him so that he might not suffer in the death camps. Art reports, "After the war my parents traced down the vaguest rumors, and went to orphanages all over Europe. They couldn't believe he was dead" (*Maus II,* 15). We cannot believe it either: the indeterminacy of the dedication photograph means that this child could be any of us. Because of its anonymity, this photograph, and many others like it, refers to the anonymity of the victims and corpses represented in photographs of concentration and extermination camps. At the end of the volume, Art becomes Richieu and Richieu takes on the role of listener and addressee of Vladek's testimony, a testimony addressed to the dead and the living. "So," Vladek says as he turns over in his bed, "Let's stop, please, your tape recorder. I'm tired from talking, Richieu, and it's enough stories for now" (*Maus II,* 136). Richieu is both a visual presence and a listener—and, as he and Art merge to transmit the tale, he is neither. The child's photograph, visible in other frames portraying Vladek's bedroom, itself becomes the ultimate witness to the survivor's tale. In this role Richieu, or his photograph,

confirms the interminable nature of the mourning in *Maus,* and the endless-
ness of Vladek's tale, a tale subtitled "And here my troubles began." This
is a phrase Spiegelman takes from Vladek's narrative, an ironic aside about
Auschwitz. Reading *Maus II* we realize not only that his troubles began
long before, but that his troubles (and his son's) never end.

If the child's photograph at the beginning of this volume is the emblem
of incomprehensible and unacceptable death, Vladek's photograph at the
end works as a sign of life that reconnects Vladek and Anja after the
liberation (Figure 1.7). "Anja! guess what! A letter from your husband just
came!" "He's in Germany . . . He's had typhus! . . . And here's a picture of
him! My God—Vladek is really alive!" (*Maus II,* 134). Reproduced in the
next frame, but at a slant, jumping out of the frame, is a photograph of the
young Vladek, serious but pleasant, standing in front of a curtain, wearing
a starched, striped camp uniform and hat. He explains the picture: "I passed
once a photo place what had a camp uniform—a new and clean one—to
make souvenir photos." Just as Vladek keeps pictures of the deceased Anja
on his desk, he asserts that "Anja kept this picture always." The photograph
which signifies life and survival is as important, as cherished, as the one
signaling loss and death. But this photograph is particularly disturbing in
that it *stages, performs* the identity of the camp inmate. Vladek wears a
uniform in a souvenir shop in front of what looks like a stage curtain; he
is no longer in the camp but he reenacts his inmate self even as he is trying to
prove—through his ability to pose—that he survived the inmate's usual fate.

1.7

In Anja's eyes the uniform would not call into question the picture's message: "I am alive, I have survived." She last saw Vladek in Auschwitz and would certainly have noticed the difference between this clean uniform and the one he actually must have worn. The uniform would signal to her their common past, their survival, perhaps their hope for a future. It is a picture Vladek could have sent only to *her*—someone else might have misunderstood its performative aspect. For readers of *Maus* this picture plays a different role: it situates itself on a continuum of representational choices, from the authenticity of the photos, to the drawings of humans in "Hell Planet," to the mice masks, to the drawings of mice themselves. This photograph both is documentary evidence (Vladek was in Auschwitz) and isn't (the picture was taken in a souvenir shop). This picture may look like a documentary photograph of the inmate—it may have the appearance of authenticity—but it is merely, and admittedly, a simulation, a dress-up game. The identity of Vladek, the camp survivor, with the man wearing the camp uniform in the picture is purely coincidental—anyone could have had this picture taken in the same souvenir shop—any of us could have, just as perhaps any of us could be wearing uniforms in our dreams, as Art is. Certainly, any of us can wear the horizontally striped shirts Françoise seems to favor (another visual pun?) only further to blur the lines between document and performance. Yet, like Helen Epstein's family pictures, Vladek's photo is also a very particular kind of document, appropriate to a history we cannot "take in."

Breaking the frame, looking intently at the viewer/reader, Vladek's picture dangerously relativizes the identity of the survivor. As listeners of his testimony, as viewers of Art's translation and transmission of that testimony, we are invited to imagine ourselves inside that picture. Like Frieda's picture, Vladek's photo, with all its incongruous elements, suggests a story and *Maus* is that story. With Art and with Vladek, but without Anja, the reader is in what Dori Laub calls "the testimonial chain":

> Because trauma returns in disjointed fragments in the memory of the survivor, the listener has to let these trauma fragments make their impact both on him and on the witness. Testimony is the narrative's address to hearing . . . As one comes to know the survivor, one really comes to know oneself; and that is no simple task . . . In the center of this massive dedicated effort remains a danger, a nightmare, a fragility, a woundedness that defies all healing. (*Testimony*, 71–73)

*Maus* represents the aesthetic of the trauma fragment, the aesthetic of the testimonial chain—an aesthetic that is indistinguishable from the documentary. It is composed of individually framed fragments, each like a still picture imbricated in a border that is closed off from the others. These frames are nevertheless connected to one another in the very testimonial chain that relates the two separate chronological levels, the past and the present, that structure the narrative of *Maus* relating teller to listener. But, once in a while, something breaks out of the rows of frames, or out of the frames themselves, upsetting and disturbing the structure of the entire work. The fragments that break out of the frames are details functioning like Barthes's "punctum"; they have the power of the "fetish" to signal and to disavow an essential loss. Anja Spiegelman, because of her missing voice and her violently destroyed diary, is herself one such point of disturbance, made more so by the photograph that is included among the stylized drawings. And embedded in those fragments—in spite of the conventional fairy-tale ending of the second volume where Vladek and Anja are reunited and Vladek insists that "we were both very happy and lived happy, happy ever after," in spite of the tombstone that enshrines their togetherness in the book's last frame and establishes a seemingly normalized closure—the nightmare, the fragility, the woundedness remain. The power of the photographs Spiegelman includes in *Maus* lies not in their evocation of memory, the connection they can establish between present and past, but in their status as fragments of a history we cannot assimilate. Utterly familiar, especially in the context of the defamiliarizing images of mice and cat drawings, these photographs forge an affiliative look that enables identification: they could be any of ours. At the same time, this same context—both the story of the Holocaust and the cartoon drawings in which they are embedded—makes them strangely unfamiliar, opaque.

*Maus I*, subtitled "My father bleeds history," shows us that this bleeding, in Laub's terms, "defies all healing," and the subtitle to Volume II, "here all my troubles began," shows that they are never absorbed. The three photographs in *Maus*, and the complicated marginal narrative of unassimilable loss that they tell, perpetuate what remains in the two volumes as an incongruity appropriate to the aesthetic of the child of survivors, the aesthetic of postmemory. Like those ghostly images of the former Jakubowicz families, of Chana's lost siblings, they reinforce at once incomprehensibility and presence, a past that will neither fade away nor be integrated into the present.

2

# REFRAMING THE HUMAN FAMILY ROMANCE

The family is an image we seek so desperately.

E. ETHELBERT MILLER

The people in the audience looked at the pictures, and the
people in the pictures looked back at them. They recognized
each other. A Japanese poet has said that, when you look into a
mirror, you do not see your reflection, your reflection, sees you.

EDWARD STEICHEN

*guests*

On February 3, 1993, the sports page of the *New York Times* featured a
touching human interest story, "Riddick Bowe Has Family in Scarsdale":
"They remembered him as a laughing boy, sweet and bright, who graced
their home for two weeks one summer. And then he came back into their
lives as the heavyweight champion of the world." It seems that in the
summer of 1975 the Goldstein family hosted a 7-year-old African-American
child from Brooklyn in their Scarsdale home through the Fresh Air Fund.
Eighteen years later, when they recognized his name on television and in
the newspaper, they contacted him. The reunion revolved around a familiar ritual: perusing the family photograph album. "We gave him a few
photographs of himself, and this was something I never realized about our
middle class values, but he just didn't have many photos from his childhood. He looked at one photo and he said, 'Gee, that looks just like my
daughter.'"[1]

  The Goldsteins identify the impetus for participating in the Fresh Air Fund
as the "sixties ideals" they hope never to lose, and the article celebrates their
generosity, quoting the world's heavyweight champion's memories of "seeing lots of trees" and finding a family who was "very nice" to him: "Being

a little kid, you don't hear much about racism. You figure everyone's the same."

Although I live in Vermont among a lot of trees, I have never participated in the Fresh Air Fund, but I can identify with the Goldsteins' "sixties ideals." Thus, in the aftermath of the Gulf War with its images of Iraqi children hurt by American bombings, my family "adopted" a Bolivian child through an international organization. The advertisement to which we responded featured a photograph of a little Indian girl with beautiful sad eyes, and informed us that for only $60 per quarter, we could make a real difference in a child's life somewhere in the world, a world we saw as profoundly endangered by American military technology. We didn't know much about the particular organization we chose, but their multi-purpose approach to international aid—combining personal sponsorship with family and community assistance—was appealing.

On the form we received, we checked that we wanted to support a male child of our 8-year-old son Gabriel's age, intending to encourage in him fraternal feelings of identification transcending the borders of class and nationality. We chose a Bolivian child for the same reasons—we had recently visited Bolivia with Gabriel; his father Leo was born in Bolivia and has some childhood photos that depict him playing with Aymara age-mates; we knew Spanish, and the landscape of our "foster child's" surroundings would be familiar. Remembering how shocked Gabriel had been when he saw abandoned boys his age roaming through La Paz trying to earn a living by shining shoes, we knew it would not be difficult to get him interested in a "foster brother."

When we received the name, address, and photograph of Secundino Callisaya, from the Altiplano above La Paz, we immediately wrote in Gabriel's name in Spanish about our family, Gabriel, his school and interests, and we included a picture of Gabriel and his brothers, Oliver and Alex. The response soon followed. The polite letter in awkward English, translated (from Spanish? Aymara?) and typed by a member of the organization's Bolivian office, told us about Secundino's life on the Altiplano, his family and his school, and assured us that Secundino's mother and his much-older brother both worked very hard. Our subsequent contact has remained similarly mediated, including the quarterly reports about improvements that our dollars are making possible in the Altiplano clean-water plan, in the local clinic and immunization programs, and in the Callisaya household. Gabriel has remained interested in Secundino and would have liked a more direct and informative correspondence.

I have begun to understand the determining role of the mediating organization with its ready-made communication kits. But I have been unable to let go of my ambivalence and discomfort with the philanthropic role I am playing, nor of my questions about whether our modest contribution actually benefits Secundino and his community. Thus, when a personalized letter subsequently arrived asking us to adopt another child—a beautiful 5-year-old Indian boy whose glossy photograph, staring intently at its addressee, was included in the envelope—I politely, though painfully, declined.

What does this gesture of "adopting" a disadvantaged child into the middle-class nuclear family and its family album mean—the Goldsteins' impulse to become a Fresh Air Fund host family and mine to participate in the international sponsorship program? What ideologies underlie it and why do they appear so suspect to me? And how can photographs help us to read the complex feelings and motivations determining these experiences?

Looking closely at the Goldsteins' photographs reproduced on the *New York Times* page I find a more complicated narrative than the upbeat human interest story suggests. The four slightly overlapping pictures on the page display, in fact, some of the same, perhaps inevitable, failures of connection that have characterized Gabriel's relationship with Secundino (Figures 2.1–2.4). The first shows the smiling African-American boy posing in a back yard on a bicycle. It is a counter-illustration to Sandy Goldstein's story about Riddick's very first ride on a bike, when he ran into a fence, leaving dents in her son's bike and the fence. According to the article, the accident left Michael "slightly ticked off" to this day. But what happened to Riddick, I want to ask?

The other pictures focus on the two boys: "If racism isn't taught," Bowe is quoted as saying, "you're just a black kid and a white kid together," and the pictures seem to illustrate just that. But do they? In the second picture, taken at the zoo and featuring fences and bars, the two boys are looking at a peacock. But while the young guest politely looks at the bird, the host child climbs on the fence and faces the camera, thus subtly asserting his centrality in the family image. The third photograph is the only one in which the two boys stand close to each other: their legs are far apart though their upper bodies lean into the center of the image, as though they had been told to pose together. But a subtle competition dictates this pose as well: Michael puts his right hand on the garden hose which is positioned between the two arms with which Riddick hugs his own waist—perhaps indicating that the guest has no claim on this household object? In the last image Michael sits

2.1

2.2

2.3

2.4

on a bike, smiling brightly at the camera; Riddick looks down at the picnic table, his hands just barely holding on to the handlebars of a bicycle, perhaps illustrating his memory in the article that "when I left, for the first time in my life, I cried."

As I study these pictures probably more attentively than any of the participants themselves would, it seems to me that the desire to believe that "everybody's the same" is quickly qualified for the young Riddick. These photographs, after all, until very recently graced only the Goldsteins' album and constructed their memories, not Riddick Bowe's. I wonder, therefore, what layers of feeling are suppressed beneath the drawing of a smiley face that the adult Bowe gave to Michael Goldstein: "Bowe signed a magazine cover to Michael 'from your old buddy Riddick' and he drew one of those smiley faces. The Goldsteins got a kick out of a large man who hits people for a living drawing a smiley face."

But could my skeptical reading of these photographs be dictated by the same "middle-class values" which left Sandy Goldstein so surprised at the absence of photos in the history of an inner-city child? Could the awkwardness that I see in the poses be explained more simply by Riddick's unfamiliarity with photographic conventions and the codes of posing, codes which the young Michael seems to have mastered so well? Only the first photograph of Riddick, in fact, corresponds to the conventions of the family album: a smiling boy, central in the frame, displaying one of the necessary accoutrements of middle-class childhood, the bicycle. Having to share the frame with a child of longer-standing training in these conventions would then make his pictures more hesitant and tenuous, his return look in them less direct. Sitting on the bike, Riddick can look out at the camera and the viewer, but, lacking any visible possessions in the later photographs, he looks down: there is no available look for the temporary guest from the inner-city neighborhood, no easy space for integration into the middle-class Scarsdale family album and family romance.

I find it equally difficult to read Secundino's look in the photographs which were no doubt taken by the organization's officer. Secundino, standing in front of a whitewashed wall, unsmiling, his arms hanging down, stares out quite intently at an unknown world beyond the camera lens. In another image, standing next to his smiling mother in front of a building that could not be his own house, he has no distinct space of his own. He does not look into the lens; his look does not engage us, the return look it invites is not familial, not identificatory, but neither is it disidentificatory or anti-affiliative. There may be a shared desire to relate familially, but no obvious way to do so. Even if our family albums were up to date, I doubt that we would have remembered to include Secundino's picture.

The conventions of family photography, with its mutuality of confirming looks that construct a set of familial roles and hierarchies, reinforce the power of the notion of "family." The pervasiveness of these conventions opens the family image and album to the possibility of broad-based identification and affiliation I have already discussed. Paradoxically, however, these very same conventions and practices can also support the antidemocratic aspects of photography, drawing borders around a circumscribed group and strengthening its power to include and thus also to exclude. It is not simply a question of class: box cameras have been available to working-class families throughout much of this century, as the work of Jo Spence and Valerie Walkerdine and the texts of many working-class writers and photographers attest. It is that representational conventions consolidate family and group identity—with its dreams, fantasies, and aspirations—whatever the particular group might be. In the case of the Goldsteins' pictures and mine, they admit the outsider but visibly as a temporary guest. Through his marginal presence and through his subtle difference, he helps to delineate the central group with its elaborate systems of representation, from which he is, and to some extent remains, excluded. Or, if he is admitted into the particular bourgeois family romance of the family album in the mid- to late-twentieth-century United States, it is to support the ideologies that undergird it, that is, as the desiring other, fantasizing that "everyone's the same," and thus supporting the dominant desire to veil inequality and exclusion.

How does the family album represent otherness? How much diversity can it accommodate, and how does that negotiation between difference and identity shift at different historical moments? Through certain common strategies, attributable to the powerful idea of "family," the family album, in our historical moment particularly, can transform difference into specular mirroring in order to include children like Riddick Bowe and Secundino Callisaya and to promote the fantasy that "everyone's the same." But this transformation is never uncomplicated, for the family album does not forget to reassert its boundaries of difference at certain strategic moments. The structure of the family album and of the familial gaze—the affiliative and specular looks it constructs—can suggest what happens when, in this way, diversity is reconfigured as familiality. It can expose the relationship between family photography and the ideological structures of—in this case—the American family romance with its ever shifting meanings.

## the human family

If one instrument helped construct and perpetuate the ideology which links the notion of universal humanity to the idea of familiality, it is the camera and its by-products, the photographic image and the family album. Jo Spence and Patricia Holland go so far as to claim that "Cameras and film have been developed with the family in mind."[2] Pierre Bourdieu has demonstrated the integral connection between the ever-spreading practice of photography and the ideology of the modern family: "photographic practice only exists and subsists for most of the time by virtue of its *family function* or rather by the function conferred upon it by the family group, namely that of solemnizing and immortalizing the high points of family life, . . . of reinforcing the integration of the family group by reasserting the sense that it has both of itself and of its unity."[3]

But the widely accepted sense of photography as a "natural language"—a 1989 Kodak advertisement claimed, for example, that "150 years ago a language was invented that everyone understood"—helped to extend photography's familial gaze beyond the nuclear family's domestic domain and to endow it with vaster and more global ambitions. Thus photography could support an expanded notion of a *human* family, a liberal ideology of universalism that has remained powerful throughout the post–World War II period and that is exhibited on a very small scale in the Goldsteins' family album and in the strategies used by many charitable organizations.

In thinking about how the ideology of the family and the technology of photography support and reinforce each other during this historical moment, I began to wonder about how family albums treat images of "others."[4] Thus I came to look at a rather unusual set of "family pictures," those of the 1955 Museum of Modern Art exhibition *The Family of Man,* curated by Edward Steichen, then the Director of Photography at MOMA. It is no coincidence that the first "blockbuster" museum exhibit should connect family with photography, or that it should superimpose familiality with universality. *The Family of Man* attracted 270,000 visitors to MOMA in its first fifteen weeks, more visitors than any other exhibit had seen until that time. Following the show at MOMA, the 503 images from 68 countries then toured 37 countries in six separate editions. The equally successful book, deliberately produced in inexpensive editions (one cost one dollar) could be found in most middle-class American living rooms in the 1950s and 1960s. Many treasure this book even now. As Steichen claims in his introduction, his exhibit "is the most ambitious and challenging project photography has ever attempted . . . It was conceived as a mirror of the universal elements and emotions in the everydayness of life—as a mirror of the essential oneness of mankind throughout the world."[5] Steichen and his assistant Wayne Miller chose the 503 photographs from among 2 million which were sent to New York "from every corner of the earth . . . from individuals, collections and files." The 273 photographers were "amateurs and professionals, famed and unknown."

Several ambitious ideas and generous impulses underlie Steichen's conception of the exhibit. In his autobiography, *A Life in Photography,* Steichen links it directly to his own war experience as an aerial photographer in World War I and a naval photographer in the Pacific in World War II, and to his attempt to use photography as an instrument with which to prevent war. After organizing three exhibitions of war photos at MOMA—the last on the Korean War—he felt he had failed. "Although I had presented war in all its grimness in the three exhibitions, . . . I had not incited people into taking open and united action against war itself . . . I came to the conclusion that I had been working from a negative approach, that what was needed was a positive statement on what a wonderful thing life was, how marvelous people were, and, above all, how alike people were in all parts of the world."[6] Stressing what one of Steichen's assistants called the "universal brotherhood of man," the *Family of Man* exhibit allowed him to envision the power of the medium in a new way: "Photography can be a moving force in the world as I saw it in the war. It can lift individuals as subjects from the humdrum and turn them into symbols of universal humanity," the assistant quotes him saying.[7]

Photographic images could thus represent the universality of human experience and, because of the particular qualities of the medium as Steichen saw it—its "natural" communicative abilities and its powerful illusion of unmediated and "truthful" representation—they could be effective instruments of that universality as well. In an article published in *Daedalus* in 1960, Steichen stresses that possibility: "Long before the birth of a word language the caveman communicated by visual images. The invention of photography gave visual communication its most simple, direct, universal language." It may have been to stress this universal form of communication, often also attributed to music, that Steichen chose the image of the Peruvian Indian boy joyfully playing the flute as the emblem of the exhibit to punctuate its sequence at many intervals and to serve as the cover illustration of the book. Steichen's claim for the universal comprehensibility of the photographs seemed to be corroborated in the response enjoyed by the *Family of*

*Man* exhibit: "The audiences not only understand this visual presentation, they also participate in it, and identify themselves with the images."[8]

In the aftermath of World War II and the Korean War, in view of an escalating Cold War and an increasing nuclear threat, and in the midst of growing movements of national liberation and decolonization, the invocation of human universality had the force of a powerful political statement, particularly emerging from the United States. To demonstrate an overriding human equality was to reinvoke Enlightenment notions of a universal brotherhood that directly contradicted all-too-recent Nazi ideologies of racial hierarchy which denied humanity to the greater part of the earth's population. The exhibition was an attempt to assert close human bonds across increasing political divisions between East and West, capitalism and communism, colonizers and colonized, rich and poor.

Appealing to the most compelling aspects of American liberalism, *The Family of Man* used the camera, the museum, and the book as tools of change aligned to political institutions such as the United Nations, which is itself prominently featured in the exhibit, "determined to reaffirm faith in fundamental human rights, in the dignity and worth of the human person, in the equal rights of men and women and of nations large and small" (184).

If today the familial humanism of Steichen's *Family of Man* appears naive in its too easy erasure of particularity and difference, we must remember the political context in which difference had so recently been used as a justification for genocide. Today, in the aftermath of the Cold War, the hopes of decolonization have shattered against the rise of new forms of racism and persecution. The memory of the Holocaust has become a postmemory. As American and Western European intellectuals continue to search for a usable discourse of commonality and difference and for forceful roles for the United States and Europe in a shifting global map, new humanisms and universalisms and new invocations of Enlightenment values are emerging. New photographic exhibits repeat the strategies Steichen made so successful. The familial photographic representations of *The Family of Man* might provide a measure of the contradictory grounds for this renewed interest in humanistic discourses.[9]

The key to *The Family of Man*'s appeal lies in the familial gaze it focuses on the global sphere with the aim of revealing points of intersection between familial relation, on the one hand, and cross-racial and cross-national interaction, on the other. A familial gaze can transform diversity into specular mirroring and can reshape global issues into domestic concerns.[10] It can undo the seemingly irreconcilable differences between Spiegelman's mice, cats, and pigs, revealing these diverse creatures with competing interests to all be equally and interrelatedly "human" instead.

The familial gaze emerges out of the elements of family photography. The illusion that photographs simply record a preexisting external reality, the fact that still photographs freeze particular moments in time, and the ambiguity that results from the still picture's absent context all help to perpetuate a mythology of the family as stable and united, static and monolithic. The photograph's perceived transparency and universal comprehensibility, combined with its pervasive presence within family life, at least in the West, enable Steichen to promote a liberal humanist agenda based on familiality. The positivist modes of reading that photography engendered, moreover, serve further to disguise the exhibit's intricate ideological constructedness. Thereby the exhibit and, with it, the institution of the museum itself, is encoded within the realm of everyday life. Inasmuch as it could be photographically recorded and disseminated, universal humanity can thus be normalized and made available as "real." On the level of representation itself, then, domesticity and transparency subsume the layered contradictions inherent in aesthetics and politics.

To use the notion of family as its primary instrument of universalization, *The Family of Man* needs to represent an image of familial relations that would be widely recognizable, applicable, and exportable. In Alan Sekula's terms, it "universalizes the bourgeois nuclear family, suggesting a globalized, utopian family album, a family romance imposed on every corner of the earth."[11] In doing so, it follows and popularizes the prevalent familial theories of the 1950s—Talcott Parsons's structural functionalism and Claude Lévi-Strauss's universalized incest taboo. Parsons universalizes the nuclear family as the most advanced and, in his terms, differentiated and progressive of familial organizations, based on strict gender divisions into male instrumentality and female expressiveness. One could argue that Steichen follows Parsons in promoting the patriarchal bourgeois nuclear family as the norm and standard against which other arrangements are measured. And one could see, as well, a reflection of Lévi-Strauss's structural anthropology. The incest taboo, Lévi-Strauss's universalized Oedipus complex, as well as the system of reciprocal exchanges of women, and the universally present relations of consanguinity, alliance, and descent, demonstrate the characteristics of the modern nuclear family to be structurally equivalent to other arrangements rather than specific to industrial capitalism.

Sekula usefully invokes the Freudian notion of the family romance to underscore Steichen's universalization of one prevalent familial model. Freud's "family romance" is a shared individual fantasy of mythic origin: the child's dream of parental omnipotence and infallibility which, when shattered, becomes the fantasy of replacing the father with a different, a richer and more noble one, in Freud's terms, a king or emperor.[12] This is more than a sexual fantasy encouraging oedipal desire: it is also a fantasy of class aspiration, an economic fantasy of enrichment. The family romance is primarily a narrative structure, making narrative space for the ways in which the family becomes a locus for intersecting dreams of sexual fulfillment, property, and social status. Located in childhood, it reveals a point where public and private, social and psychological structures can collapse within one another. Photographs enable us to locate some of these fantasy structures in the visual and to read, through the monocular lens determining the image's structure, the circumscribed direction that fantasy takes.

*The Family of Man* disseminates the fantasies of Steichen and his contemporaries, located in a specific space and time and articulated from a particular viewpoint. It can be read as a narrative of the idealization of the bourgeois nuclear family and its social, psychological, and economic foundations. Including the culturally and economically "other" in the exhibit undergirds the power of the exhibit's author and organizer as both the subject and the object of his own fantasy. Victor Burgin's 1990 digital work "Family Romances" invokes Steichen's *Family of Man* in just this spirit:

> Identification with the perfect parents in an international arena underlies the 1955 photographic exhibition *The Family of Man*. Prevalent opinion in the United States during the immediate post-war years saw the country as being in a tutelary position of benevolent authority towards the rest of the world. Appropriately, the particular version of 'the family' which this exhibition projected into every part of the globe was the domestic ideal of the Eisenhower years.[13]

In the conception of Steichen's exhibit, the family functions as an idealized haven of potential protection from discord and war. At the same time the family becomes an instrument of political intervention: in its role of fragile space itself in need of protection from the dangers of global politics, it attempts to act as an effective sphere of influence and transformation. If Art Spiegelman uses family pictures to reveal the ironies of this familial mythology in the face of war and genocide, on the one hand, and the family's own Oedipal psychodramas, on the other, Steichen tries to revive this same traditional familial mythos as a means of positive political action. But can it still be workable "after such knowledge?"

## the familial gaze

Steichen's "family album" progresses thematically from love and marriage, to birth, childhood, adolescence and courtship, adulthood, and branches out to consider aspects of adult life, such as work, dancing, singing, eating, religion, death and mourning, war, loneliness, politics and justice. It returns to childhood at the end, opening out toward new beginnings. While some of the images conform to the conventions of familial snapshot photography, others are more akin to ethnographic photography, documentary photography, and art photography. Steichen's album, moreover, does not just have the function Bourdieu associates with the family album, that of "solemnizing and immortalizing the high points of family life" (*Photography*, 19). Although "happy" and poignant images predominate, there are also pictures of hunger, begging, war, loneliness, and grief, even a few images of domestic discord. Steichen does not attempt to suppress the underside of his "universal brotherhood." If this is a family album, it is clearly one that stretches the limits of the genre, not least because of the diverse cultures and physiognomies it includes: couples from France and the USA kiss or marry next to couples from Japan, Czechoslovakia, India, Sweden, and Mexico; children from India, South Africa, Botswana, Austria, and the USA play near one another; farmers from Iran, Indonesia, Japan, China, Italy, Ireland, and the USA till the land in the same exhibit space.

In his exhibit Steichen had to create an identificatory, familial look which would effect the affiliative mutuality and specularity to which he aspired: "They recognized each other." He had to suture his viewers into images most of which are bound to diverge radically from their own self-representations and their own habitual processes of recognition. The spectatorial look invited by the exhibit and album had to be able to transform a global space of vast differences and competing interests into a domestic space structured by likeness and specularity.

It is my argument that the family is in itself traversed and constituted by a series of "familial" looks that place different individuals into familial relation within a field of vision. When I visually engage with others familially, when I look through my family's albums, I enter a network of looks that dictate affiliative feelings, positive or negative feelings of recognition that can span miles and generations: I "recognize" my great-grandmother because I am told that she is an ancestor, not because she is otherwise in any way similar or identifiable to me. It is the context of the album that creates the relationship, not necessarily any preexistent sign. And when I look at her picture, I feel as though she also recognizes me. We share a familial visual field in which we see even as we are seen. When Barthes finds the winter-garden photograph, he knows his mother and also wants to be known by her. When Artie looks at Richieu's picture, he both sees and wants to be seen, desiring thus to bridge an unbridgeable distance and to undo the effects of death and separation. As Steichen puts it, "in corroboration of the words of a Japanese poet, 'When you look into a mirror, you do not see your reflection, your reflection sees you.'"

When Barthes omits the winter-garden photo of his mother from his book, he delineates the boundaries of the familial look and excludes his readers from it. Steichen tries an opposite strategy: he subsumes a complex set of intersecting gazes and looks under an overarching affiliative look of familiality. The subjects photographed look at one another within the picture and at the photographer who looks at them, and the reader and museum visitor observe this interaction, usually through the photographer's lens and perspective.[14] In *The Family of Man* these looks are mediated by enormous cultural, economic, gender, and racial differences, and by the institutional gazes of ethnography, anthropology, tourism, journalism, or art photography. But, in Steichen's conception, they are also mediated by a familial gaze of mutual recognition which is meant to override these alienating forces dividing subject from object. What specific strategies and principles of selection did Steichen devise in order to further and expand this transcendent recognition, investing it with global proportions? How does his human family metaphor work and what can it tell us about the family's representational frames?

Reading the exhibit, we can identify several predominant strategies, strategies that allow us not only to understand the workings of *The Family of Man* but to explore, as well, some of the more troubling aspects of familial looking: individualization, naturalization, decontextualization, differentiation within identification, and the universalization of one hegemonic familial organization. Some of these strategies have been identified and virulently criticized by commentators at various moments since the exhibit enjoyed its monumental success. These critiques, in themselves—most notably by Roland Barthes in the 1950s, Edmundo Desnoes in the 1960s, and Alan Sekula in the late 1970s—form an integral part of the story of *The Family of Man*. In looking at what makes Steichen's vision work so powerfully for his audiences, one inevitably encounters, as well, the problematic strategies he used, and these critical readings inform my reading of Steichen's exhibit. Interestingly, however, the 1980s and 1990s have given rise to more

2.5

recuperative and sympathetic readings such as Eric J. Sandeen's effort to "recover some of that founding power"—perhaps an echo of the new humanisms of this, our, moment.[15]

The specularity that Steichen envisioned—to produce the sense that "everybody's the same"—had to occur on the level of the individual and of
relations among individuals, and, in fact, the album's images are predominantly limited to individuals and couples, removed from their social, political, and economic context. Thus, the album begins with a series of couples
of diverse origin, hugging and kissing, in various poses of erotic attachment.

Robert Doisneau's famous picture is emblematic, I believe, for the entire
album (Figure 2.5). The picture is clearly taken in Paris on the banks of the
Seine. In the foreground a small child stands on a bench looking left, beyond
the frame; a policeman stands in the center, looking at a woman sitting on
a bench at frame right. She contemplates, quite intently, a kissing couple

barely visible through the bars of the fence that divides the two planes of the photograph, because they are standing behind the three central figures on a lower level of the park. The kiss completely absorbs them, but evades the authoritative gaze of the policeman and that of the child. Only the woman sees them, whether judgmentally, longingly, or approvingly, we don't know. The kiss occurs on a different visual plane, outside the space of the social, challenging the nuclear family structure that dominates the foreground, with its mother, father, and child figures. These seemingly "private" candid images, which give the erroneous impression of occurring outside of the space of the camera's surveillance or intrusion, make the position of the camera inherently ambiguous and contradictory. Love conquers all, love attracts our spectatorial look, deflecting our attention from the public life depicted in the rest of the image. Global, legal, and social issues are addressed on the individual and the familial levels: the background of the image moves into the foreground and absorbs our look. Like the woman, we conspire with the couple against the policeman. Eroticizing the social with her/our desire, we arrive at Steichen's "brotherhood": a seemingly singular, individual connection, forging familial ties, across private/public divides.[16]

The fantasy that structures the entire exhibit is this fantasy of the hug and the kiss with which it starts, the fantasy that global, legal, and social problems might be resolved as we hug, kiss, and make up. The primary unit of interaction in Steichen's family is the couple: heterosexual courting or married couples, two children playing, two women talking, two men working together. "We two form a multitude" is the recurring phrase that runs over several pages depicting a diverse series of couples. But we must consider that the many couples, enacting this friendship and marriage fantasy throughout the album, are all, with the exception of one image of two young boys, heterosexual and of the same race or ethnicity: no chances are taken in this familial solution to global strife.

To consolidate the individual affiliation and identification between the people in the audience and the people in the pictures, the exhibit invokes nature over culture, thus diminishing, if not erasing, pronounced differences due to culture and history, and also thus naturalizing and sentimentalizing the institution of the family. Roland Barthes points this out in one of the most scathing of his *Mythologies* devoted to the Paris showing of "La Grande Famille des hommes" in 1956: "This myth of the human 'condition' rests on a very old mystification, which always consists in placing Nature at the bottom of History."[17] The exhibit is framed by majestic images of sky, stars, and oceans, risking that the important distinction between "nature" and "human nature," between the biological and the social/psychological will be blurred. Thus, within this frame viewers experience human "nature" as pervasive, as common to all, as undifferentiated, like the ocean and the sky. To place human life on the level of nature, Steichen needs to tease out the most fundamental elements of human ritual, recognizable and acceptable to everyone in their sameness and repetition as universal.

The strong emphasis on nature and its broad definition, covering human nature as well, carries the risk that events represented in the album will be ascribed to human nature, thus erasing historical agency. For example, viewers might attribute the images of hunger, deportation, devastated cities, war, and violent death, as well as the images of strife within the family, to a constant human nature. And if the album indeed implies that war is as natural and as universal as kissing and singing, then it might also appear to be as inevitable, directly contradicting Steichen's explicit purpose of invoking universality to prevent war. The risk, for example, is that viewers might read the large transparency of the H-bomb explosion which took up an entire room at the end of the exhibition as "natural."

Could it be that agency and political change, clearly among Steichen's primary goals, are actually antithetical to the familial look the album fosters, a look based on the elevation of nature over culture and history, and that, in fact, Steichen's means do not ultimately support his ends? If the exhibit expresses a wish or desire, a utopian aspiration on Steichen's part, thus encouraging intervention to make his utopia a reality, he may well be hampered by the indexical and iconic aspects of photography, by the fact that photographs tend to be read as mimetic representations of what is rather than as wishful constructions of what might be.

Perhaps the most troubling aspect of *The Family of Man* is the decontextualized exhibition of the images. Although the country of origin is provided on each photograph, they are not dated, which gives the impression of synchrony, the antithesis of the possibility of change—Matthew Brady's civil war image is next to images of World War II, for example. If this juxtaposition is meant to emphasize a reassuringly unchanging continuity in family relations and human nature to support the universality of the album it also serves to underscore the perpetuity of hunger and war. If this repetition and continuity are inherent in the recognition of the familial look, they also directly contradict the possibility of intervention and transformation, especially because this familial look represses its disidentifications and the specificity of its temporal and geographical location, and thus further isolates itself from agency.

By radically de- and recontextualizing the images, Steichen exerts strong authorial control over the reading process, invoking and cultivating an affiliative look that underscores similarity and relationship, even as it ultimately represses agency and change. As Barthes concludes: "I rather fear that the final justification of all this Adamism is to give to the immobility of the world the alibi of a 'wisdom' and a 'lyricism' which only make the gestures of man look eternal the better to defuse them" (*Mythologies*, 102).

Even granting that Steichen's strategies of individualization, naturalization, and decontextualization serve the larger purpose of constructing an effective familial spectatorial gaze, however, I look at some of the album's pages and, where I should see specularity, I begin to see subtle differences. Even as the family album is enlarged to include diversity, a centrally North American gaze asserts reassuring limits. Let us consider, for example, the images of four extended families consciously posing as units for the camera (Figures 2.6–2.9). They are all rural farming families and thus similar to one another. But while the Sicilian and the U.S. family are shown in indoor settings, the Japanese and Botswanan families are outdoors. And only the members of the U.S. family, though agricultural, participate in a tradition of representation: they are surrounded by family portraits that grace their walls. Such a subtle play with difference within identity might serve on the one hand to establish the specularity desired—*the Bushmen have families like us they are farmers like us*—even as it confirms, on the other, Western museum-visitors in their own distinct identity: *We, unlike them, have our distinct domestic spaces, we have pictures on our walls*. From this insight only a small step leads to the next—*We can admit their picture into our album, onto our coffee table without threat, because their difference has been acknowledged. They do not threaten to invade our space; they can become like us, but we don't have to become like them*.

The exhibit and the album shape an ultimately reassuring dissimilarity even within their overriding universalizing frame, assuring the implied European and the European-American viewer that their humanism is, in Etienne Balibar's terms, a "humanism of differences" and not a "humanism of identity" or of "absolute civic equality."[18] Two photographs of mothers, each with two small children, illustrate this (Figures 2.10, 2.11). In the picture taken by Wayne Miller in the USA, a young white mother is lying on a bed looking into space, just past the little girl to her right, who is cradling a small baby. The three figures form a closed and close triangle: their bodies are interconnected in the traditional iconography of Madonna with children. The camera is clearly a familiar object that does not intrude on the intimacy of the scene: it should not surprise us to learn that this is a picture of the photographer's wife and children. Maternity is sentimentalized in the soft-

2.7

2.8

2.9

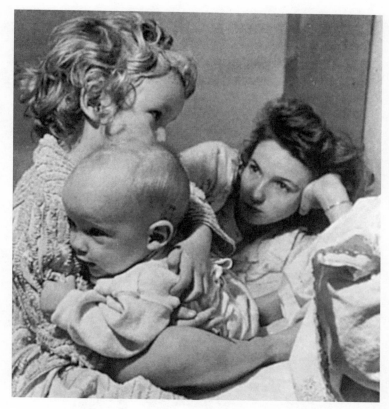

2.10

ness of the pose and the light, and is seen to pass down from mother to daughter-apprentice. The figures are comfortably settled in a protected domestic space and iconographic representation that both seem to disguise the mother's distracted unfocused look, the absence of a visual interaction between her and her children.

An entirely different image also from the USA is Consuelo Kanaga's best-known photograph and Steichen's favorite in the entire exhibit. Photographed from a very low angle, it depicts a tall and very thin black woman standing in front of a white brick wall, resting one arm on a small boy at her right side while a little girl stands to her left. The three figures look not at each other but at the camera. The woman is wearing a much-too-small sweater with two safety pins in front, and a scarf tied into a turban. The children are healthy-looking and cleanly though poorly dressed. Their looks are intent but not easily readable: the mother looks tired and resigned to a

2.11

tough life, the children look confrontational, perhaps suspicious or curious, maybe intrigued by the large camera and the itinerant white woman who came into their community to take pictures. In spite of the protective gesture with which the mother holds the children close to her, there is no warmth or comfort in this picture, no domesticity or circularity. The three figures are more directly engaged with the intrusive photographer than with one another.

Whereas Miller's image fits into a long-standing tradition of mother-child representation—from Leonardo, Raphael, and del Sarto—Kanaga's echoes the ethnographic iconography of the 1930s images of the Farm Security Administration, amply represented in other parts of the exhibit. Maternity and mother-child relations are very different for these two families. Perhaps, then, we are not all the same just because we all—culturally—share maternity and childhood. The Cuban writer Edmundo Desnoes, revealing some of his own cultural prejudices, writes in 1967 of the "visual lies," such as this one, which structure *The Family of Man*: "an indigenous New Guinea couple is hugging next to couples from Italy, North America and France; love in the jungle and in ignorance is not the same as in civilization and among commodities."[19] Roland Barthes's comment is even more biting: "But why not ask the parents of Emmet Till, the young Negro assassinated by the Whites, what *they* think of *The Great Family of Man*? . . . It will never be fair to confuse in a purely gestural identity the colonial and the Western worker (let us also ask the North African workers of the Goutte d'Or district in Paris what they think of *The Great Family of Man*)" (*Mythologies*, 101–102).

But is not the establishment of difference, albeit unconscious, as essential to the exhibit's success as the cultivation of similarity? Does not the African-American mother in her very contrast, in her external unspecified location, confirm the white mother in her domesticity and specificity? That contrast is necessary to the European-American museum visitor's look, a look which must mix a mirroring recognition with a sense of distinct identity. Barthes and Desnoes object by invoking the excluded look of Emmet Till's parents or of the guest-worker from the Goutte d'Or. As left-wing intellectuals, they are trained to perceive the omissions that Steichen's strategies disguise. Contrary to what Steichen might have desired, the look that is cultivated in *The Family of Man* is the look of the middle-class European and European-American museumgoer. If it is a familial look, then it illustrates how the familial look operates in relation to disidentification as well as identification, how it invokes alterity as well as identity, how it insists on drawing up boundaries that ultimately enclose it.

Steichen inadvertently admits this in one of his most ambiguous narratives about foreign showings of the exhibit: "On the final day of the exhibition [in Guatemala City], several thousand Indians from the hills of Guatemala came on foot or mule back to see it. An American visitor said it was like a religious experience to see these barefoot country people who could not read or write walk silently through the exhibition gravely studying each picture

with rapt attention" (*A Life in Photography,* ch. 13). If this is "like a religious experience," it is clearly that of the American visitor and not the
Guatemalan Indians. For him it would confirm the fact that even though he
could read and write and they could not, photographic images offered a
shared medium of communication. But what did the Indian visitors see? Did
they recognize themselves, did they recognize their similarity to the European subjects, or the European subjects' similarity to them? Did they enjoy
seeing themselves as represented by others, a decentered and therefore
potentially illuminating look?

The images themselves would make that difficult, for even though South
American native populations are represented along with many other non-
Western subjects, those images are overwhelmingly attributed to European
and American photographers and originate in journals or photographic
services such as *Life, Magnum, or Rapho Guillumette.* In the photographs'
original contexts of production, the camera gazes tended to belong to
European and American photographers who created images from their own
perspectives, mostly for their own viewers. For example, we see Guatemala
through Lisa Larsen's image published in *Life* (p. 29), Cuba through Eve
Arnold of *Magnum* (p. 31), Botswana through Nat Farbman of *Life* (p. 35),
and South Africa through Constance Stuart of *Black Star* (p. 34). There are
exceptions: most of the Russian photographs are from the Soviet service
*Sovfoto;* many Mexican images are by Mexican photographer Alvarez-
Bravo; and the Polish images are by Roman Vishniac. Still, 163 of 273
photographers are from the United States and approximately 88 of the
503 pictures originated in *Life* magazine. Just as Steichen self-confirmingly
quotes the line of "a Japanese poet" but does not name him or her, so the
exhibit's images grant a more developed subjectivity to the Western subject
and viewer.

Even if the Guatemalan Indians might enjoy seeing themselves as they are
seen by others, they could not help noticing the power differentials, and the
overwhelming control of the medium exercised by a specifically located
European or European-American gaze. How are we to imagine these encounters between the photographers and their subjects? What kinds of
power and economic relationships does the exhibition's familial discourse
suppress? I thought about this when, in 1995, I visited the Isla del Sol on
Lake Titicaca between Bolivia and Peru. As we tourists disembarked for a
brief visit of the island and a climb to the spring that is said to be the source
of Inca civilization, we were accosted by a group of native women and
children eager to sell us inexpensive hand-made souvenirs: woven bracelets

and hair ribbons, flowers and herbs. It was clear that this isolated population depended on the tourists for their livelihood. An economy of dollars, Bolivianos, and pesos had developed there with tourists acting as money changers as well as consumers. But visits seemed to be infrequent and, that day, the tourists were tired from their long trips over the mountains and were unwilling participants in the exchange. As a last resort many of the local women, dressed in the colorful dresses and the bowler hats of the Andes, brought up another suggestion: "Fotografia! fotografia! con niño! un dolar." "Take my picture, with my baby, for a dollar."

In selling their own image along with other souvenirs, the women on the Isla del Sol expose the economic underpinnings of a relationship the tourists wish to perceive as mutual. The women expose the inequities that the tourist industry and the ideologies of *The Family of Man* try to disguise. When North American or European visitors, whether ordinary tourists or art photographers, come into a context like the Isla del Sol and the local inhabitants become flat images to be shown off in albums or exhibited in museums they will never see, then the relationship between photographer and model becomes a relationship of unequal exchange which must be compensated, financially or otherwise. The women of the Isla del Sol know something that the producers of *The Family of Man* and many generations of tourists have wished to forget. And Steichen's exhibit works powerfully to disguise this knowledge.

## the traffic in photographs

The high point of Steichen's exhibit was its visit to Moscow as part of the large American Exhibition in 1959. *The Family of Man* went with Steichen and his brother-in-law Carl Sandburg to represent the United States along with automobiles, model homes, toys, and voting machines. Like other foreign showings, this one was sponsored by USIA and Coca Cola.

"I stood in one spot . . . and photographed the people as they looked at the section devoted to parents and babies," Steichen writes about the Moscow showing. "I decided that, if I were to say the snapshots had been made in Wisconsin or Iowa or New England, the statement would be accepted without question" (*A Life in Photography*, ch. 13). Proud of Moscow's overwhelming response, Steichen dismisses *Pravda*'s review: "The satire was expressed in complaints that the exhibition did not reveal certain 'necessary' statistics. For example, we should have given the figures on how many more babies died in Timbuctoo than in New York or Chicago." He also dismisses the controversy around George Silk's image of the little Chinese boy with an empty rice bowl which, at the insistence of the Soviets, had to be removed, although the Americans argued that it was just "a universal image of hunger."[20] And he neglects to mention the incident in which a Nigerian student, reinforcing the unidimensionality of the family-romance structure, tore down several pictures because, as he said, "the collection portrayed white Americans and other Europeans in dignified cultural states—wealthy, healthy, and wise and American and West Indian Negroes, Africans, and Asiatics as comparatively social inferiors—sick, raggerty, destitute, and physically maladjusted."[21] Needless to say, the image of a lynching, prominent in the United States exhibit, was eliminated from all foreign showings and from the book, just as the H-bomb explosion was not shown in Japan.

In the late 1950s, when I might have seen the exhibit, I was geographically closer to Moscow than to New York. But as far as I know *The Family of Man* did not travel to Rumania, where I grew up. There is only one image from Rumania in the album, a tiny picture on a page devoted to dancing children from many countries. The Rumanian image, by Werner Bischof of *Magnum Photos,* depicts a number of little girls wearing traditional headscarves, dancing the *hora* in a very disorderly circle. In the book, the picture is small; I study it with my magnifying glass. The girls seem to be of the age I would have been in the late 1950s, about 7 or 8. Had I seen the exhibit at the time—and I am sure that had it come to Bucharest, my parents and I would have gone, as we hungrily attended every foreign movie, exposition, or fair—would I have recognized myself in this picture, or in any other? Would I have felt included in *The Family of Man*'s visual field? Yes and no.

Sadly, I realize that although these are my age- and country-mates, these little girls are not like me. The exhibit's Rumania is a folklorized timeless representation (the picture is not dated, of course)—an eternal girlhood that might or might not have coincided temporally with my own childhood. Its unspecified countryside location diverges radically from my urban life in Bucharest, and only a few girls I knew would have worn the huge head scarves worn by the little girls in the picture. This image is not representative of my urban life in Rumania, except perhaps for the large white fence which, if I stretched a bit, I could read as an metaphor for the Iron Curtain behind which we felt so trapped.

Had my family and I seen the exhibit, however, we would certainly have identified with its message of "universal brotherhood": my parents' Austrian-Jewish upbringing on Heinrich Heine and Stefan Zweig, their recent history of persecution, and our minority status as German-speaking Jews in Rumania would have made us ideal visitors to *The Family of Man*. Even the contradictions in our mentality would have been reflected in the images: the belief in human equality, on the one hand, and, on the other, our own sense of cultural superiority as "Western Europeans" displaced in the Balkans, surrounded by what we secretly thought of as a backward peasant population, as well as our fragile bourgeois comfort, all correspond to the mentality of Steichen's "human family." The space of identification is the space enjoyed by the Western European and European-American bourgeois nuclear family, a space to which we were close enough that, by the logic of the family romance, we could imagine, desire ourselves into it. In the aftermath of the Nazi deportations, the image of a close-knit nuclear family would itself have inspired us as an alternative to external strife, a sanctuary to be cherished and protected. An ideal made up of humanity, familiality, and universal communication would surely have found resonance.

What we would not have found in these representations are the barriers that separated us from the West, the intense desire for Western goods and consumer items and for the mobility that the exhibit itself enjoyed. For me, on the other side of the Iron Curtain, the Cold War was not ruled by fear as much as by curiosity, material desire, and a sense of imprisonment and deprivation. In the absence of television and of glossy picture magazines, *The Family of Man* would have seemed a window on the world. But it would not have resolved the ruling paradoxes, the contradictory affiliations and warring ideologies, the ambiguous locations in which I was raised. I would have found only a part of myself because, in relation to *The Family of Man*, I was sufficiently *other* and, as Paula Rabinowitz has said in her trenchant critique of James Agee, "The story that seeks to 'know' through what it can 'see' of the other finds, not the other, but itself."[22] I would like to think that, even then, I might have been a skeptical and resisting, though still a sympathetic, viewer of *The Family of Man*.

## looking back

If *The Family of Man* is, in Alan Sekula's terms, a "guidebook for the collapse of the political into the familial" ("The Traffic in Photographs," 95), the camera, the family picture, and the family album are effective instruments of this collapse. The appeal of large-scale exhibits and coffee-table books such as *The Family of Man* has never waned. Several new such books have appeared in the 1990s, for example, the expensive *The Circle of Life: Rituals from the Human Family Album,* edited by David Cohen (1991), with images of rites of passage from different cultures throughout the world. The rationale for this book, uncannily reminiscent of Steichen, is articulated through the words of the anthropologist Barbara Myerhoff: "Given the fragmented, complex, and disorderly nature of human experience, rites of passage are more important than ever to orient and motivate us during life crises" (142). More recently, the United Nations Population Fund sponsored *Material World: A Global Family Portrait,* edited by Peter Menzel, featuring a series of images of families from around the world depicted with all of their material possessions spread out all around them.[23] The book's inside cover reproduces currency bills from many countries signaling that the global family is differentiated economically and that, indeed, money will shape the images and their content. The text reproduces statements by the different photographers, outsiders who selected the families in different countries and spent a few days with them in their homes to take these unusual pictures of people and things. Although *Material World* is a great deal more self-conscious about the complex factors shaping global interactions than *The Family of Man* and although its images are carefully contextualized and historicized, it still fundamentally seems to hold to a notion of a universal humanity, suggesting that if we only had the same amount of money we might all be the same. Its very format—the large-scale global exhibit based on individual families representing their individual countries and enacting cross-cultural relationships—disallows any deeper political or ideological analysis.

A parody of this genre can be found in Christian Boltanski's 1995 exhibit and book, *Menschlich (Human),* which includes all of the images Boltanski has ever used in his work: images connected to World War II and the postwar world in Europe.[24] They are images of victims and perpetrators, Jews and Nazis, French and Swiss, children and adults, guilty and innocent, all together, undifferentiated, represented singly and in groups. The images invert *The Family of Man* in more than content: grainy and not glossy, unaestheticized, they are printed on cheap paper and they are often identity and newspaper photographs that frustrate the viewer's desire for recognition or positive reflection. Flat, uninviting, forbidding, they do not allow viewers to see themselves in them: these pictures are not-us.

In the exhibit of *Menschlich* at Marion Goodman Gallery the undifferentiated images were crowdedly and inelegantly hung all over the four walls of the gallery: in the center of the room, however, low-hanging lamps with bare bulbs obstructed the viewer's approach to the walls themselves—one had to find one's way in between them as they uneasily swung all around. Illumination is difficult, the exhibit seems to imply, and even though many lights are provided, pictures alone cannot make for us the discriminations that we might like to make. *Menschlich,* the human family, includes lost and orphaned children and, next to them, those who murdered their parents—but how can we tell who is who? The familial look elicited by these family pictures too quickly leads to a deceptive notion of a human family that disguises agency and historical change. In Boltanski's representation, the human family is a trap.

But even though Boltanski's *Menschlich* makes its viewers conscious of the false identifications photographs can effect and of the deceptive attractions posed by the glossy notion of universal humanity based on familiality, he himself duplicates the very universalization he critiques. Like Steichen's, Boltanski's pictures are also not dated or contextualized. In their free-floating invocation of the notion of "Menschlich"—even in its inverted form effected by the grainy prints—they still fall into the seductive snare of the familial look. As viewers peruse the faces, they will find, willy-nilly and perhaps against their better judgment, some areas of commonality, of affiliation and projection. And they will not find any tools of discrimination or differentiation.

No simple notion of a "human family" can hold in the 1990s. Even the new universalism of theorists like Tzvetan Todorov wishes to find the "universality of the human race" through a systematic scrutiny of particularities, not in a simple specularity. Todorov's integrationism, like Jürgen Habermas's Enlightenment humanist community, does not erase otherness and power, but wishes to respond with ideals of civility and mutuality, a recognition of fundamentally shared values and a model of responsible citizenship.[25] In this spirit, the family still serves as an operative unit of these new humanisms and universalisms.

The key question posed by any humanism or universalism is point of view. I wonder, for example, what if the young Riddick Bowe had been able to record his own version of his encounter with the Goldsteins? Would the pictures look the same? And what if the Guatemalan Indians who saw *The Family of Man* had provided some of their own images for Steichen's exhibit? What if Secundino could himself record his life on the Altiplano, rather than posing, again and again, for the annual photo that the organization sends us—the latest featuring him, smiling more confidently, in a Norwich, Vermont, baseball cap that used to belong to Gabriel? When we undertook the long drive and walk to see him and his mother in his distant hamlet, our brief visit, overseen by the local staff of the agency, revolved around the photographs we took of the boy and his mother, their house and sheep. In the pictures he holds the gifts we brought him, and we hold the three fresh sheep cheeses his mother made for us. But when we leave, the digital watch we gave Secundino, like our encounter, is off by an hour, still on U.S. time: none of us has figured out how to reset it. Could I have given him a camera? Where would he get film, how would he get the pictures developed in a small hamlet on the Altiplano? The obstacles are insurmountable and yet, I wonder: what would Secundino's own representations show? would their cultural difference be readable to me?

Jamaica Kincaid's 1990 novel *Lucy* offers just such a radical shift of focus, as it places the camera into the hands of the Caribbean servant in the United States household, exploring her images of the United States family and her place in it.[26] Although Lucy does not say that "everyone's the same," her perceptions and images do probe obsessively the boundaries of cultural difference and similarity, of what is shared and what remains divergent. Like anyone traveling from one culture to another, Lucy needs to see comparatively, to measure her discoveries by the standard of the world she knows, and to be ready for surprise, shock, and disappointment:

> I did not know that the sun could shine and the air remain cold; no one had ever told me. What a feeling that was! How can I explain? Something I had always known—the way I knew my skin was the color brown of a nut rubbed repeatedly with a soft cloth, or the way I knew my own name—something I took completely for granted, "the sun is shining, the air is warm," was not so. (5)

But in representing the white U.S. family through the look of the Afro-Caribbean *au pair*, Kincaid drastically refocuses images such as the ones promoted by *The Family of Man*. Furthermore, she offers a trenchant critique of the very metaphor of the human family.

If Lucy's perceptions differ radically from those of her host family, it is most often because of the power structures distinguishing colonizer from colonized. The individual relations they share are embedded in a larger historical and economic plot. A simple natural scene, such as Lucy's first encounter with daffodils, emerges as a complicated social and political drama, "a scene of conquered and conquests; a scene of brutes masquerading as angels and angels portrayed as brutes" (30). Whereas the employer Mariah sees the flowers as beautiful objects to which she feels deeply connected, the servant Lucy sees them through her memory of being made to learn Wordsworth's poem about daffodils and being unable to relate to it: "nothing could change the fact that where she saw beautiful flowers, I saw sorrow and bitterness. The same thing could cause us to shed tears, but those tears would not taste the same" (30). When they have dinner on the train, the meal is different for Lucy, who has to be aware that "the other people sitting down to eat all looked like Mariah's relatives; the people waiting on them all looked like mine" (32). When Mariah admires the beauty of a plowed field, Lucy is grateful not to have had to do the plowing.

Lucy and Mariah have predictably distinct and competing perspectives on difference: Lucy, the Caribbean worker, notices and reveals it, whereas Mariah, the European-American liberal humanist, denies it and wishes to include Lucy, in uncomplicated fashion, into her family life. "She [Mariah] acted in her usual way, which was that the world was round and we all agreed on that, when I knew that the world was flat and if I went to the edge I would fall off" (32). As a result, Lucy challenges the comfort of Mariah's worldview, the invisibility of her privilege: "Mariah wanted all of us, the children and me, to see things the way she did" (35–36). Kincaid's bold move is to decenter Mariah's perspective—the humanist view of *The Family of Man* which simply records the world's roundness—and to offer us Lucy's instead.

At the same time, Mariah and Lucy converge in their complicated familial relation: "The times that I loved Mariah it was because she reminded me of my mother. The times that I did not love Mariah it was because she reminded me of my mother" (58). Lucy finds many continuities between her island life and her life in New York: people's smells, the taste of boys' tongues, men who remind her of her father. While at times she watches her hosts from a distance, marveling how anyone can be the way they are, at others she finds them to be a lot like herself. But she never forgets her status as a servant and the power distinctions that separate them.

Modulating similarity and difference, Lucy is able to see with distinct clarity the upper-middle-class U.S. family and its self-representations: "The husband and wife looked alike and their four children looked just like them. In photographs of themselves, which they placed all over the house, their six yellow-haired heads of various sizes were bunched as if they were a bouquet of flowers tied together by an unseen string. In the pictures they smiled out at the world, giving the impression that they found everything in it unbearably wonderful" (12). Lucy is not included in these photographs, and her relationship to the family romance they represent is full of ambivalence. The self-confirming mutuality of looking that creates pictures such as this one can be blinding. Moving about their house, the family members see only reflections of themselves, wherever they look. If they wish to include Lucy it is because they do not acknowledge the significance of her difference. But Lucy—in the traditional voyeuristic position of the domestic servant—can see their self-deceptions, and she is the first to recognize Lewis's betrayal of his wife. Taking nothing for granted, she can identify the conventional aspects of family life through family photography, and she can perceive how photographs are used to promote sham images of familial happiness, while they are unable to represent the tensions of familial interaction:

> I thought of Mariah and all those books she had filled with photographs that began with when she and Lewis first met, in Paris in the shadow of the Eiffel Tower or in London in the shadow of Big Ben or somewhere foolish like that. Mariah then wore her yellow hair long and unkempt, and did not shave her legs or underarms, as a symbol of something, and was not a virgin and had not been for a long time. And there were pictures of them getting married against their parents' wishes, behind their parents' backs, and of their children just born in hospitals, and birthday parties and trips to canyons and deserts and mountains, and all sorts of other events. But here (Lewis kissing Mariah's best friend) was a picture of something that no one would ever take—a picture that would not end up in one of those books, but a significant picture all the same. (79–80)

Nevertheless, Lucy often visits the museum, voraciously peruses photography books, buys her own camera, and learns how to develop her own work. How does photography negotiate the cultural, racial, and class encounter in which Lucy is engaged? Is it that her camera enables her to reverse the power differential that distinguishes her from her employers, that it enables her to assert her vision, or her "truth," over Mariah's? Or is it that the camera itself enables her to see differently, to define her own and their perspectives as equally contingent, thereby reenvisioning the power struggle in which she finds herself immersed and engaging differently with the visible?

The photographs Lucy likes are "photographs of ordinary people in a countryside doing ordinary things, but for a reason that was not at all clear to me the people and the things they were doing looked extraordinary—as if these people and these things had not existed before" (115). Rather than providing her with a way to record her "truth," it seems that photography, as Lucy describes it, offers her an instrument of the relativity she experiences as she lives in an alien world. Thus she wants the pictures to help her see. She wants them to reveal to her the ways in which to see is to invent something that does not preexist the act of perception: "Why is a picture of something real eventually more exciting than the thing itself? I did not yet know the answer to that" (121). Photographs are exciting and helpful because of their ambiguity, because of the reading they demand, because they do not transparently offer a single truth. As a photographer, Lucy is deeply, personally, and sensually engaged with her world: she looks intently, she sleeps with the man who sells her the camera, she relates to the boy in the picture through the memory of a smell. At the same time, photographs contain and communicate the mystery and uninterpretability of the world she encounters. As she approaches photography with the look of the outsider, the marginal, she finds in it the conflicts and contradictions, the unreadability that shapes her encounter with the United States. And as she wants to master her world, the photographs she takes resist mastery and foreground a continuing indeterminacy and opacity:

> I mostly liked to take pictures of people walking on the street. They were not pictures of individuals, just scenes of people walking about, hurrying to somewhere. I did not know them and I did not care to. I would try to make a print that made more beautiful the thing I thought I had seen, that would reveal to me some of the things I had not seen, but I did not succeed. (160)

Lucy's photographs are personal acts of engagement, records of an outsider's look freed from the predictable gazes of convention. They record the inevitable cultural conflicts she suffers, the incommensurability of her difference, her painful disconnection from the people who surround her and about whom she cares. Perhaps Steichen had pictures such as Lucy's in mind when he planned his exhibit: pictures that reveal the humanity of their subjects but that allow for a variety of looks through which they might be seen, for a multiplicity of interpretations; pictures that record more than the transparent world of the visible. Such an exhibit might not have offered the European and European-American viewer a space of comfortable self-reflection, but might instead have decentered the European eye. It might have shown the contingency of each picture, its situatedness and relativity. For Lucy, each print is only one version of a negative, and she develops each with a consciousness of its tenuous relation to its negative and to the object photographed, and with a consciousness, as well, of her own ambivalent investments in the product, of the projections that shape the result.

The wall of Lucy's room is her own "family" album, depicting "photographs I had taken, in black-and-white, of the children with Mariah, of Mariah all by herself, and of some of the things I had acquired since leaving home" (120), photographs that reverse the gazes of *The Family of Man* and its ideology. For Lucy these "family" pictures are a way to disentangle herself from her own family ties, to loosen those invisible strings, and to explore how family functions. Family, in Kincaid's novel, is the site of desire, longing, and nostalgia, and the "millstone around your life's neck" (8). It is the space of a love so strong that one can die from it, and it is the space of pain, betrayal, and tears. It is the site of anxiety, resistance, projection. Kincaid reveals the politics embedded in the familial and therefore demystifies its power to stand as a model of human interaction. Family pictures, Lucy suggests, need not disguise the internal politics of the family. To become more apt instruments of vision, they merely need to be seen in their contradiction and ambiguity and to resist transparent readings.

*The Family of Man* ends with a figure of hope and rebirth embodying the very notion of family romance—Eugene Smith's well-known image of a little boy and a little girl, photographed from the back and from a low angle, walking out of an undifferentiated forest: a close-up of the ocean is on the facing page. Their fragile infancy, protected through maternal nurturing and paternal authority on surrounding pages, signals the rhetorical power of conventional representations of the family.

At the end of her book, Lucy ends up outside of all familial relations. At least outwardly, she is "alone in the world. It was not a small accomplishment" (161). She writes a line in her journal and then washes it away with her tears. It is a line full of desire and longing, embodying the mythologies of the family romance: "I wish I could love someone so much that I would die from it" (164). But as she cries, the words end up as "one great big blur." For Lucy plots and photographs are contingent—they can be altered, manipulated, washed, and changed. But their contingency is painful, leaving her unanchored and uprooted.

Lucy negotiates difference more in the terms developed by recent postcolonial theorists—Homi Bhaba's hybridity and interstitiality, Françoise Lionnet's métissage, Edward Said's cultural multiplicity and interconnection—rather than Steichen's liberal humanism or the new universalisms of Todorov or Habermas.[27] Materially performing her engagement with U.S. culture, photographs enable Lucy to try out many types of seeing, to tell a multiplicity of stories with possibly conflicting interpretations. In Kincaid's novel, photographs can be instruments of a cultural hybridity embodied in the photographic look with which Lucy, the traveling photographer, represents her white subjects and measures her resistance to their ways of seeing. Hers is a look that insists on difference *and* interconnection, on conflict *and* commonality. It still invokes a familial gaze, but one that has complicated the very notion of the family and has radically reframed and opened up its boundaries.

# 3

# *M*ASKING THE SUBJECT

The autobiographical moment happens as an alignment between
the two subjects involved in the process of reading in which they
determine each other by mutual reflective substitution.
PAUL DE MAN

## *mother/daughter images*

While I was working on my book *The Mother/Daughter Plot,* I spent much
time fantasizing about its cover.[1] Although I did look at paintings by women
of mothers and daughters, especially those by the ubiquitous Mary Cassatt,
my fantasies of what the cover might look like revolved around a picture
my mother had in her photograph collection, an old studio photograph of
her mother and older sister, taken about ten years before my mother's birth
(around 1908). There were actually two pictures, both probably taken on
the same visit to the photographer, and my mother and I disagree about
them. The one she preferred and I rejected is a classic profile shot of the
mother (in the background) and the little daughter (in the foreground). Their
faces are touching, they are looking out into space; there is nothing individual in either the faces or the pose. They could be any middle-class European
mother/daughter pair in the early years of the century. Only their general
traits matter; only their resemblance identifies them as mother and daughter.
The picture I chose instead was to me very different: it had a story to tell,
and I realized that it was a story I had been trying to decode since I was a
child, without ever feeling that I had been successful. It touched me in a
way I could never verbalize (Figure 3.1).

Here is my grandmother dressed in an elaborately embroidered, full-
length gown that shows off a thin corseted waist and a stately bosom, standing next to what looks like a Japanese screen and in front of a mysterious
half-drawn tasseled stage curtain, holding a curious feather fan in her right
hand. Her left hand is wrapped around her daughter's knee as the little girl,

dressed in a delicate white gown and white tights, stands very daintily on an ornate square stool so that her head is at the same height as her mother's and her arms, covered with embroidered sleeves which reach down to her fingers, can be wrapped around her mother's neck. My grandmother is standing on a thick animal fur, perhaps a seal, that is laid out on top of a thin patterned carpet. The two clear faces are looking squarely at the camera: my grandmother just barely smiling, her head proudly tilted upward; the little girl exceedingly serious, almost sad, as she lays her hands ever so delicately around her mother's neck without, however, clinging to her.

As I have looked at this picture over the years, so many questions have occurred to me. Who are these people and what is their relationship to the two women I knew half a century later: my old and wrinkled, yet always surprisingly strong Omama, wearing modest black dresses; and the stately gray-haired Tante Fritzi, wearing thick glasses, a brilliant, worldly and energetic, yet deeply sad and angry woman who moved around with difficulty owing to a sudden paralysis? Worlds seemed to separate them from this photograph, yet they are—I am told, and I believe it—the same people.

What is the occasion for this photo session—why did they have this picture taken and why was my grandfather absent from the scene? What is behind that curtain, like Boudinet's, an emblem of the photograph's frustrating flatness? What is their world like and how could that prewar world—Czernowitz, a German-speaking largely Jewish city in the Bukowina, an outpost of the Austro-Hungarian empire—disappear so completely before I was born? How, over a lifetime, had they been able to deal with the drastic changes brought by two wars, the shift of nationality from Austria-Hungary to Rumania to Soviet Union, the emigration to Rumania, the shifts in style and, it seemed to me, in being?

And what about their relationship: those hands interlacing the bodies, the faces separate, not touching, yet tilted along the very same angle? Had my aunt's heart condition already been diagnosed, and does this account for her adult expression, for her melancholic look? Most important for me, perhaps, where am I in this picture: are there facial resemblances to my mother, who in my memory did not at all look like her sister, and is there a likeness of me? What, in this picture, has touched me so strongly that I claim its familial relation to me, even though I don't actually *recognize* the individuals represented?

These questions emerge from the familial look with which I have always confronted this photograph, and which placed them and me, and my visually absent mother, into close familial relation defining identity squarely as fa-

3.1

milial. As for Barthes, this "exchange" of looks structures both the individual and the familial: my grandmother and aunt looking at the camera, and perhaps at my grandfather, almost eighty years before I look at their picture, a picture that has been looked at, and thus also shaped, by the mediating presence of my mother.

Part of the picture, also, is its history. My mother told me that before the war it had always been displayed on a drawing room wall in a beautiful silver frame, but that during the war it had been ripped out of its frame, which was sold with most of their other valuables. This accounted for the obvious cracks and for the unfinished upper edge of the picture, which then survived, frameless, mounted on its original photographer's black paper. Until it reached my desk, it was never displayed again but was kept in a box, first in my grandparents' rooms and apartments and later in my mother's.

If I so wanted this picture for the cover of my book, if I was so pleased when the designer agreed to use it, it must have been because I did recognize myself in it, or in its history. But that became clear to me only when the actual cover reached me and I saw my name printed in large white letters right under the picture of my grandmother and aunt. In 1989, when *The Mother/Daughter Plot* was published, I was already almost ten years older than the adult woman in the picture, my grandmother, who had died at 83, thirty years earlier. At that time my children were older than the little girl, my aunt, who had died in her sixties, more than twenty years earlier. Their clothes and their facial expressions could not be more different from mine, yet something about my name under their photo seemed just right. It seemed, in fact, much less strange than my name on the cover of this book that I had written but that, quite unexpectedly, I could *own* only by way of this picture which, through multiple displacements, made *The Mother/Daughter Plot* mine, a space of reflection, a kind of autobiographical act. And it is the absence of this picture, and the substitution for it of a black-and-white rose, as much as the unfamiliar language, that makes it difficult for me to recognize the Japanese translation as my work.

Although, of course, no woman critic writes a book about mothers and daughters without some personal investment, *The Mother/Daughter Plot* was for me about women's literature and about feminist and psychoanalytic theory. The cover was to be just that, a decoration, at most a proto-narrative that would comment obliquely on the contents. Yet the cover picture I selected unmasked for me and for my mother the book's deep connection to us and our relationship. Through this picture, which is and is not a self-portrait, I declare myself as the subject of my book, which is not an autobiography or a memoir, but a literary and theoretical study of mother-daughter relations. Or is it? Like Barthes looking at his mother's childhood photo, I am sutured into this image by the familial look which overrides the enormous temporal, spatial, and cultural distances that otherwise separate me from it, and overrides, as well, the lack of visual recognition, of coincidence between the people I see and the women I remember.

Through this familial look I define a boundary between inside and outside, claiming these women as a part of the story through which I construct myself. This inclusion is an act of adoption and an act of faith determined by an idea, an image of family: it is not an act of recognition. It is fundamentally an interpretive and a narrative gesture, a fabrication out of available pieces that acknowledges the fragmentary nature of the autobiographical act and its ambiguous relation to reference. Photographs are fragments of stories, never stories in themselves. It may well be that I wrote a book on mothers and daughters in part to "open the curtain" in that picture, to assemble the parts, and to reach into the recesses of that emblematic family relationship.

To me, then, this picture is the product of a process of *familiality* which it illustrates—the exchange of looks that structure a complicated form of self-portraiture which reveals the self as necessarily relational and familial, as well as fragmented and dispersed. Just as the family picture can be read as a self-portrait, so the self-portrait always includes the other, not only because the self, never coincident, is necessarily other to itself, but also because it is constituted by multiple and heteronomous relations. The self-portrait's double-edged otherness—combining multiplicity with alterity—is well-characterized by Philippe Lacoue-Labarthe's term *allo-portrait* (from the Greek *allos* meaning *other, different*).

In the previous chapter I looked at the visual relationship between self and other through images of cultural "others." Here I propose to limit myself to the space of the subject's own constitution which occurs within a relational group that most often takes the shape of what is called "family." Difference or otherness, in this conception, is not an external difference, but an otherness within—within a circumscribed cultural group, such as a family, and, also, within the self, reflecting the subject's own plurality over a lifetime, the intersubjectivity that is subjectivity. Inside this closely drawn if permeable frame, the notions of the familial look and gaze can be explored and illuminated through the genre of the photographic auto/allo-portrait.[2]

Autobiography and self-portraiture share with photography a presumed referential basis and proximate relationship to truth which disguises their

3.2

mediated and constructed qualities.[3] The illusion of the self's wholeness and
plenitude is perpetuated by the photographic medium as well as by the
autobiographical act: both forms of misrecognition rest on a profound
misprision of the processes of representation. Autobiography and photography share, as well, a fragmentary structure and an incompleteness that
can be only partially concealed by narrative and conventional connections.
Naively, I keep trying to learn something about my grandmother and aunt,
about my mother and about myself, by staring at their portrait. Might it
not be more productive to see in the photograph an analog of the process
of the subject's construction which occurs—as it does in autobiography—
relationally in response to discursive practices? In the case of the family
picture, a plural exchange of familial looks filtered through multiple cultural, ideological, and historical screens produces a subjectivity which remains familial and relational.

It is from this perspective that I can now look at my own first identity
photo, taken in 1961 on the occasion of my family's emigration from
Rumania (Figure 3.2). With the permission to emigrate, we were issued not
passports but "Certificates of Travel," valid only for the passage from
Rumania. "My" identity picture was actually a picture of me with my
mother: since I was only eleven we shared one travel certificate. It is a tiny
photo in which my mother and I pose in front of an illuminated curtain in

the photographer's studio. I am wearing my school uniform, a black-and-white checked cotton dress with a starched white collar and a black apron. My mother is wearing a white blouse with the identical round collar, and a dark jacket. Our expressions—clearly composed for the occasion—are identical. We are very serious as, leaning toward each other with our heads touching, we earnestly and bravely, though sadly, face the photographer and prepare for the many officials who will examine and stamp our travel certificate, and as we also confront our uncertain future abroad.

Even in this official conception of identity, relationship is stressed—at least for mother and child. My father's certificate includes a more conventional identity picture of him alone, although looking at the two certificates together, I can imagine, if not recall, a joint session at the studio and the shared feelings of anticipation and displacement that constitute the shifting selves we see in the pictures, constructed in relation and according to particular institutional frames in specific historical circumstances.

In deliberately conflating the self-portrait with the family picture, I aim to explore the continuum on which these genres uneasily define themselves. This continuum between self-portrait/allo-portrait and family picture traces the subject's constitution in the familial and the family's visual reflection of the individual subject. It defines the process of subject-formation in the field of vision and it makes the taking and reading of photographs central to its contemporary manifestations. I would like to bring this process into focus by looking not so much at actual family pictures such as my grandmother's and aunt's or my identity picture, as at imagetexts which constitute a commentary on them. Thus, I turn to Lacoue-Labarthe's striking *Portrait de l'artiste en général* (1979) in order to explore more closely the ramifications of the shift from the self-portrait to the allo-portrait: the portrait of the other, defined as the other within.[4]

My readings of this work and of the imagetexts which follow—Ralph Eugene Meatyard's *The Family Album of Lucybelle Crater* and Cindy Sherman's portraits—invoke both literal and metaphoric notions of masking. On the one hand, the mask is a metaphor for the photograph's power to conceal, for the frustrations of the photograph's surface. On the other hand, we can see the mask as a metaphor for the semiotic lenses or screens through which we read photographs, and through which the images themselves are constructed as objects of social meaning.[5]

This particular use of masking echoes Barthes's suggestions about the signifying structures of photography: "Since every photograph is contingent (and thereby outside of meaning), Photography cannot signify (aim at a generality) except by assuming a mask. It is this word that Calvino correctly uses to designate what makes a face into the product of a society and of its history . . . the mask is the meaning, insofar as it is absolutely pure (as it was in the ancient theater)."[6] Barthes sees this purity in Richard Avedon's portrait of "William Casby, born a slave": the caption produces a certain reading of the portrait in which we project our understanding of slavery onto the face in the picture which then reflects that understanding back to us. Masks, Barthes maintains, are social roles containing allegorical or mythic power, thereby enabling political readings. As we pose, we assume particular masks; as we read photographs, we project particular masks, particular ideological frames, onto the images. Familiality can be thought of as such a mask. But Barthes's reading of the mask of signification as pure meaning, corresponding to the structure of allegory, is too straightforward for the complicated exchange of looks and gazes, filtered through multivalent screens, that construct the photographic masks of familiality. The readings that follow reveal a more multilayered conception of masking.

### allo-portraits

Lacoue-Labarthe's unusual "portrait of the artist" is a response to Charles Baudelaire's condemnation of photography as the antithesis of art, as the reproducible, exposable, simple-minded, and anti-imaginative copy of the real.[7] "L'art peut-il s'identifier?" Can art *identify* itself? Lacoue-Labarthe asks. The portrait of the artist he will construct in response to this inaugural and unanswerable question is a multipersonal one which focuses not only on the abstraction of "art" but also on the more concrete notion of "s'identifier." Identification inheres in the familial process of subject-formation, and it is in this context that Lacoue-Labarthe discusses the portrait of the artist.

*Portrait de l'artiste* is, in fact, a commentary on a series of nine self-portraits by the Swiss photographer Urs Lüthi, exhibited by the Stadler Gallery in Paris in 1974, and embedded between the nine short chapters of Lacoue-Labarthe's text. Representing the individual subject, these portraits enable Lacoue-Labarthe to reflect on what he characterizes as a crucial interconnection between art and subjectivity, on art as a form of *self*-expression. Following Baudelaire, Lacoue-Labarthe equates the identity of art, or painting, with the identity of the human subject.

Lüthi's photographs are preceded by the English title "Just another story about leaving" and the English epigraph "you are not the only who is lonely." With this direct address, in the second person, Lüthi's pictures engage the viewer/reader in a paradoxical dialogue which establishes relationship by way of an identification through at once an invocation and a refusal of solitude: *you are not the only who is lonely.* Lüthi's epigraph is signed in his handwriting, but the book can offer only a photocopy of his signature, placing in doubt the identity of the signer as well as the subject of the nine photographs. But this multiple reproduction and dissemination of the signature, this central plurality, is already implied in the epigraph's omission of the crucial word "one": "you are not the only [one] who is lonely." Omitting "one" opens the space for an infinite multiplication and reflection of subjectivities. "You are not the only *one,*" Lüthi assures his viewer, thereby engaging us not only in dialogue but in a complicated self-reflection. If "you" or "I" are/am not (the only) one, then how can we talk about the subject? Lacoue-Labarthe's book responds to this question by way of its very form. His "portrait de l'artiste" is signed Philippe Lacoue-Labarthe on the cover and the first page, but Urs Lüthi on the second and third pages. Each of the nine brief chapters is preceded by a (self-) portrait (initially read by readers, I imagine, as either Lacoue-Labarthe's or Lüthi's) and by signed epigraphs of nine other interlocutors: Baudelaire, Blanchot, Diderot, Nietzsche, Benjamin, Valéry, Hegel, Rank, and Freud. Quotations in the text are often unidentified, and thus authorial identities typically merge and blur.

"Only with difficulty can we speak of self-portraits," says Lacoue-Labarthe, and indeed, if the authorial "self" is multiple and dispersed, as we have seen, so is the visual "self" of the portraits. "Whose face, exactly, is being 'photographed?'" (24), asks Lacoue-Labarthe. If Lüthi's pictures tell a story, it is a story of the "progressive degradation," the "aging," of the "same" face (29), in that sense a story about "leaving" (or "living"): a life-story. The sameness and repetition, and the changes and variations among the nine poses, are striking, for Lüthi is playing not only with the variable of age but also with that of gender and sexuality: the portraits allow him both to age and to trace an oscillation between "masculine" and "feminine" appearances: "here is a man no doubt but one who displays the woman in him," says Lacoue-Labarthe (30; Figure 3.3). Through a range of experiments with makeup and hair dyes, Lüthi is able to engage in a series of metamorphoses and transvestisms that allow him simultaneously to simulate "youth" and "age," "masculinity" and "femininity."

Lüthi's portraits address directly and overturn several essential elements of photography: its illusion of mimetic representation or the effect of the real (on which Barthes so insists), its construction in time, and its embedded-

**3.3**

ness in relationship. Although the pose and the angle from which the face is photographed vary only slightly throughout the nine images, the variations in the subject's appearance foreground staging and simulation, rather than realistic portrayal, as central to these pictures, thus challenging the referential myths of self-portraiture. These are studio images—images printed on cloth, thereby quite directly simulating painting—artificially lit and shaded. Their subject faces the viewer frontally or at a very slight angle. Only the top of the face is clearly lit, leaving the peripheral areas of the image in mysterious darkness. There is no curtain here, no tease or suggestion that the picture might yield a greater depth. The frame is drawn closely around the head and half torso.

If the photograph captures and freezes one moment in time, then these images challenge this aspect of photography by giving us nine moments, each completely individual, but related and placed into diachronic progression through play on repetition and variation but not through narrative connection. In their relation to one another, these photographs constitute an album, a story of aging and change "over time," figured in nine stages that allude to the nine months of gestation. But in its obviously staged artificiality, this temporal extension becomes conflated again into several synchronous moments, perhaps somewhat like *overlays* revealing different aspects of the subject not as they develop over time but as they coexist at the same temporal moment, filtered through different screens.

It is here that Lacoue-Labarthe's notion of the allo-portrait becomes useful. The subject exists in time always as "other" in one of several ways. On the one hand, the subject constitutes himself visually by way of a false identification with the misapprehended imaginary "other" of Jacques Lacan's mirror stage—the mistaken jubilant belief in the bodily wholeness and self-identity apprehended in the mirror. On the other hand, the subject constructs what Lacan calls the "moi," the self as externally, socially, given and recognized—as a projected and therefore absent self/other, a *personne* in the double sense of *person* and *no one*.[8] Third, existing in time, the subject is also always temporally other, that is, always, in addition to the present self, a previous or subsequent and anticipated self. By selecting one instant out of the subject's temporal existence, the photograph stages the subject's own specular self-encounter as an encounter with otherness: the subject represented in the photograph is always *other* to the one looking at the picture. Lüthi's pictures perform this apprehension of otherness by self-consciously and artificially staging change and variation along the intersecting axes of age, gender, and sexuality. Recognition is always misapprehension: the subject is never identical with himself. "De la naissance à la mort, *et inversement,* tel est le trajet de la reconnaissance spéculaire et de l'identification: alternance sans repos de deux visages où le sujet cherche le 'sien'" ("From birth to death, and inversely, such is the passage of specular recognition and identification: a tireless alternation of two faces in which as subjects we search for 'ours'") (91). The result is a fundamental ambiguity as to the identity of the "real" Lüthi's age, or gender, or sexuality. If we ask such questions, the images will only confound us.

In Lacoue-Labarthe's reading, however, other "others" circulate in and constitute the self-portrait, as well. In his gender ambiguity, Lüthi reveals the relationality inherent in photography as well as in subjectivity. In the "old" pictures, for example, he is, Lacoue-Labarthe insists, identified with both his mother and his father, with both maternal and paternal expression (Figure 3.4). His identity is both specular and affiliative, his auto-portrait is also an allo-portrait in the sense that it includes in his self-representation the familial others and the ways in which the subject is constructed familially. Mother and father are literally *in* the face he constructs and photographs. As Lacoue-Labarthe suggests, glossing Blanchot, his look is *fascinated* and *fascinating:* Lüthi glances with fascination at himself, in his very otherness, that is, at his own maternal and paternal identities. He reflects—literally—the familial gaze and looks that construct his pose and his subjectivity. In this sense, each *individual* image is an overlay of mutual looks. Together, then, the nine images are overlays of overlays, conflating a lifetime, an array of gender and sexual positions, and a set of familial relations into a series of captured instants.

By way of the familial gaze, Lacoue-Labarthe can identify Lüthi's pictures as art: "the true subject of painting," he says, glossing Hegel, "its *ideally* determined content and its essence, in its proper truth, is *feeling* as such" (82). That feeling, he maintains, is love and, essentially, maternal love. In Lacoue-Labarthe's oedipal argument, the ideal painting is either the painting of madonna and child or the painting of the *mater dolorosa;* the essence of art is Christian iconography. By conflating child and mother in the same persona, Lüthi offers Lacoue-Labarthe a "myth of the origin of art" (87). But in so doing Lüthi also suggests "*another story* of identification," one that has evolved from a Christian to a Freudian mythology: the myth of the constitution of the subject of psychology, constituted through identification in familial relation. "The artist, or art, in general" Lacoue-Labarthe concludes, "constitutes itself and unmakes itself, (de)constitutes itself, *interminably,* between father and mother" (91).

But could we not say the same of the subject *in general?* Why limit this analysis to art and the artist? Does not the move from painting to photography, from Baudelaire and Benjamin to Freud and Lacoue-Labarthe, invite precisely this further *general*ization? If Baudelaire needed to limit the intangible and the imaginary, the ethereal and the immaterial, to art and to separate them from the industrial and therefore the photographic, does not Lüthi show precisely that photography also represents the imaginary and the intangible? Does he not show that photography offers an allegory of the constitution of every subject—because, after Freud, we see that every subject houses both the real and the unreal, the conscious and the unconscious, the material and the immaterial? By making Lüthi's self-portraits into family pictures, Lacoue-Labarthe engages in a double, inherently self-confirming move: first he transforms the self-presentation of the lone artist into a record of relationships, and then he uses those relations to construct the persona

**3.4**

of the universal artist who has the power to express universal feelings and thereby to identify and to confirm the work emanating from those feelings as art.

The Stadler Gallery's catalog of Urs Lüthi's "Just Another Story about Leaving" includes the nine images preceded by the two title pages, and framed by a cover photograph of an industrial landscape. There is no supporting text, not even a biography of the artist, no list of other works or exhibitions. Lacoue-Labarthe's elaborate reading of these images, and his insertion of them into his own book, facilitated by the absence of any contextual information, is an act of appropriation and incorporation. Do the images themselves support the theoretical and narrative superstructure to which they are subjected in *Portrait de l'artiste*? What are we to make of Lacoue-Labarthe's use of Lüthi as an example of the *artiste, en général,* and of the story Lacoue-Labarthe tells in order to be able to do so? And what can we say of the relationship established between the theorist and the artist, both of whom appear as twin subjects of the written/photographic portrait? In what terms can we, as readers, interpret the pictures or evaluate Lacoue-Labarthe's reading?

Barthes's famous characterization of the photograph as "a message without a code" clearly does not hold for photographs that are as highly coded as Lüthi's.[9] Far from portraying "the scene itself, the literal reality," far from teasing us with the referentiality promised by the portrait or the self-portrait, these images engage in elaborate play with accepted conventions. Yet the codes they embed are surely less explicitly determined than Lacoue-Labarthe's overdetermined reading allows. His search for the "général" leads him to favor a specific narrative, specific theoretical formulations, and to read the images so that they support those formulations over others. The images in themselves, or in another context, may well suggest different readings to different readers.

In discussing Lacoue-Labarthe's text, I am tempted to argue with his interpretations. I am tempted first to dismiss his distinction between art and photography and to suggest that Lüthi's images are not the equivalent of art but allegories of photography, supporting my own argument about the familiality of the photographic look and gaze. Contemplating the pictures more closely, moreover, I am tempted to question the family romance Lacoue-Labarthe finds at the core of Lüthi's self-portraits and at the mythic origin of art. In inscribing Lüthi's metamorphosis into the narrative of maternal and paternal identification and into a mythic invocation of maternal love, Lacoue-Labarthe seems to be normalizing the subversive and disturbing aspects of Lüthi's gender ambiguity.

It is equally possible to see Lüthi as staging an emancipation from a familial narrative, rather than a projection into it. In this reading, Lüthi's queer identity would appear as a blurring of gender that transcends and bypasses dualisms rather than an enactment of masculinity and femininity. The familial framework in which Lüthi remains in Lacoue-Labarthe's myth of artistic origin has the risk of undercutting another meaning of the negotiation between the missing "one" in Lüthi's epigraph, "you are not the only who is lonely," and the "just another" of the title: the subject of the portraits may well be not "one" but "just another"—perhaps, as Marjorie Garber defines the transvestite, a "third."[10] In her reading, the third is not a third sex or a third term, but a "mode of articulation" and a "space of possibility" which challenges, puts into question established gender categories. This questioning would be both a product of and a way of transcending the familial: it is a mode of familial *dis-identification,* a challenge to familial ideology—a resisting relation to the familial gaze. Lüthi, we might say, elaborating on Lacoue-Labarthe's family romance, structures his portraits in response to the looks and gazes of familiality but to such excess that he is able to question and to transcend the category of the familial.

This reading is neither more nor less valid than Lacoue-Labarthe's: Lüthi's photographs, like all photographs whose context is unspecified, bring us to a point of limit in interpretation. If we are going to use them to further a theoretical inquiry, we must see that we are doing just that. The different theoretical frameworks through which Lacoue-Labarthe and I look at Lüthi's enigmatic work, the *general*izations to which we subject it, are a further layer in the series of overlays that the images constitute, screens that reflect our spectatorial encounter with the images.

But Lacoue-Labarthe's and my encounters with Lüthi's pictures are perhaps not so different from Barthes's reading of his mother's childhood picture or my encounter with the photograph of my grandmother and aunt. It may be that self- or family portraits are images of a particular kind, eliciting specifically relational forms of reading, a specific form of what Victor Burgin terms "intertextuality." How, as readers, do we insert ourselves into the network of identificatory and disidentificatory looks and gazes that structure the images? Barthes and I certainly do not know much more about the context of our remote family pictures than we know about Lüthi's staged images. Yet Barthes's claim to so individual, so unreproducible a relationship to his mother's photograph relegates the picture itself to the space outside his book, where he alone will read and interpret it.

The work of reading isolated images necessarily becomes a work of overreading, determined by the particular familial or extrafamilial relation we hold to them. Recognizing an image as *familial* elicits, as I have argued, a specific kind of readerly or spectatorial look, an *affiliative look* through which we are sutured into the image and through which we adopt the image into our own familial narrative. Akin to Barthes's move from the studium to the punctum, it is idiosyncratic, untheorizable: it is what moves us because of our memories and our histories, and because of the ways in which we structure our own sense of particularity. What I see when I look at my family pictures is not what you see when you look at them: only my look is affiliative, only my look enters and extends the network of looks and gazes that have constructed the image in the first place.

Thus Lacoue-Labarthe's familial reading of Lüthi's self-portraits may well be the result of such an affiliative look rather than an imposition of a familial screen or gaze, it may be the result of a personal investment that remains unspoken in his discussion, masked by the *general* question, not his but Baudelaire's, about the subject of art. If this is so, then Lacoue-Labarthe's *Portrait de l'artiste* becomes a family album or, at least, a double portrait, testifying to a familial, perhaps a fraternal, or a homoerotic relation between its two authorial figures, Lüthi and Lacoue-Labarthe.

In *Portrait de l'artiste,* the self-portrait becomes, through the mode and content of Lacoue-Labarthe's reading, a kind of family picture. But what of the inverse case, a family album that also constitutes a very particular kind of self-portrait? Ralph Eugene Meatyard's *The Family Album of Lucybelle Crater* can be read as a commentary on the construction of the photographic subject in relation to the gaze of familiality.[11]

### masks

If any text succeeds in laying bare and challenging the most obvious conventions and rituals of family photography—and thereby in elaborating the notion of the familial gaze and looks—it is Meatyard's *Family Album of Lucybelle Crater,* published posthumously in 1974. This is an album of sixty-three black-and-white plates, each depicting two masked figures in various middle-class indoor and outdoor suburban domestic spaces: typical living rooms, houses, cars, gardens, back yards, fences. One figure, Lucybelle Crater—wearing a grotesque female mask with two protruding teeth, and a variety of informal, mostly feminine outfits—is present in all the pictures. The afterword informs us that she is really Madelyn Meatyard, the photographer's wife. The other figure varies—a number of men, women, and children wear the same transparent mask which appears to change slightly with the head shape and size of the wearer. The pretense of informal family-snapshot photography is maintained through the unvarying perspective and distance of the camera: the figures always face frontally, filling the frame. The poses are deliberate and naive, and the lighting appears to be natural so that some of the faces are in the shade. Only two pictures are labeled, the first, reading "Lucybelle Crater and her 46-year-old husband Lucybelle Crater," and the last, reading "Lucybelle Crater and close friend Lucybelle Crater in the grape arbor" (Figures 3.5, 3.6). Some of the images republished in other catalogs duplicate this gesture of name repetition, for example "Lucybelle Crater & 20 yrs old's 3 yr old son, also her 3 yr old grandson—Lucybelle Crater" (Figure 3.7). Thus the figures in the family album share not only the same two "faces" but the same name.

3.5

The source of this name is Lucynell Crater—the name of two characters, a mother and a daughter, in Flannery O'Connor's story "The Life You Save May Be Your Own."[12] There are obvious connections between the images of familial relations put forth by Meatyard's album and O'Connor's short story. Both, in fact, can help us to reflect further on the relationships defined by familiality.

The story begins with an older mother and her mute 30-year-old daughter who sit in their yard. A one-armed drifter, Mr. Shiftlet, introduces himself into their household, marries the daughter, then immediately abandons her and drives off with their car, which had served as a kind of dowry in the

3.6

marriage negotiations. Mother and daughter are trapped in the familial relation of sameness underscored by the name they share, and the ambiguity of the proposal that "You and her and me can drive into town and get married." As mother looks at daughter on the wedding day and exclaims, "Don't Lucynell look pretty? Looks like a baby doll," it becomes clear that Shiftlet will not be included in their familial look. "Mr. Shiftlet didn't even look at her." Marriage for him is a business deal involving the car and not Lucynell. With his disregard of human over material relation and his inherent shiftiness, he remains outside the self-reflexive address of the haunting highway sign he repeatedly encounters as he drives away: "The life you save

**3.7**

may be your own." Identity and relation in this story are reduced to a sameness that can be constraining and terrifying, as well as exhilarating and visionary. The injunction to safe driving emblematizes the hermetic inter-connection of individuals: you and I are actually the same. The only escape is Shiftlet's irresponsible drifting and the pain he causes, parallel to the story he tells about the doctor who cut out a human heart. Is this not what Shiftlet has done by separating and then unthinkingly abandoning the two Lucy-nells? Is not their separation akin to the dismemberment he himself has suffered in losing his arm?

Familiality has the same sort of constitutive and, at the same time, terrifyingly hermetic quality in Meatyard's family album. Identity is no longer individual but is defined by the mask of familial relation and of photographic convention. Meatyard's pictures are an ironic comment on the conventions of family photography like, for example, Julia Hirsch's remark that "profiles . . . are seldom used in family photographs because entire faces show family resemblances more fully."[13] When we are photographed in the context of the conventions of family-snapshot photography, Meatyard's pictures suggest, we wear masks, fabricate ourselves according to certain expectations and are fabricated by them.[14]

These subjects are constructed by their relationships and by their photographic representation, by the click of the camera, representative of the familial gaze. The masks are protective screens and disguises, hiding the individual faces and expressions inscribing them into a conventional narrative. But they are also ritual masks uniting the characters in the rites of family life, constituted through the camera into magic moments with mysterious, haunting, and lasting power. The figures in the photographs play out the codes of the encounter between self and other, in which self is already other—othered by the facial and name repetition established between the figures in the entire album and by the familial gaze that places the masks on the faces. Thus, every image is an allo-portrait. The album mocks the search for "lineage" that Barthes in *Camera Lucida* highlights as an element of reading family photographs, by giving us not facial resemblances but the sameness of the two masks, echoed in the sameness of Lucybelle's name. Familiality is made grotesque, surreal, comic, yet the every day quality of the poses, the shabby informal clothes and the subtle tenderness of some of the gestures, do suggest that beneath the excessive performance of convention there may be stories of affiliation or conflict that the masks, and the conventions of family photography, will not reveal.

Like Lüthi's pictures, Meatyard's images play with the temporal dimension of the photograph. The masked faces lack expression and so truly connect the singular moment in time to a timeless moment of unchanging quality, denying the effects of aging, change, and loss. At the same time, they conflate diachronic development into synchronic representation as they show children's bodies with adult masks, and old bodies with youthful masks. An earlier photograph of Meatyard's illustrates this strategy as it depicts a young boy climbing a rock and carrying two different masks on his belt as though they were subsequent faces he might yet grow into.

Meatyard's images, like Lüthi's, challenge and overturn expected elements of photography, mimetic representation, for example, and—for family photography—its reliance on identifiable roles and positions. Inherently antimimetic, the masks are the obvious indices of the images' constructedness. Gender roles are as relativized as generational positions, moreover, with men and women, children and adults, interchangeably wearing the clear mask.

If the masks in the family album disguise the figures' faces and expressions, they also hide their eyes. There is no actual return look that the viewer can perceive. If there is a familial look that structures the images beyond the more distant gaze of familiality, then, it must be either the photographer's or the viewer's. These are the relationships that structure the images: the photographer who serves as the spectacle's director, and the viewer who shares the camera's angle of vision. But can we assume a photographer, or a viewer, who is not implicated in the effects of masking, a spectator who can remain separate from the spectacle? "Am I looking at a mask or am I the mask being looked at?" Meatyard asks in the epigraph, underscoring the specularity, reversibility, and interchangeability that are basic to the conception of his family album and to his assessment of family photography.

Where is the photographer in these images, and where, as viewers, are we? The context of the album's production helps to define the photographer's role. Meatyard made this album of photographs in the two years that followed his cancer diagnosis and preceded his death. The individuals wearing the masks were all relatives and close family friends, people Meatyard is said to have loved and to have wanted to connect with one another before his death. He himself serves as director and authorial presence to the spectacle, shaping the encounter and determining the poses. He adopts the gaze structuring these pairs into familial relation, a gaze reflected in the screen of their masked presences. This is clear in one picture where the photographer's shadow is literally reflected in the figures represented.

But, relinquishing the gaze, the photographer also appears himself—as Lucybelle Crater, of course—in the first and the last images, taken with a self-timer.[15] In the first (Figure 3.5) he is identified as Lucybelle's 46-year-old husband and he is named, Ralph Eugene Meatyard, in the list of illustrations. But that list fails to name the "mystery people" on the last page (Figure 3.6). This is the only picture in which Madelyn Meatyard, in men's clothes, wears the transparent mask and Gene himself wears a dress and the grotesque female mask. Apparently this picture was taken toward the very end of Meatyard's life and developed posthumously. He had lost so much weight during his cancer treatment that his body had become thin and feminized, whereas Madelyn's, in comparison, looks solid and masculine in her pants and workshirt. The caption identifies the two as "close friends," sharing the same name, one leaning gently on the other. The masks hide the struggle with illness, the mourning preceding death: they exhibit the same expressions we have been studying throughout the album. But here not only the face and the name but the bodies themselves—as well as illness and health, life and death—have become interchangeable. Whereas the masks and the clothes disguise the individual bodily materiality, the bodies hint at another story. But that story can only be read contextually, through the grieving testimony of his surviving friends.

Meatyard's posthumous pictures document the limitation of family photography, that which it cannot record or tell. At the same time, in their temporality, they hauntingly inscribe the irreversibility of the photograph's relation to its referent and that referent's own presence in the picture only as an already absent—dead—other.

Read contextually, in relation to his illness and impending death, Meatyard's family pictures are all pictures of him, family pictures which become allo-portraits and thus self-portraits. In this reading, Meatyard as photographer is completely implicated in the scene of his photographs. But in their masked anonymity, these are also generic family pictures, engaging every viewer in a scene of recognition and a relational connection. Like the highway sign in the O'Connor story, the conventions exposed here interpellate the viewer, suturing us into these strange images. On some level, we are each affiliated with this "family" and represented by it—each of us could be, each of us is, Lucybelle Crater. What we recognize, with a smile, is a sense of human familial interconnection in which the family is suffocating and grotesque, and, at the same time, touching and engaging even in its erasure of individuality and expression.

We recognize the construction of the subject in the familial, and the way that the familial is the ideological. For these figures are deeply interconnected not just with one another but with the material scenes and objects which surround them—the interiors, back yards, and cars of the 1950s and 1960s suburban culture of the United States—all structured by a familial gaze. With the alienation effect of his masks, Meatyard can demonstrate, even as he criticizes, how, in the words of Jo Spence, "visual representation privileges the nuclear family by naturalizing, romanticizing, and idealizing family relationships above all others."[16]

*screens*

The gaze that shapes Meatyard's family album and is represented in his photographs is a familial gaze. Thus Meatyard's photographs can provide a playful illustration of the way in which the individual subject is constructed relationally through an elaborate and multiply inflected process of looking. The external gaze of the ideological Other, in this case, the gaze of familiality, positions these subjects in relation to one another and to the ideologies that interpellate them. In picture after picture, Meatyard's album creates a cumulative and repetitive narrative of this process which we can read by referring back to our own familial experiences, for his masks are anonymous enough to be broadly inclusive. The familiality of the gaze is readable in these pictures through its excessive performance, its parody of the all too familiar conventions of the family album, evoked in the title.

Jacques Lacan's writings on visuality theorize the important role of seeing in the formation of the subject and, read in relation to Meatyard's images, can provide some useful terms for our discussion of family pictures. In Lacan's mirror stage, the subject first apprehends him- or herself as a coherent image, a misrecognition which disguises the profound incongruities and disjunctions on which identity is necessarily based. The visual sense of self that results is a false one, but it provides a welcome antidote to the fragmentary bodily experience of the child. The mirror self is an ideal self, a projection.[17] Looking, then, is a complicated process, a form of cognition that is not to be trusted, that is and must be inflected by other psychic, epistemological, and ideological forces as the imaginary is redefined by the symbolic.

Even at this point, in the imaginary, the symbolic intrudes through the workings of the gaze, the determining Other that shapes the image as well as the looking process. In our common conception, the camera becomes a metaphor for the gaze, the instrument through which we can try to visualize and understand it. "In the scopic field," Lacan says, "the gaze is outside, I am looked at, that is to say, I am a picture. This is the function that is found at the heart of the institution of the subject in the visible. What determines me, at the most profound level, in the visible, is the gaze that is outside . . . Hence it comes about that the gaze is the instrument through which light is embodied and through which . . . I am *photo-graphed*."[18] In the "mirror stage" the subject conceives of her/himself as an image, but at the same time the subject is also seen/constituted as an image from the outside by the Other, photographed by the gaze.[19] Looking into the mirror, the subject depends on the confirming look of the other, usually the mother's look which enables the process of image formation. The moment of seeing, which is also the moment of being seen, is a moment of interconnection between exteriority and interiority, and between self and other, usually a familial other who thus inflects the image the subject incorporates as a self-image. Looking is thus inherently relational.[20]

The visual exchange between members of the familial group takes place within the ideological field of the gaze. Meatyard's photographs clarify the exteriority of the gaze that shapes the visual interaction of familial subjects; they demonstrate the family's implication in the social, the economic, and the ideological, in the narrative of health and illness, life and death. The camera's gaze, Meatyard implies, not only records but structures these moments of exchange, repositioning the subject, again and again, throughout a lifetime, in the familial, thus defined.

Meatyard's album suggests that we all function as *subjects and as objects* in a complex visual field not entirely determined by the gaze, but also the product of a series of more individual, local, and contingent looks, which are mutually constitutive, reversible, and reciprocal. "I see only from one point, but in my existence I am looked at from all sides," Lacan explains (*Four Fundamental Concepts,* 72). In addition to being subject to the familial gaze, these looks are mediated by other elements of visuality highlighted by Lacan. The *image* and the *screen* intervene between the subject and the object of the look, structuring the system of representation in which looking takes place. The image/screen is the space where the visual field is localized and historicized, where light is refracted and filtered. It is, as I have argued, the space of ideological determination, and thus it is also where looking is redirected and thus possibly altered.

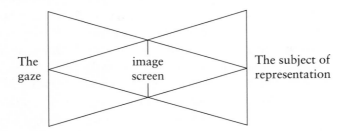

In Lacan's third diagram illustrating perception, subject and object are mutually reflective and interchangeable as light bounces off each and reflects back to the other. But they become visible only through the mediation of filtering screens. In her rich readings of Lacan, Kaja Silverman specifies the ideological status and the potentially subversive meanings of the screen. Subjects are constituted and differentiated in relation to a screen that is informed and shaped by a variety of parameters—class, race, gender, sexuality, age, nationality—that determine the ways in which they see and are seen. As it is filtered through these screens, the familial gaze is historicized and contextualized—marked by race, class, historical moment, location, nationality, ethnicity, sexuality, among other determinants.[21] If the gaze and look cannot constitute subjectivity except through the grid of the screen, then the screen becomes the space of the subject's active intervention— through mimicry or masquerade—in the imaginary relationship. Here Silverman attributes agency to the looking subject, thus opening the space for resistance, for the image/screen is culturally generated and therefore can also be culturally manipulated, resisted, or contested.

I would argue that Meatyard's masks—like Lüthi's elaborate makeup and dress-up, like Spiegelman's mouse masks—function as image/screens which interpose themselves between the camera (or the look that guides the pencil) and the object of representation, reflecting, and thereby constructing, the image that will be represented and explicitly demonstrating thereby the act of manipulation that the image/screen enables in response to the gaze. Meatyard's family album, moreover, makes visible what is inherent but masked in the very activity of perception—that we both look and are looked at, and that the subject is installed in the social through that double, mutual, perceptual relationship which makes every spectator also a spectacle.[22] Clearly, the looking subject is always already *in* the image, shaping it with his or her own reflection or projection. The winter-garden picture of Roland Barthes's mother acquires particular significance only through the son's projection of his own desire to be seen by her. Looking and being looked at are identical processes for Lacan—when you look you are also seen; when you are the object of the look you return it, even if only to reflect light back to its source: "things look at me and yet I see them" (*Four Fundamental Concepts,* 109).

That mutuality and specularity of looking, as well as that fundamental masking and misrecognition, are nowhere more constitutive than in the space of the family. They are fundamental to the familial look, which is institutionalized through the screen or mask of a culturally and historically specific familiality, so graphically represented in Meatyard's photographs. Inserting itself between the hegemonic familial gaze and the individual, local, and often resistant familial looks, the screen of familiality, like Meatyard's masks, makes visible the functioning of familial ideology, even as it provides the space where that ideological function might become the object of play, reversal, or dispersal. In its very reversibility, the mask of familiality is also the space of possible contestation: "The life you save may be your own."

The mystery of Meatyard's pictures elicits readerly investment and provokes a series of questions and responses that do not erase the enigmatic character of the images but fill in narratives around them—narratives that, in their opacity, they will necessarily challenge and resist. In pushing the familial gaze and screen to an extreme impersonality where, surprisingly, the personal returns with all its moving tenderness and in all its aversion, through a series of familial looks provided by the viewer, Meatyard begins to chart an oppositional visual discourse, as well as a visual meta-discourse.

## "i am photo-graphed"

A few months after the publication of *The Mother/Daughter Plot,* the *Dartmouth Alumni Magazine* asked me to write a short article on the book and on my course about mothers and daughters. The article was to be accompanied by a photograph and a biographical sketch about me, but since the editor knew my mother, she suggested that we use a photograph of me with my mother. I was pleased: here would be a chance to create an image of our own parallel to the one on the book's cover. But the photo session in which we posed for this picture was more complicated than either my mother or I expected.

The magazine's staff photographer, Jon Gilbert Fox, came to my house late on a spring afternoon. He placed us in one of the few sunny spots in the living room; I was perched uncomfortably on the wooden arm of a couch and my mother was leaning behind me. We tried serious and smiling poses, but in every case we felt stiff and uncomfortable. I realized that we were expected to act out our relationship, project some of its depth, but the constraints of the occasion made that very difficult: as the author of the article, I was supposed to occupy the foreground of the image, with my mother posing in the immediate background. At the end of the session, we asked the photographer to take some more "natural" poses for our own albums. Here we stood next to each other, or my mother sat down while I stood behind her with my arms around her. We felt freer to smile, even to laugh. It was a tender moment, though I know we were both confused about what it might mean to each of us, and hoped the prints would reveal that meaning.

3.8

For the article, the photographer and the editor chose an image that both my mother and I felt quite unhappy about—one in which we failed to recognize ourselves—but of which the photographer was deservedly proud (Figure 3.8). In fact it earned him many compliments, and he later exhibited it in a show of his work. For Fox, the image illustrated the mother/daughter relation: he liked the intertwined hands, the merged faces, the multiply interlacing bodies, the soft blurry trees in the background. Why were we so miserable with this choice? I don't think it was because we didn't "look good" in the photograph, or that we "looked old," or that my mother's wrinkles were showing, or my double chin. Turning our familial looks to read this image, we feel dissatisfaction, as though the photographer had failed to deliver a picture that we might want to publish and publicize. Perhaps this picture tells a story of a relationship we do not want to claim.

But what exactly is the story it tells? What do the overlapping unsmiling faces and interlacing hands reveal? Having just participated in the process of its construction, we nevertheless read the image as a record, we read it against some notion of truth value. And as such it remains, at most, the occasion for a repeated conversation between me and my mother—our continuing unhappiness with it, our unconvinced reassurances, an uneasy irresolution repeated each time the picture comes up in conversation, the desire at once to display and to suppress it.

I realize as I study this picture, as well as the others we purchased in which we smile and look happier, that I wanted them to reveal to me aspects of our relationship I didn't know about, I wanted them to tell me a story I could add to my collection of familial narratives. But I stand before it as puzzled as before Meatyard's masks, or before the photograph of my grand-mother and aunt. Although these photographs were taken at divergent moments in the history of photography, involving completely different proc-esses of posing, I find the expressions on the faces in them equally inscru-table, equally difficult to read, equally masked by an opaque screen of familiality, another curtain I have difficulty opening. Its codes are visible to me, the look I apply to them is the familial look I am trying to describe in this book, but its masks will not be lifted. Perhaps it is the familial look itself that makes it difficult to read this picture which will not reveal any identifiable truth. It will only leave me conscious of all that it cannot show, or all that I cannot see in it. It can illustrate, abstractly, the workings of the familial gaze of the photographer's camera, filtered through the image/ screens of our particular circumstances, of our own desires and projections. It can record one of the many *photo-sessions* in which I continue to be inscribed/to inscribe myself as a familial subject. It can offer food for reflection and conversation, it can encourage particular readings of its de-tails, but, as a visual representation of a relationship, it can only frustrate.

There are, nevertheless, many ways I can use this image to explore and perhaps to contest the familial gaze. I can use it to ask questions, for example, rather than accepting it for fact. I can see it as fluid rather than fixed; I can read it against other images, against other narratives, I can read it with and against my memories and desires, my longings and fears. I can read it alongside those other photographs, that of my grandmother and aunt and our old travel certificate picture, and I can produce a dialogue between these images, separated by eighty and thirty years yet strangely mirroring one another. I can begin to see how certain images repeat themselves in our lives in overdetermined ways, and I can wonder about the sources of these repetitions and the "unconscious optics" that structure the life of every family. And in this process of reading—a process that is personal and analytic, visual and discursive—I am both spectator and spectacle, both subject and object. These pictures are allo-portraits and family pictures: the process of reading them is deeply affiliative, relational, familial, yet it is also aesthetic, political, and theoretical.

As I think about these photographs, however, I realize that one of the primary elements of the familial look is that it occurs within a closed circle. What happens when that circle is enlarged to include other viewers and readers? Meatyard's images invite both affiliative and alienated looks: we recognize ourselves in his masks, even as we rush to disavow that recognition. But what is my readers' relationship to my family images? What kind of look mediates between the protective circle of the familial and the public scrutiny of academic writing? What are the ethics, what are the politics, of this "exposure," this public reading of images that generate their meanings in the private realm?

The conventions of family photography, like Meatyard's masks and Barthes's refusal to show us his mother's picture, are designed to keep the family's secrets and to protect it from public scrutiny. Family albums include those images on which family members can agree and which tell a shared story. Pictures that diverge from the communal narrative tend to be discarded as "bad" or "unrepresentative." But even within the album, images remain opaque, objects of a quick glance but not objects of scrutiny, reading, or interpretation—lest looking beyond the surface of the image, or outside its frame, might upset the delicate balance of agreement on which the construction of the album and the narrative of family rests. Victor Burgin's description of reading photographs applies most pertinently to family pictures: "To look at a photograph beyond a certain period of time is to court a frustration; the image which on first looking gave pleasure has by degrees become a veil behind which we now desire to see."[23] The curtains often figured in the images are the emblems of this frustration. Going beyond the surfaces, telling the stories surrounding the images, attempting to open the curtains, might offer a way out of the hermetic circle of familial hegemony. But the complicated configurations of gazes, looks, and image/screens exchanged within the familial makes any real exposure impossible: family pictures, including self-portraits, will continue to resist understanding.

My reading of my family photographs in this chapter has been an explicitly intertextual one, in dialogue with Lacoue-Labarthe, Lüthi, and Meatyard's meta-discourses. Their imagetexts reveal for me some of the conventions of self-portraiture and of family photography, and their interconnection. This practice of reading continues to be based on affiliation and familiality. Jo Spence, however, asks: "How can we begin to change the portrait, to change ideas of what should and should not go into our family albums?"[24] Her challenge is a difficult one. Even Lüthi's strange and subversive images do not provide a way out of the circle of familiality, as Lacoue-Labarthe's reading demonstrates. Even Meatyard's critical masks cannot disguise the tender familial feelings he projects onto his images. At this point we need perhaps to turn to the very peculiar "self"-portraits of Cindy Sherman, which demonstrate more graphically and disturbingly, I believe, than Lüthi or Meatyard what it might entail to "change the portrait." Sherman's work does indeed take the familial subject to its very limit, subjecting it to gazes and screens that might remove it from the familial altogether, challenging us to imagine a subject that defies the familial gaze.

## *performances*

"They're not at *all* autobiographical," says Cindy Sherman about the characters she enacts and represents in her photographs.[25] Yet, from her black and white film stills of the late 1970s, to the color images of the 1980s, to the recent history portraits and images of objects and body parts, Sherman's project is, as Lisa Phillips has said, "connected to the question of identity."[26] Although, as photographer, director, makeup artist, designer, actor, and protagonist, she is fully the subject of her photographs, Sherman calls into question any received notion of subjectivity or identity as presence, emphasizing instead its performative and theatrical character, the self as, in Henry Sayre's terms, an "endless 'acting out.'"[27] Parodying the illusion of mimetic representation that still dominates our conception of the photographic genre, Sherman unhinges, more fully than Meatyard or Lüthi, the connection I have made between the construction of the photographic and the familial subjects. Through endless variation of makeup, costume, and cultural citation, Sherman relinquishes any connection between image and referent, and thus resists any possible familial or affiliative look (Figure 3.9).

"But are we so certain that autobiography depends on reference, as a photograph depends on its subject or a (realistic) picture on its model?" Paul de Man asks.[28] Sherman's pictures are admittedly simulacra, reproductions of reproductions. They refer only to a world of images and stereotypes of women ranging from cinematic to historical representation, from Marilyn Monroe to Marie Antoinette. The pictures, Sherman suggests, "should trigger your memory so that you feel you have seen it before" (Nilson, 77). If indeed we have seen it before, it is in the movies, on billboards, or on television. Each of the scenes presented is a performance of a performance. There is no return of the dead here, and no mourning.

But this postmodern play with simulation is also a tease: "Her hall of mirrors," says Lisa Phillips, "her masquerade conceals her real identity: Cindy Sherman is hidden in her self-exposure" (16). But is there a "real identity," is there a Cindy Sherman beyond the makeup, the masks, the costumes, the prosthetic body parts, the celluloid of the film? If Sherman's pictures are "allo-portraits"[29] par excellence, it is not because they exist in any kind of relationship—they assert the absence of relation, the accomplishment of isolation. The only "real" self, I would insist, is coextensive with the mask, the makeup, and the costume. It is constructed in relation only to other performances, other artifacts, and thus it is itself always *other*, scattered through and among the debris of our culture.

Sherman can provide a useful lens through which to reconsider the enactments we have seen in Lüthi's and Meatyard's images. There are many similarities: all three photographers overturn photographic expectations, all use staging devices, masking, makeup, artifice. Yet Lüthi's and Meatyard's image sequences suggest and evoke a story, fragments of a narrative, an illusion of depth, even as they remind their viewers of their artifice: they teach us how we look at images and how we tend to invest them with story and with meaning. Sherman's photographs, in contrast, arrest their viewers on the flatness of their surfaces; their performances are completely self-contained. They do not draw us in, they do not evoke our curiosity. Most of the poses do not address a spectator but stare blankly into a space that is neither inside nor outside the frame. If there is a body here it is a static, frozen, dead body, continuous with the fake breasts and buttocks, the innards of the late 1980s, early 1990s series.[30]

It is impossible to find a familial look in Sherman's images: no familial subject exists in these pictures. In placing the "question of identity" and even the body into the larger arena of cultural artifacts and representations, eventually even into the space of recycled debris, Sherman takes it out of its familial origin and out of its relational, affiliative construction. In doing so,

3.9

she offers a definitive answer to Baudelaire's question about art and to Lacoue-Labarthe's meditation on it. As Rosalind Krauss suggests, "For the play of stereotype in her work is a revelation of the artist herself as stereotypical."[31] This could not be further removed from Baudelaire's standard of art.

Critics who write about Sherman's work rarely single out a particular image, but tend to discuss the work in its totality, grouping the images into different periods.[32] Her images can be contemplated; their references can be discussed and analyzed, they can be seen as allegorical or symptomatic, as tools of feminist resistance or objects of cultural appropriation. But, as much as they are composed out of the stockpile of stories that surround us, it is difficult to tell a story about or around them. All of Sherman's images are untitled, merely dated and numbered. They refuse to participate in the narrative frameworks with which we are comfortable and instead insist on existing in the space of their production. In my own reading, the look viewers apply to these pictures is neither identificatory nor disidentificatory; it is certainly not affiliative, for the images themselves repel affiliation. There is no space into which the viewer can move in these images: they are constructed outside of the social or familial spaces that we are used to inhabiting and the gestures they make toward those spaces are multiply mediated and excessively parodic. As Cathy Davidson argues, "there is no self, no soul, but the photograph."[33]

*Untitled Film Still* #14, for example, like many of the others, includes a number of frames within it: the mirror, the door visible in the mirror, the picture frame on the dresser, the cabinet hanging on the wall behind the woman (Figure 3.9). In her domestic setting, surrounded by images of herself and caught in the midst of a drama that includes a glass of wine, a jacket signaling her imminent departure, the scared look that indicates someone may have just surprised her, and holding a mysterious object in her outstretched hand, this woman is enclosed in a mystery that leads to no depth, to no story. She is encased in self-reflections that suggest no relations except to cultural myths and stereotypes. The mirror and the photograph duplicate her on the same level as the mirror reflects the candles, the plant, or the wine glass.

Sherman's work suggests that outside the possibility of the familial gaze and look we can find no depth, not even an illusion of depth. Can we intimate from her images that familiality and sociality alone provide the space of interiority, memory, relationship, continuity? The flatness and opacity of Sherman's photographs, their refusal to reveal a subject, their absent affect, may well constitute part of their postmodern appeal. It may take such an extreme departure from our ways of looking to extricate the subject, once and for all, from the closed circle defined by the familial gaze and by familial looks, by the image/screens of the familial. It is unclear, however, if what remains is a human subject in any recognizable or identifiable sense.

# $\mathcal{U}$NCONSCIOUS OPTICS

To a great extent then, the inexpensive home-camera may have invented an important part of what we've come to mean in America in the twentieth century by family and by all the tangled feelings evoked in the echoes of that most loaded of human nouns.

REYNOLDS PRICE

The camera introduces us to unconscious optics as does psychoanalysis to unconscious impulses.

WALTER BENJAMIN

Whose version of family life do you inhabit in your family? How do you know anything about your own history—most of all the history of your subjectivity, and the part that images have played in its construction?

JO SPENCE

## *freud's gaze*

We have very few photographs on display in our house. There were none until a few years ago when my husband Leo's mother, Rose, died and we placed three pictures of her into two frames on his dresser. One was taken at a family reunion some years earlier and shows this diminutive woman surrounded by her six grandchildren, some of whom tower over her, while the youngest, our son Gabriel, then still a toddler, is squirming on her lap. Another picture, in the same frame, shows Rose a month before her death with two of her sons and three grandsons, now considerably older. I took that photograph on her last visit to us; it was the Seder, everyone was dressed up, we were going to celebrate with friends. The third was taken of her with her four children at her seventieth birthday party almost exactly a year before her death. She has a different hairstyle in each, but otherwise she looks equally comfortable, equally happy, surrounded by children and grandchildren, each time taking up so much less space in the image than any of her descendants.

Once those pictures appeared on the dresser, signaling the fragility and the preciousness of familial togetherness, others came to join them around our bedroom: first some images of my parents and one of the informal pictures of me and my mother taken by Jon Gilbert Fox for the *Dartmouth Alumni Magazine,* and then, when my son Oliver started taking photographs, a few of his pictures, such as a close-up of his brother Gabriel and a casual picture of Leo and me outside on our deck. As I arrange and rearrange the photographs, I try to ensure that everyone in the family is represented. Still, I fail: "There's no picture of me on this dresser," Oliver remarked just as I was trying to find one of him and his older brother Alex to display, reminded of their absence by the work on this chapter. "Where's your father?" one of my friends asks me as she surveys the dresser, and I show her some pictures that are waiting for the right frame. The process of display is self-conscious, unnatural. The pictures don't quite fit that setting, edged out as they are by knickknacks, jewelry boxes, and cologne bottles.

I always have pictures on my office bulletin board, pictures of my children and my husband, of friends' children, of me with women friends, of my parents. On my desk at home, I display the picture of my grandmother and aunt that I used on the cover of *The Mother/Daughter Plot* and the portrait of my mother and me published in the *Dartmouth Alumni Magazine.* I look at them frequently, placing them in an ever-changing dialogue with one another. I particularly like keeping the same images for as many years as it takes to make them iconic and thereby more and more unnoticeable and invisible.

Thus, as I start writing this chapter in a temporary office during my sabbatical at the National Humanities Center in North Carolina, I have put up the same pictures of my children that were on my office bulletin board during my last sabbatical at the Bunting Institute in Cambridge eight years earlier. In these photos, the kids were eight years younger than they are now, and my work space acquires a comforting continuity by this repetition of a former setting. But there is also a strange dislocation in their smaller and what now seems like their "cuter" presence. What was I thinking years ago when the children were small, when I looked at these pictures on that bulletin board day after day? How different am I now, when my children are so clearly, so measurably altered? How do their images affect my thinking and writing? I wonder what these pictures tell me about who my children are and who I am, about how we look at one another and through these looks construct our relationships and ourselves. And I wonder about what these pictures cannot tell me.

Why, if photographs play a significant role in my work space, are they marginal, almost absent, in my living space? Our house has many other objects on display: some contemporary paintings, exhibition posters gathered by one or the other of us during the last thirty years, a number of treasured African and Afro-Brazilian masks and sculptures collected by Leo on research trips to Africa and Brazil, and many pieces of folk art from other travels. I often think of the origins of these objects, of their displacement, and of the links they establish between various spaces around the world and our house in the woods of Vermont. I have a more intimate relationship with the objects I brought into this marriage—the 1966 poster of Magritte's stone bird, for example, the first I ever bought, or the still life on a poster for a Picasso lithograph exhibition at the Boston Museum of Fine Arts in 1968. I think of them tacked up or taped on the walls of previous rooms and apartments, eventually dry-mounted, some of the cracks and holes still showing, finally framed, and I appreciate the continuities they forge among my living quarters, relationships, marriages.

Two posters are particularly arresting, even determinative in our family and social life. When you walk into our house from what in Vermont is known as a mudroom, the first thing you see is a finger pointing at you in a Roy Lichtenstein image on a poster from a Swedish op art exhibit. It might take you a while to notice that the finger follows you as you walk around the room, pointing directly at you insistently and relentlessly. I have always been intrigued and amused by the trick in the picture, curious about but not understanding how it really worked. I feel addressed every time, although I wonder which ideological systems and structures might be seeking me out as I walk through the kitchen on a given day.

Equally striking to me is the Valerio Adami lithograph of Freud (the red and purple version of his "Sigmund Freud in viaggio verso Londra") which used to hang across from the Lichtenstein, but which now hangs in our new bedroom. It's a schematic drawing of a face wearing enormous glasses of pure glaring white and a large hand that thrusts a mysterious object (a fly?) into areas of bold purple, red, blue-green, and black. It is as amusing and as disturbing to have Freud staring at me in the bedroom as to have a finger point at me as I walk around the kitchen. In both cases, I feel the effect of the gaze of the Other, in both I know I am interpellated by discourses and structures "out there" that have made their way—that I have invited—"in here," humorous, though also perhaps necessary, reminders of the public nature of domestic life, of the ideologies that structure and determine the private and familial. I even take some comfort in Freud's patient surveillance of my waking and sleeping and bathing and lovemaking, for he stands for all that I don't know and don't see, all that remains unexamined, as I, too, often hurriedly, go through the motions of my life. Static and immobile, unlike Lichtenstein's more interactive finger, a disembodied face made up almost entirely of stark white eyes, Adami's Freud reminds me that even as I see, I am seen. As Lacan would say, "I am a picture . . . I am *photographed.*"

Adami's Freud has become a structuring image for me, an icon of the familial plots in which, unthinkingly, we all participate and which, often, we try to resist. The family pictures that are beginning to spring up around the room are also monitored by Freud's gaze and make his presence all the more necessary as he organizes them into the conventional familial narratives to which every one of them is subject, but which each one, in its particularity, exceeds or subverts. In their interaction with Freud's gaze, they reveal to me how inescapable a condition visuality is in domestic space: the photos are records, documents of the looks and gazes which order and organize familial relations, of the often unconscious and seemingly invisible patterns structuring familial interactions, of the screens through which we define ourselves responding to and resisting the familial gaze. This inescapability may explain my hesitation about putting family pictures into the space in which the family lives, but not into my work space. If Freud's gaze makes me too uncomfortable as I dress in the morning, I can always suspend my awareness of the lithograph's production or acquisition, of its role in the story of our lives, and concentrate instead on the full purple or red in his image, on the ways the skylights are reflected in it, or on the bursts of color in the room. But family pictures allow no such evasion.

## unconscious optics

How does vision structure the day-to-day practices of family life? How does it produce family relations and form family memory? An inquiry into familial looking must begin by exploring the ways in which the family is inscribed within a system of representation that inflects its construction. It needs to examine the elements of such representational systems, the particular historical circumstances and conventions that shape them and their power to uphold or contest dominant familial ideologies, to construct competing familial narratives. Close readings of commonplace visual images, such as family pictures and other domestic objects, as well as particular scenes of looking and particular photo sessions within a family's history can illuminate the workings of the familial gaze and familial looks. Such readings can also reveal the particular social and cultural screens that mediate these looks, inflecting the familial gaze with racial, ethnic, class, and sexual difference. In this book I use such close readings to build a supple theoretical vocabulary that can help us understand the psychological layers of this visual process. In this chapter I propose to adapt Walter Benjamin's term "unconscious optics" to elaborate on and perhaps to clarify the Lacanian notions of the gaze, look, and image/screen within the family's visual dynamics.

The family as a social construct depends on the invisibility of its structuring elements. Inasmuch as visuality functions as such a structuring element determined by the familial gaze, its workings must to some degree remain unconscious if familial ideology is to be perpetuated and imposed. In this chapter I ask: What are the elements of the family's "unconscious optics," and through what means might we explore them? I propose, through readings of several family pictures and stories, to sketch this relation of visibility and invisibility, conscious and unconscious in the family's field of vision.

Benjamin wrote of the "Optisch-Unbewußte" in his 1931 essay "A Short History of Photography" and in both versions of his 1936 "The Work of Art in the Age of Mechanical Reproduction." In all three accounts he is concerned with the invisible that is present inside the visible, those bodily movements that are too minute to be discerned by the human eye and too automatic to impinge on human consciousness. Edward Muybridge's series of still images of horses running, women walking, or men wrestling must have been in his mind. The camera reveals these movements:

> Evidently a different nature opens itself to the camera than opens to the naked eye—if only because an unconsciously penetrated space is substituted for a space consciously explored by man. Even if one has general knowledge of the way people walk, one knows nothing of a person's posture during the fractional second of a stride . . . Here the camera intervenes with the resources of its lowerings and liftings, its interruptions and isolations, its extensions and accelerations, its enlargements and reductions."[1]

Clearly, Benjamin means to focus on the minutest physiological processes, but his analogy for the workings of the camera is psychoanalysis, and the notion he invokes is the unconscious: "The camera introduces us to unconscious optics as does psychoanalysis to unconscious impulses." The camera is like psychoanalysis. There are optical processes that are invisible to the eye: they can be exposed by the mechanical processes of photography. The camera can reveal what we see without realizing that we do, just as psychoanalysis can uncover what we know without knowing that we do: what is stored in the unconscious. The camera can expose hidden dimensions of our actions and movements through its artificial techniques of making strange ("its lowerings and liftings, its interruptions and isolations, its extensions and accelerations, its enlargements and reductions"), just as psychoanalysis can reveal unconscious content through the formal and precise techniques of the therapeutic encounter.

"Unconscious optics," like the repressed content of the unconscious, disturb and disrupt our conscious acts of looking. Like any psychic process, looking is complex, multilayered, compelling. Perhaps, in establishing this analogy, Benjamin was thinking of the elaborate analogy Freud develops in his *Interpretation of Dreams* for the translation between the conscious and the unconscious mind:

> Everything that can be an object of our internal perception is *virtual,* like the image produced in a telescope by the passage of light rays. But we are justified in assuming the existence of the systems (which are not in any way psychical entities themselves and can never be accessible to our psychical perception) like the lenses of a telescope, which cast the image. And if we pursue this analogy, we may compare the censorship between two systems to the refraction which takes place when a ray of light passes into a new medium.[2]

What passes between the unconscious and consciousness functions like an optical instrument: a telescope, or perhaps a camera.

For Benjamin, photography is too transparent, too mimetic an art, one that disguises its own inability to represent.[3] By producing what appears to be a too straightforward or faithful reproduction of the photographed, the picture actually accentuates its own infidelity to a complicated and layered real. Together, increased mimetic illusion and mechanical reproduction rob photographs of the "aura" that characterizes the authentic work of art: the greater the technical advances, the closer the image is to the "real," the further removed the photograph becomes from the auratic and the more implicated it becomes in a realism that for Benjamin has dangerous, possibly fascistic, ideological implications. Benjamin's notion of "unconscious optics" intervenes in this development of photography in paradoxical ways. On the one hand, unconscious optics are the result of technical advances that offer ever greater mimetic possibilities. On the other, they expose or at least hint at the invisible behind and inside the transparently visible, not just the unseen but that which is unavailable to sight. Therefore they end up revealing precisely what Benjamin fears will disappear: the inability to represent that which must remain at the core of our technologies of representation. And, if we follow Freud's image of the telescope that mediates between unconscious and conscious, the processes of this revelation are multiply mediated and refracted.

Benjamin's convoluted argument gets at the basic tension in the photograph that we have encountered again and again in this book—the tension between the photograph's flatness and its illusion of depth, between the little a photograph reveals and all that it promises to reveal but cannot. His notion of unconscious optics is particularly resonant in the familial field. It is in the family, after all, that structures of repression operate most fully and forcefully and that the familial gaze, familial looks, and various screens of familiality intersect in unacknowledged ways both to reinforce and to challenge those structures.[4] But, as I argued in the previous chapter, looking occurs in the interface between the imaginary and the symbolic. It is mediated by complex cultural, historical, and social screens. Photographs may capture some of this process, but, as the opaque and masked images of Lüthi, Meatyard, and Sherman demonstrate, they alone do not allow us to read its many dimensions.

Family pictures, in particular, offer conventional surfaces resistant to deeper scrutiny. They say more about family romances than about actual details of a familial life. Since they say more through their absence than through their present content, they can illustrate the workings of an optical unconscious. Only the narratives that take shape in relation to the pictures can provide insight into the actual workings of unconscious optics: the confrontation of a family romance and the particular circumstances through which it is mediated within a given family, the interaction between individual familial looks and the familial gaze, by way of the screen—the unspoken, unacknowledged interrelations and intersubjective bonds that shape familial subjects and relationships—and, most poignantly, the persistence and resistance of certain patterns of looking and interaction within family groups.

This chapter is a reading of three texts that offer different approaches to the hidden but determinative dimension of looking that I am calling unconscious optics. The first, Sue Miller's *Family Pictures* (1990), is a novel which explores thematically the mechanisms of family photography.[5] The second, Jo Spence's *Putting Myself in the Picture: A Political, Personal and Photographic Autobiography* (1986), is a radical inquiry, in personal essay form, into the conventions of photographic practice and familial narrative conventions.[6] The third, Carrie Mae Weems's "Untitled (Kitchen Table Series)" (1990), is a family story constructed through a series of staged and stylized photographs featuring the photographer herself, accompanied by a written narrative.[7]

These three texts, like the works of the previous chapter, blur the boundary between self-portrait, allo-portrait, and family picture, but these highlight more fully the verbal-narrative dimension of the photographic imagetext. In spite of their generic differences, we can look at them here as different kinds of family chronicles or three unusual family albums, representing three families from radically different social contexts. Thus, while the masked images kept us on their surfaces, these narratives at least appear to invite us into recessed depths, thus providing some access to the unconscious optics that structure family ideology. But that invitation, that point of access, is differently marked as the familial gaze itself is contextualized and refracted through the screens of class and race.

## domesticating freud

Sue Miller's 1990 novel *Family Pictures* explores the constitutive role certain images can play in family life and family memory. Miller's family pictures are not just the photographs the daughter and narrator Nina takes as she grows up to be a professional photographer; they are also the scenes and images Nina, her parents, and her five siblings look at in their domestic life together, images that shape their memories and their narratives. The novel's description of these pictures and the stories it tells about them expose the functioning of visuality in family life and, particularly, its central role in the construction of the familial subject. We can read this novel and this particular family, then, for clues as to the workings of the unconscious optics operating within family structure more generally.

Although conventional in its fictional form—the multipersonal family chronicle—*Family Pictures* breaks its diegesis with the insertion of "prose pictures" and thereby challenges its own narrative mode. Thus, it resembles the family picture itself: the most conventional of images nevertheless has the capacity to operate on several levels at the same time and to subvert the very structure it so solidly upholds. Even though the text itself contains no actual images, the inscription of prose pictures into the novel opens it up to a visual as well as a verbal reading, forcing us to confront different ways of telling family stories. Although family photographs and the family chronicle in themselves can support and perpetuate a traditional family romance, Miller puts the two genres together. Thus she suggests that a redefinition of both photographic and narrative techniques—of how we look and how we tell our stories—might redefine our fantasies and expectations.

*Family Pictures* is a chronicle that reconstructs thirty years in the life of a white middle-class Chicago family, from the 1950s to the 1980s. David, a Freudian psychoanalyst, and Lainey, his Catholic homemaker wife, have six children. They separate, get back together, finally divorce. Assembled by the fourth child, Nina, the first-person narrator of several chapters, the story is told through the alternating perspectives of Nina herself, both parents, and the oldest son, Macklin. At the center of their history and their memories is the third child, Randall, an autistic boy who is sent to a boarding school at the end of the novel's first part and dies in a car accident at the beginning of the second. Randall's mysterious and silent existence structures David and Lainey's marriage and reveals their opposing Freudian and Christian world views. Macklin's development and Nina's need to understand her family, her use of photography as an epistemological tool, also derive from Randall's determining place in the family.

Most of the family's story can be read through the images on the kitchen wall of their house, a wall Nina eventually appropriates and reconstitutes in her own apartment. The foundational images on the wall are visual analogues to the chapters of the novel: the family's history exists in their pictures as well as in their words and thoughts. Lainey offers the first reading of the wall:

The walls were hung with the children's drawings and paintings, bright blobs of running colors, which Lainey loved; and with newspaper and magazine clippings and photographs of Lainey's heroes: Joseph Welch in a prim bow tie, Adlai Stevenson resting his worn-out shoes on a table in front of him during his losing campaign.

David had hung a photograph of Freud up with them—the famous portrait—but its piercing stare had frightened Nina. When she noticed it, she would cover her own eyes and say, "*No man!*"—would sometimes even whimper. When Lainey had found another picture of Freud, in an

old copy of *Life*—a slightly overexposed photograph of him and his wife
in a garden—she had substituted it . . .
   "We needed a more domestic Freud," she said . . . "The other one scared
Nina." (34)

The children's drawings and paintings share a wall with photographic
images that introduce a public history and a dominant ideology into the
household: Welch and Stevenson on the one hand, Freud on the other. The
violence of this intrusion of the public image into the domestic space can
be measured by Nina's fear of Freud's piercing gaze and her mother's need
to "domesticate" Freud, to reduce his gaze to a more domestic and circum-
stantial look: "Freud looked puzzled in the photo. He was frowning into
the sun" (34). Nina's initial fear of Freud develops into a stronger defiance
which is one of the sources of her photographic career. She later explains
to her sister Mary that taking pictures is her "little victory over all those
Freudian processes" (377) like repression or sublimation, though she eventually has to concede that visuality may also be governed by unconscious
processes.
   Although the composition of the kitchen wall changes over the years,
Freud's image remains central. Here is David's reading of the wall when he
returns to the family after some years of separation:

> The picture of Freud with his family in the garden was still there, spotted
> and browned with age. There was a clipping of JFK laughing, a photo-
> graph Nina must have taken of Randall and Mack together. There were
> three art postcards, two of annunciations . . . and one of Paul as a
> Harlequin, by Picasso. Underneath all of this someone had taped a three-
> by-five card with a recipe for Rice Krispies Treat. (208)

Lainey comments on the "crazy" choice of two annunciations, the "classic
and peaceful" Fra Angelico, as opposed to the more sexual Botticelli whose
Mary resists "as though part of her is wanting to run" (225). Except for the
smiling JFK, who has replaced Welch and Stevenson, and the commercial
intrusion of Rice Krispies, this arrangement circles around Randall—seen
in the Picasso harlequin, twinned with Mack whose life is completely determined by his brother's disability, "explained" differently by the annunciations and by Freud.
   But when the images reappear in Nina's own apartment, she reads them
with reference to herself:

> I began thinking of them as elements in a Rock-Scissors-Paper game, which

contained the mystery of my childhood. Which had the most power? Freud? That analytic version of my parents' life, which insisted that Randall—and their misery—had its source in my mother's wackiness and should be struggled against, fought, cured? Or the annunciations, which said, in effect, that Randall was holy, that the failure was my father's in not accepting what was a given, what was fate—as both of the annunciation Marys did in separate ways, as Mack did in his twinship with Randall. (379)

Nina supplements these images with a picture of her pregnant sister, also a Mary, representing "perhaps the reality of gestation and birth, which should have taken over the argument anyway with its simple, pressing insistence on life" (379). Later Nina adds an enormous family photograph she took professionally at an unknown couple's sixty-fifth anniversary party because it "seemed connected somehow" (383). Eventually she realizes that these images are not alternate explanations of her family's mystery, challenging her to choose the correct one, but that they are in themselves a puzzle whose connections are different for any given family member, just as each element of the puzzle would vary by another selection. Nina claims that for her, in particular, "the family photograph held the answer. That it was really a portrait of a kind of reckless courage, a testament to the great loving carelessness at the heart of every family's life, even ours. That each child represented such risk, such blind daring on its parents' parts—such possibility for anguish and pain—that each one's existence was a kind of miracle" (384).

Nina's conviction that her version of the family story is uniquely hers is contradicted in the course of the novel, as certain images and narratives acquire collective fetishistic power for all. The kitchen wall was there for all to see, and its images may well be as formative as other family stories which form the focus of the individual chapters: the day Mack cuts his foot, or the day Lainey's mother dies, or the day Randall hits and injures Lainey. Certain images remain constant: Mack is obsessed with Randall's resemblance to him and calls him his twin; Mack's graduation photo of the entire family group, taken by David, resembles Sarah's birthday photo, taken by Nina, or the picture Nina took of them all by the Christmas tree. The large family picture Nina takes at the end recalls all of these as it affirms familial bonds and organizes a completely unwieldy group into coherence and hierarchy. Any of the Eberhardts could have this insight: "He had an image, then, of what they must look like, pressed together, their heads leaned in, their faces presented. A family" (196). When Nina takes her pictures and looks at them, she is merely recording and exposing, inadvertently bringing to consciousness, the family's ways of engaging with one another visually, mostly around the mystery of Randall: "I used to think that you were trying to get some handle on him by taking his picture over and over. That you were trying to solve some mystery," Lainey tells her (335). Nina shares with her parents and siblings the attempt to "solve some mystery" about Randall. In control of the camera and of a part of the novel's verbal narrative, she can go further than they in her effort to expose the family's unconscious optics—the interaction between their different familial looks and perspectives and the familial gaze.

The family relationships often remain nonverbal and are expressed only in exchanged looks: Nina looking soberly at her mother's rage; David's look of "pure cold hatred" for Lainey; Mack's sense that his mother has been watching his own sexual initiation; Nina's shock at not being seen by her father on the street; the children watching from the landing a fight that leads to their parents' separation. There are other, more voyeuristic scenes of familial looking such as the many moments when any of them might discover Lainey sitting in the kitchen in the middle of the night with the sleepless Randall. These looks organize familial interaction and negotiate relationships nonverbally, often unconsciously. They reinforce roles and mediate power struggles; they solidify bonds as well as fragmentations; they instantiate the workings of the gaze.

One of the most disturbing things about Randall's autism, in addition to his inability to speak, is his failure to return other people's looks, his failure to see: Randall is "unseeing," he "rides on, looking neither left nor right" (17). He is thus unable to participate in the familial drama and, in his parents' and siblings' interpretation, he demands a completely different form of relation, a different kind of parental love, different treatment: "Randall lived safe from neurosis. He'd escaped Freud" (171), Lainey thinks as she lies down next to him to watch him sleep. She watches him, but, as she sees it, he cannot look at her and thus has a sexuality separate from desire, innocent of oedipal feelings. No wonder she is so utterly shocked by his masturbation: never able to perceive his sexuality, she could also deny the erotics of her feelings for him.

By not looking Randall also cannot be seen in the same way as others; he can puzzle Freud or evade his gaze altogether. He thus cannot acquire any recognizable subjectivity: there is neither mirror stage nor photo session for Randall. He can internalize no image of himself, nor can he serve as an image to be appropriated. He has no memory and therefore no history; the visual memories that constitute his siblings form no coherent picture in his mind, as far as they know. For Randall there is neither recognition nor misrecognition; he stands outside the system of signification and representation that constitutes subjects in the visual and in the familial. Unseeing, he is seen. Always in the place of the other, he transforms every portrait into an allo-portrait. In relation to Randall his parents and siblings can constitute themselves as "normal." But each does so in a different way.

Pictures serve not only to construct the individual subject but also to constitute and reconstitute a family unit that is forever in question. Who is in the family? Who is out? Are Liddie and Mack the "real" children, with the other four (or three) as what the father cruelly calls the "afterthoughts" or the "last straws?" Should Randall be at home or should he be away? Who has a room in the house and who doesn't? How can Randall, who has no space of his own, nevertheless be the central presence? Should he be included in the graduation scene? Should David? How can Nina be in the picture if she is the photographer? Maybe David should take the picture? How can they get away from home? How can they get back into the picture?

The family's ways of looking, perhaps unconsciously imprinted on them all, actually translate themselves into Nina's photographs and even into her photographic style. When Nina shows her pictures to her father he comments on the "gimmick" that defines them: "In many of the photographs, I'd been experimenting with a technique that results in a central sharp image around which the background appears to swirl in dizzying motion. I liked it because it recalled the way life felt to me when I was young, when you focus on what's important to you so clearly that everything else swims out of your consciousness" (14). If David sees these as a gimmick, he may only be trying to deny or suppress his own disturbing participation in this form of looking, made evident to him the day he realized that there was something wrong with Randall: "As he looks, it seems the other children, the parade itself, the adults watching, all swirl and blur, are only color, motion, like the background in a photograph" (17).

Nina's technique repeats David's central, foundational realization, a moment that changed his life, even as it gave expression to the rest of the family's engagement with their visual world. Invariably, Randall, whether present or absent, alive or dead, returns to the center of their perceptual spaces, and when he does, other things around him begin to blur. And as they see him, they also see themselves as different from him. Their look is fully focused and thereby it becomes disidentificatory, distanced and distancing. For David, his realization is a relief of "letting go of all the denial" (17). Seeing Randall "stripped of the illusions of normalcy they've spun around him" is for David a reassuring moment for it restores coherence, understanding, order; it reestablishes a distance that he had lost, that Lainey cannot regain. He needs to recognize Randall's difference in order to define himself.

But this form of looking also denies repression: as all things around the object in focus blur, the interconnections and affiliations that connect all family members disappear into the background and each can enjoy his or her own, illusory, separateness and particularity. What get repressed are the messy interrelations of family life, the mutual implications, the reflections and mirrorings that emphasize the ways in which Randall and the rest of the family do indeed live in the same domestic space.

It is from his own distant perspective that David records his impersonal and clinical observations of Lainey and Randall, referred to as L. and R., in a fateful journal he keeps as a result of his realization about Randall's autism. The analyst/father's journal makes the rest of them subjects of scrutiny of the unrelentingly Freudian familial gaze. Critics have argued that the camera gives Nina the same visual mastery and thus clinical distance from the family that David has enjoyed and allows her to disidentify from and contain the maternal, aligning herself with the paternal.[8] "Look at Nina, making us get little and unimportant in her magic lens," Lainey complains. Nina grins behind the camera. "It's true. You're shrimps. A million miles away" (175). Nina's first interest in photography arises in response to her own invisibility, her indistinguishability from her two younger sisters. Thus, instead of going to summer camp, she stays home to take a photography course, asserting her age and maturity in opposition to them.

But for Nina the camera is not only a way to see and thereby to be distant, to analyze, it is also a way to be seen: paradoxically, from behind the camera, she can attract attention and become more visible. This also repeats David's evolution from the impersonal and sarcastic observer in the journal to the one who offers his journal, and thus also himself, to be read. Realizing that the journal is neither "that horrible diary about how crazy [Lainey] was" nor "about Randall," David sees that it is about himself: "It's really just a young man's very philosophical discussion about which came first, the chicken or the egg" (362). Like Nina's pictures, the journal is both a product and an object of the look, it both observes and analyzes, and in itself it needs to be read and analyzed. If Nina's pictures repeat her father's ways of seeing, then his gift of the journal to her repeats her offering of her photographs to him.

Family memory, then, has this shared, tentative, and vulnerable quality. Its inherent visuality and contingency is exposed in pictures. In the visual, based on the fragmentary remnants that are photographs, one generation's memory is indistinguishable from another's. It is passed down from parents to children, from older to younger siblings. The novel begins with Nina's "wrong" memory of Randall's words at Mack's fourteenth birthday party. Liddie insists that this was her own much earlier memory, appropriated and altered by Nina to suit her needs. To Nina "it seems as clear . . . as a picture I might have taken" (4). Memories say as much about the present as about the past. They say as much about the person remembering as about the person remembered. More important, they comment on the shared and often unconscious preoccupations of the family or social group. Nina, like all the others, needs the memory of normalcy, of a "before" Randall's disturbing presence, which defies all available familial narratives, and which "escaped Freud." For the person born "after," such a memory is by necessity what, in relation to a familial or cultural past marked by trauma, I have called a postmemory. Photographs can be primary documents of postmemory, structuring its shape and its content: "it seems as clear as a picture I might have taken."

Nina's postmemory conforms in part to David's insight about Randall—each of them needs to normalize his or her world, to make it coherent through a form of self-definition in which Randall stands as truly other, and for each of them this need shapes familial memory and postmemory. Initially the camera plays this distancing role for Nina, but its function gradually shifts.

Nina's role in the novel is, in fact, to negotiate between, to revise, and to reframe her parents' memories and obsessions, their different ways of seeing. Having appropriated as her own primal scene David's moment of distance and separation—the moment he saw Randall as no longer "normal" but as autistic—and having repeated that moment for herself in her own visual work, Nina becomes interested in another primal moment derived not from her father's memory but from her mother's. As a child, she eavesdropped on her mother talking to a friend about having children: "For me, the air was suddenly thrumming over the beckoning cries of the game. This was it, then. The mothers were talking about *us*! About their children" (249). They were not just talking about raising children but about having them, what Mrs. Gordon calls "the goddamned labor." Lainey admits that she must have been "quite mad" to have six children, and Nina begins to see herself and her siblings as her mother's "symptom, the shape of her madness" (249–250). This scene of eavesdropping interrogates not paternal analysis but maternal impressions of deep and mysterious intersubjectivity. Nina thinks about conception and birth as a scene of origin, a primal scene that requires the imagination of postmemory for its visualization. As we will see, the birth she most wants to imagine is not her own but Randall's.

Nina is fascinated with pregnancy and labor, primarily with their visual qualities. In her teens a suspicion of pregnancy makes her run away from home. A later miscarriage breaks up her first marriage. She takes rolls of pictures of the very pregnant Mary: "We talked of everything inconsequential as she lay back in the tub, her feet propped against the wall above the nickel faucet, her belly rising solid as an island out of the lapping water, white and immense and taut. I was sitting on the toilet seat. I had trouble not staring at her. I actually thought I saw, once or twice, the moving pressure of a tiny heel or fist pushing her flesh from within" (376). This is the ultimate moment of intersubjective interconnection, fascinating and confusing as the maternal body is submerged in the tub the same way that the fetus swims in amniotic fluid, both almost too large to fit in the water, yet both still comfortable there. This symbiotic maternal/fetal body is meant to be the object of repression, but Nina's photographic practice wants to circumvent "all those Freudian processes" (377).

Pregnant in her own second marriage, Nina finds a way to end her story by imagining her mother's third pregnancy and incipient labor, just preceding Randall's birth. Based on some pictures David had taken that were included in the family album, this becomes another instance of Nina's postmemory: "And there's one of her alone that always fascinated me. Her mouth and eyes are peculiarly rounded, like a Kewpie doll's. She's feeling a contraction, a sharp one that almost makes her groan, that makes her think perhaps this baby means business after all" (386). Through the photograph Nina can see and feel what generally cannot be shared—the pain of a contraction, the instant prior to disconnection. She can be present at a moment that precedes, that initiates, not only her own birth but the entire family's course. In choosing this site as another of her own primal scenes, she opts for an example of confusing interconnection to oppose to David's privileged moment of separating insight. She chooses the maternal over the paternal. But in attempting to record that moment photographically she finds a way to incorporate David's way of seeing with Lainey's: he was, after all, the author of the initial picture (Daley, 22).

Nina's photographic work and her narrative are structured around primal fantasies attempting to resolve "the puzzle of who I was, the puzzle of what I wished to make of my life" (384). They are also attempts to resolve "the mystery of my family." Through an elaborate optical process, both conscious and unconscious, Nina can constitute a personal and familial narrative that includes a number of perspectives in addition to her own. In her pictures and her story she records and exposes the circulation of looks that constitute familial relations and follows them back in time to discover and thus to record what cannot be seen. This work with pictures and words is akin to a psychoanalysis in that it goes further and further back, throwing up images and memories, both personal and collective, both individual and cultural. Like analysis, it is a performative process in which fantasies get reenacted, as Nina imagines both her father's and her mother's responses and feelings. But in allowing Nina to negotiate between the maternal and the paternal modes of understanding, to negotiate between connection and separation, it redefines the traditional romance of family life and thus refocuses the familial gaze. In exposing the family's unconscious optics in her photographic images, Nina finds in the medium an interconnective (here a maternal) as well as a distancing (here a paternal) mode of interrelation.

Both through images and through the stories they elicit and contain, photographs reveal looks that circulate in multiple ways among different familial subjects and thus offer a point of entry into the family's unconscious optics. Pictures enable us to see the constitution of the subject in relation to mother, father, and siblings, to non-oedipal as well as to oedipal processes. They stress separation, distance, and misrecognition as well as mutual recognition as fundamental aspects of subject-formation and familial interaction.

Nina's scene of looking is not the classic scene of voyeurism in which Freud's patient observes his parents' intercourse and thus his own conception. Instead Nina juxtaposes two scenes, one in which the father realizes that there is something "wrong" with his son, an insight which leads to his own self-definition as the analytic father; the other, a scene of mother/child interconnection that precedes birth but not conception. Negotiating between these stereotypic perspectives, however, Nina does mediate her parents' "marriage"—or, at least, the "marriage" of their modes of seeing and knowing.

In her effort to refocus the familial gaze through her photography, to inflect it with a more located, individual, and mutual series of familial looks, and to reveal the dominant screens of religion, politics, and psychoanalysis that shape them, Nina comes back to the centrality of the familial gaze after all. In its light, she is forever the child at the top of the landing, watching the conflict between her parents, forever the daughter walking in on Lainey and Randall in the kitchen. Pregnant, an adult professional woman, she nevertheless remains the child in her ancestral home, the child who has taken it upon herself to become the holder of the family's postmemory. As a wedding and anniversary photographer, Nina learns to arrange family members according to set hierarchies:

> The family all fell obediently into the desired shape, a widening triangle, with the grandparents at its peak, the immediate children on the first step down, then the spouses and grandchildren beginning and tumbling down the stairs. The second and third cousins were asked to form a kind of border at the edges. In three long rows on the lawn at the bottom of the triangle, standing, kneeling and then sitting, were the great-grandchildren. (382)

Nina's photographic and narrative look is not significantly different from that of the professional anniversary photographer: her representation of the family not only assumes the shape of this giant and ultimately mysterious triangle but remains within the permutations such a structure allows. Nina's familial look modifies, but does not ultimately challenge or evade, the Freudian familial gaze, figured by her father's journal to which it is, after all, a response.

### *revisualization*

For a more profound challenge, I turn to the photographic and theoretical work of Jo Spence, who reveals the workings of the family's unconscious optics through a number of irreverent and innovative techniques that break open the structures of silence and repression that tend to govern the family album.

In their 1981/82 analytic and photographic essay "Remodelling Photo History," Jo Spence and Terry Dennett also pay appropriate tribute to Freud. A picture entitled "Revisualization" features Jo Spence sitting in front of several giant film reels, reading a paperback book entitled "Sigmund FREUD on Sexuality." Wearing plastic carnival glasses with giant eyes at the end of loose springs, she is laughing hilariously, her hair windswept. The cover of the book she is reading features a photograph of Freud's face with large round glasses that echo Spence's mock spectacles: as she holds the book,

4.1

both she and Freud are looking out at the camera and not at each other. While his face is serious, almost grim, hers is amused, taunting (Figure 4.1).

Spence's "revisualization" is what the essay refers to as a form of "photo-theatre," a spectacle which ridicules prevalent theories of representation and dominant structures of seeing. Spence's homage to Freud's centrality is at the same time an appropriation of his gaze, a gaze she can turn back on him by "reading" his words through a clown's spectacles and by laughing at them.

Spence and Dennett's essay, originally published in *Screen,* is included in Spence's provocative book *Putting Myself in the Picture.* This is a collection of essays covering her life and work from childhood in the late 1930s to 1986 when the book was first published. Some of the essays were published separately and later inserted into the book's chronology, while others were specifically written to fill in the gaps of the autobiography. The essays are shaped by photographic work which ranges from her High Street wedding photography to various exhibits and installations to advertising work.

Most of the essays focus not on life story but on photographic projects and theoretical/practical issues with which Spence has been concerned: the autobiographical is expanded to include the "political" and the "photographic" on either side of the "personal." The first-person narrative and the self-portraits that underwrite it cast the autobiographical subject in a great range of roles and identities, both within and outside the family. The book promotes her lifelong effort to challenge and redefine photographic practice and the institutions of photographic work.[9] Spence manipulates both her images and her essays to reinforce one another in a massive project of subversion.

Is it possible to read the British autobiographical text *Putting Myself in the Picture* in relation to the American novel *Family Pictures* and to compare the career of Miller's character Nina with that of Jo Spence? There are certainly thematic convergences as both live through rebellious adolescences, start their careers as wedding photographers, go through divorces, sibling rivalries, and difficult family histories. Both, moreover, use family photography to reflect on family memory and postmemory, as well as on photographic practice. Both construct their narratives by means of several voices (Nina's are her parents' and siblings' and Spence includes several coauthored essays); both question and attempt to redefine the conventional gazes of photography. In addition, they both ask whether the tensions and problems of family life can be recorded photographically and end up finding in photography a route to the family's unconscious optics. However, the class difference between them makes them subject to quite different familial gazes. Their strategies to expose repressed visual memories are equally divergent: where Miller redefines the multipersonal narrative conventions of the family chronicle, Spence experiments with photo-theater, spectacle, parody, "photo therapy," theoretical reading, and analysis. Miller's Nina works through memory and postmemory in the process of telling her family's story, adopting or making space for narrative perspectives other than her own, and revealing different familial subject positions. Spence's autobiographical subject arrests and challenges narrative structure, inflecting it with the essay form and supplementing it with visual images. She works more directly with

images, constructing and reconstructing them, using them in therapy, breaking their unity and integrity and thus their illusionistic power, what she calls
their "documentary naturalism" (213). Spence thus produces a very different
imagetext, offering a radically different challenge to the familial gaze and
different strategies for exposing and analyzing the family's unconscious
optics.

I shall concentrate primarily on a central essay in the volume, originally
part of the "Three Perspectives on Photography" exhibit at the Hayward
Gallery (1979), "Visual Autobiography: Beyond the Family Album." I will
also look at several essays dealing with the process that Spence has called
"photo-therapy," including the more recent article "Shame Work," published in Spence's 1991 coedited volume *Family Snaps: The Meaning of Domestic Photography.* These essays interrogate and attempt to redefine the conventions of the family album.

Spence's interrogation of the unconscious optics of the family is based on
a clearly stated premise:

It has been suggested that the workings of the mind lead us to have only
certain conscious perceptions about the everyday world, and that the
unconscious mind (out of our apparent reach) moves across a matrix of
structures and fantasies. How does the blocking off of earlier traumas and
desires from childhood, which we still inhabit as adults, encourage us to
collude in the limited amount of stories in circulation about family life?
Just how much is the lack of image-making about the family part of this
cementing-over process? How does the family album relate to the regime
of images offered to us from birth, in learning to read, watching television,
acquiring the habits of taking for granted the "truth" of the stories on
offer in the media in general? This regime not only encourages silence from
us as individuals around the power struggles between parents, and between
adults and children, but positively invites us to enjoy the extraordinarily
few stories in circulation about that world. (213–214)

Spence's overriding project, during the twenty-five years of her photographic
career discussed in her books, is to "learn new ways of using our cameras,"
to "begin to re-imag(in)e who we are, both visually and verbally" so as to
"explore and explode the structures of shame, guilt, loss, and desire into
which we are currently stitched" (214–215).

Spence begins her "Visual Autobiography" with a list of all that is missing
from her early photographs:

> There is no record of my appalling health . . ; no record of the pointless
> years shunted around schools inside formal education . . ; no record of a
> broken marriage and the havoc this so-called failure caused me; no record
> of hard work done for countless employers; no record of trying to please
> parents and other authority figures; no record of struggles . . . Moreover,
> those "happy," "serious," "loving," "miserable," but always passive visual
> moments which do exist . . . give no indication at all of the wider social,
> economic, and political histories of our disgusting class-divided society.
> (82–83)

She tries to understand all that the photographs do not show, by "deconstructing [herself] visually." The essay is laid out like a family album beginning with two pictures: a conventional image of a naked baby on a lacy
sheet and, underneath, the same pose taken of the adult Spence on a black
sofa, captioned, "five hundred and twenty eight months later" (84). Clearly,
this essay will not just read old family pictures but will retake them, so as
to reveal their conventions, their inclusions and exclusions, the unconscious
optics they repress. The rest of the essay is printed in four narrow vertical
columns running down each page, somewhat like strips of negative film.
Each page has a black border and four squares at the edges, as though each
were a photograph in its own right. Three horizontal levels interrupt the
vertical flow: at the top of each page there is a chronological narrative and
analysis; in the middle some images are reproduced on a very tiny scale, and
below are captions commenting on the images. This structure loosens after
the death of Jo's parents and falls apart in the last pages of the essay, which
reproduce a large number of "public images" depicting various social roles
Jo tries out, various advertisements that interpellate her as a woman.

Reading this essay means negotiating images and words, story and caption, horizontal and vertical progression. These images are small and hard
to see, while their captions break out of the frame to become mini-narratives
in themselves, thereby reversing expected conventions of illustration. Although Spence's album begins with the most conventional images of herself
as a child with her mother and family, it soon challenges that type of image
in favor of different kinds of photographs. But even the early pictures
provide the ground for different readings which confront each image with
its omission, with retrospective knowledge, with irreverent questions: "I
wonder about my own mother's sex life? Did she still have one? Did she
ever have one?" (89). Spence also interrogates the gaps between the pictures,
most significantly the years of the Second World War during which, as a
child, she was evacuated to the countryside.

Most important, Spence reads and reconstructs the pictures with the eyes of feminist and class consciousness, revealing the social and political elements of unconscious optics not explicitly explored in Miller's novel. "We must learn to see beyond ourselves and the stereotypes offered, to understand the invisible class and power relationships into which we are structured from birth" (92). To see beyond ourselves is to undo a "visual rhetoric" that makes the social and ideological structures underlying our images as invisible as they make familial structures of desire. The fact that the pictures are so small and so hard to see constitutes an integral part of Spence's project: reading them is as difficult for her readers as it should be for herself as photographic subject. Pictures should not be transparent, they should not be read only for their documentary value, but as constructions to be taken apart, analyzed, and understood. Photography, as Benjamin insists, should not be mimetic, but should inscribe its own inability to represent. As Spence puts it: "This reworking is initially painful, confusing, extreme. As I become more aware of how I have been constructed ideologically, as the *method* becomes clearer, there is no peeling away of layers, to reveal a 'real' self, just a constant reworking process. I realize I am a process" (97).

As she analyzes that process, however, Spence attempts to replace psychological insights with social ones, personal factors with ideological ones: for example, she explains her sibling rivalry with her younger brother by an analysis of women's roles in the family and in society. And, as these determinants, these image/screens, become more visible in the process of reworking images with words, unconscious optics become more conscious. If "earlier traumas and desires from childhood" are exposed, they are never limited to psychosexual development, but always include social and ideological dimensions. "The point where image production in society intersects, through our snapshots, with personal memory is where a disruption can be caused, so that we never see ourselves in quite the same light again" (172). But the consciousness that can balance these different factors, that can intervene in ideological construction on such multiple levels, is never complete, never achieved. Thus Spence ends her essay with a reinscription of the conventions of the family album, conventions she has already deconstructed: "These pictures are here for no better reason than that they remind me of happy times and of people I love" (97). Whether that reinscription is straightforward or ironic, or both, remains ambiguous.

Photo therapy becomes the technique Spence develops for her continuing analysis of the intersections of photography, autobiography, and feminist and class consciousness. Through photo therapy familial roles and looks become unfixed, contingent, and interchangeable, and thus potentially liberating. Spence begins simply by "using family photos in therapy," a work she calls "a kind of 'permission giving' session in which you are encouraged to go over old stories in new ways" (142). Her essay on this process transcribes one session which, like Miller's novel, concentrates on and interrogates several determining images attempting to evoke old feelings, to understand them from the vantage point of the present: "We believe that we all have sets of personalized archetypal images in memory, images which are surrounded by vast chains of connotations and buried memories. In photo therapy we can dredge them up, reconstruct them, even reinvent them, so that they can work in our interests, rather than remaining the mythologies of others who have told us about that 'self' which appears to be visible in various photographs" (172).

Spence's photo therapy sessions, described in several essays, take this radical approach: with her partner, Spence acts out herself at earlier moments, as well as moments of her mother's life, has pictures taken of these scenes, and then spends time looking at the pictures and writing about them. As she acts out these roles, her self-portraits become allo-portraits. She shows herself as a teenager looking for boys, as a "virgin bride," as a vamp or fashion model. In one image she imagines her mother as a wartime factory worker; experiencing the mother's urge to smoke, she relates that urge to the family's poor health history. In the photo therapy sessions she describes, Spence tries to understand her mother's different sides and the different moments in her mother's life, so she represents her mother ironing, making sandwiches, cleaning the floor, "acting" the part of the martyr mother. She acts out her mother as a war worker with a life of her own, "de-stereotyped" and "fun"; she borrows the tight mouth of the older, angry, and disappointed mother (Figure 4.2). Through gesture and pose, she jogs memory: "When I take up the pose, I start to remember my relationship with her. I did not realize I had a memory of her making sandwiches for the factory. It seems so trivial that it is hardly worth thinking about. Yet it is a key thing in a Brechtian sense, a gesture that is coded into our class position" (192). But the process of photo therapy includes the subsequent reading of the pictures as well, and the feelings they evoke. "I made her really sneer at me, turning the mouth down so much that it became ridiculous and I burst out laughing and stuck my tongue out. When I got the photos back I realized that I was looking at the way in which I sneer at myself" (190). All these are the types of photographs that would rarely be taken, that would never be included in the family album.

If photo therapy is about deconstructing old images and disidentifying

**4.2**

from familial bonds, if it is about diminishing the effects of the familial gaze and refracting through different screens, it can also enable the participant to accept and identify with parts of her parents and herself, and to create, through photo-theater, parental figures who have a healing rather than merely an epistemological function. In a fantasy structure, the participant in photo therapy both acts and sees herself act. In the transactive and projective structure of analysis, she is herself and her mother, analyst and analysand, subject and object of the look. As in Miller's novel, the camera in photo therapy records the looks and gazes that circulate, often unseen, in familial interaction. But here it also has the potential of resisting and reversing those looks, of disempowering them, of undoing the work of suture. Spence is determined to balance deconstruction with reconstruction: "Basically you cannot deconstruct without a reconstruction process going on simultaneously as it does in photo therapy, where each time you deconstruct you are already at the beginning of the next phase of putting things together again" (186).

Resistance occurs precisely on the level of the screen and literally by means of the strategy of masquerade. Making conscious the images she adopts and the images that are projected unto her by various gazes, she can play with them, contest them. She can manipulate the screen situated between the look and the gaze, the subject and the other, and she can suggest some different ways of seeing. In her photo therapy sessions she can discover, or rather create, positions never before experienced by her: the benign female gaze of an accepting mother, the look of a nurturing and loving bodily father, the look of the self-accepting working-class child who understands and lets go of her envy and shame, the look of the sexual, or the lesbian mother who has explored her own sexuality, the looks of the parents who enjoy their work and have their own pleasure. By situating herself on both sides of these looks, Spence plays with them using them as a means to challenge the Freudian gaze. She exposes the screens of class, economic status, and sexual orientation in familial optics and thus multiplies possible roles and positions and available family stories.

In Spence's unconscious optics the body is revealed not only as the object of desiring looks but also as the aging, diseased, and consuming body. Spence's Health Project needs to be included in any account of her photo therapy. The body that appears in the essays that record her treatment for breast cancer is the patient's body, the object of surgery and treatment. "My aim is to try and form a bridge between work done on health struggles usually dealt with through documentary photography, and work done on body as image. An understanding of how these spheres relate seems to me essential to being healthy and well-balanced" (168). By fragmenting her body and writing on it, by showing it as the object of various treatments and surgery, and by concentrating particularly on the breast—her diseased organ as well as the object of cultural fantasy—Spence demystifies the maternal body explored in Miller's novel and glorified in the conventions of the family album:

> By applying the knowledge I had gained in higher education (most espe- cially from the work of Foucault and Althusser) I began to ask questions about the way in which the institutions and professional bodies of ortho- dox medicine used photography to help maintain the status quo, and thus retain their power over us as patients. I asked the women in my ward whether they minded if I took photographs of what was happening in the hospital. I said I wanted them for my family album. No one objected. (158)

In documenting her treatment photographically, Spence is turning the look back at the medical establishment and gaining some small control over an institution that can decide her future. In addition, she is unhinging the gazes of photographic habits and enlarging the conventions of the family album to include these very different self- and group portraits. She is also going back into her family, working through her mother's illness and death from breast cancer and the ways in which she would like to take charge of her own illness, to claim her agency, and to disidentify from a passive subject who believes that things happen to her or are done to her.

Spence's Health Project images, documentary records of a process of treatment and recovery, are shocking because they violate so thoroughly our habits of seeing: "The question is: 'Will I be a heroine or a victim?' The answer I gave myself was that I had no desire to be either; I merely wanted to be 'seen' as a person in the daily struggle to restore equilibrium and health to myself" (162; Figure 4.3). Such a record challenges photographic conven- tions that interpellate us as either victims or heroines; the look that can "see" illness and treatment needs to be developed as it has more recently been in the tradition of photographic work by and of people with AIDS.

But Spence steps out of a representational tradition which depicts the ailing person as one who copes and suffers; in her images the ill person acts. She not only graphically records her scars and her semiconscious body laid out on stretchers and monitored by X-ray equipment, she also deliberately fragments that body, thus reproducing medicine's relationship to a body in parts and exposing its disregard of the integrity of a person. Spence's body

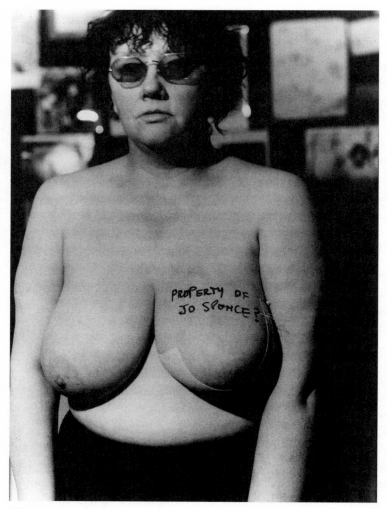

**4.3**

parts are inscribed with enormous black letters, as though they were part of a puzzle to be cut up and reassembled. Thus the "I" is written on her forehead literalizing, and thereby reversing, a subject's sense of self-defini-tion. Similarly, when she writes on her breast "Property of Jo Spence?" she is underlining the body's commodification and thereby answering negatively the question posed by the letters on her breast.

In her cancer photography as well as in her photo therapy, Spence casts herself an adult playing with images, challenging the familial gaze from an adult perspective. But often and with pleasure, she acts the part of a child and reexperiences childish feelings. The adult she has become needs to work through the looks and gazes of her family of origin in which she was a working-class girl, marked by the war, by poverty and class envy, by the ideologies of class ascendancy, by guilt, anger, and shame. But in displacing the Freudian structures of the primal scene and of nuclear family dynamics, Spence can refocus the Freudian gaze.

Where Miller gives us a puzzled Freud, Spence's Freud is subjected to what she playfully theorizes as a "female gaze." Thus she starts her book with a photo therapy picture of her adult self sitting on a potty, her panties down by her ankles as she looks intently at her genitals. Above her head in a cartoon bubble in a juvenile print, the words: "My God . . . I've got an imaginary lack!" Toward the end, in a chapter on the "female gaze," the penis appears in various forms as she photographs the photo therapy sessions of her partners Terry Dennett and David Roberts. The naked men are vacuuming, urinating, bending over, sitting with their legs far apart, tying balloons to their penises. Spence concludes: "Coming from a family which always locked bathroom doors, had silent bedrooms and forbade explicit talk of sexuality or bodies (beyond endless discussions of family illness), I always felt this to be a totally taboo subject. Perhaps, in part, this explains my desire to 'look.' Maybe I just never knew that as a girl I wasn't supposed to do so!" (199). The mocking female gaze returns Freud's familial gaze and displaces its centrality. Humor, parody, and play are the antidote, the ways in which Spence can "encourage others to use the camera for its unfixing, rather than its fixing abilities" (208).

Spence's last image at the end of her book, is a close-up of a flabby adult female abdomen, wearing cotton panties, a hand reaching deep inside them. The other hand is holding a phallic ice cream cone, as another cartoon bubble says, in a childish print: "Some day my prints will come . . ." Thus eroticizing the photographic relationship and unfixing the gaze, Spence can offer us some access to the unconscious optics that can destabilize its influence.

## untitled

Freud does not appear in Carrie Mae Weems's "Untitled (Kitchen Table Series)," but her characters are no less subject to the scrutiny of various monitoring gazes, here specifically racialized in the act of cross-racial looking. Throughout her career, in fact, Weems's project is to redefine traditional representations of blackness in American photography, to respond to the documentary images that show African-Americans as objects of the gaze, as poor and destitute, products of unstable familial and social circumstances. It is to challenge the very foundations of photographic practice, which, she maintains, are determined by whiteness: "Well, the zone system is completely constructed around what makes white people look best. It is our system and our theory—photo theory—for understanding what a good print is, and it is based on white skin."[10]

Appropriating the camera eye and the pen, Weems undertakes her work of demystification always by combining images and text and thereby creating composite narratives that engage viewers on many levels. As a folklorist, she weaves her narratives out of familiar phrases, blues songs, folk tales, colloquial expressions, clichés. Her images, in contrast, are unfamiliar, arresting, and surprising: mostly staged, formal, and static, they constitute strange and sometimes unfamiliar responses to the text. Thus image and text interact in multiple ways; never simply illustrations or captions, they illuminate each other, as one adds what the other omits. This interaction of absence and presence, this concentration on the unseen and the unsaid, offers a possible approach to unconscious optics, a notion that has particular resonance in a culture as openly scrutinized and judged and therefore as interested in opaqueness and privacy as African-American culture during the 1980s and 1990s.

Weems's first familial imagetext, "Family Pictures and Stories" (1978–1984), is an alternative family album of her own family of origin: her mother and father, sisters, brother, nieces, and nephews.[11] Seemingly the most informal and documentary of Weems's works, these images taken with a 35-mm camera have the appearance of snapshots, often unposed. Read in conjunction with their captions, however, they constitute carefully constructed narratives that break the conventions of the family album, even as they represent a black family that is warm, vital, deeply interconnected, and comfortable in its domestic spaces. As the subjects look at the camera, it is obvious that they are confronting a photographic gaze that is in deep sympathy with them: "It amazes me that even in the midst of a bunch of crazy wild kids, my sisters still manage to carry on a half-way decent conversation. I'm really impressed." Still, familial looking is never simple or unambiguous, and Weems's narrative hints at some of the hidden stories that intervene and shape family memory: "Daddy—much to the dismay of my mother—definitely has a way with the ladies. They swarm around him like bees to honey, they just love him. Man has so many women he calls them all Susie-Q so he doesn't have to remember any one name."

Just like Miller's *Family Pictures* and Spence's *Putting Myself in the Picture,* "Family Pictures and Stories" inscribes Weems as the daughter photographing her family of origin, presenting them to a public eye. In the process, she can work through her own developmental issues and provide an assessment of traditional white, middle-class representational structures. This "album" represents looks that are intricate and layered, individual and situated, even as it responds to a racialized familial gaze that has pronounced summary judgment on the black family. Weems's camera restructures that gaze. Her later text, "Untitled (Kitchen Table Series)" (1990), however, departs quite radically from this by-now-familiar script of the daughter-photographer.

"Untitled" is a series of visual and verbal tableaux. In chapter form, "Untitled" tells the story of a woman's stormy romance with a man, its breakup, and her relationships with women friends, with her daughter, and ultimately with herself. This is unequivocally a mature woman's story, unconcerned with her family of origin, focusing on the extended-family relationships she forges throughout her adult life. It is about sexual politics and the construction of black female subjectivity, and it highlights the intersubjectivity and relationality of the black female subject.

Weems herself is the principal actor in the staged and stylized images that are accompanied by verbal tableaux spinning a tale out of blues lyrics and clichéd phrases: "Looking her up, down, sideways he said: 'So tell me baby, what do you know about this great big world of ours?' Smiling, she said, 'Not a damn thang, sugar. I don't mind telling you my life's not been sheltered from the cold and I've not always seen the forest or smelled the coffee, played momma to more men than I care to remember." The text is symmetrically inscribed on thirteen panels, eleven by eleven inches. The twenty images, twenty-seven by twenty-seven inches, are taken with a self-timer from the identical camera angle in the identical setting: they reveal the back half of a plain wooden kitchen table and an overhead lamp that illuminates it. One to four figures are gathered around the end of the table: the woman and the man, her daughter, her two friends, another child.

Weems's self-portraits are always already allo-portraits; in the pictures, she is acting the part of "woman" with "man," "daughter," or "friends." Even at her most seemingly independent, the "woman" is deeply interconnected. In the different images, various ordinary objects are placed on the table and around it: bottles of whiskey and cans of beer, cigarettes, playing cards, a bowl of peanuts, a mirror, a telephone, books, and notebooks. Behind the table a back wall bordering on a closed door is variously decorated in the different images: at times small pictures or paintings are there but unreadable; one image features a poster of Malcolm X with his raised fist and a number of smaller images around it; some images have an African-looking painting or hanging, some a painting of flowers, and some an empty wall. The figures are variously smoking, playing cards, reading, sulking, putting on makeup, combing their own and each other's hair. Some images have a bird-cage in the background (perhaps a reference to Maya Angelou's memoir *I Know Why the Caged Bird Sings*); others a bare wall. Some of these objects provide the particularized cultural markings of the entire work, inscribing it clearly into a blues context: the whiskey, the peanuts, some of the objects on the wall, enable the characters to perform not only masculinity and femininity but blackness.[12]

The images expose different scenes in the main character's life, and we can read them in sequence to understand the story's progression. In the first, "Untitled (Man and Mirror)" the protagonist faces a table mirror but looks straight out at the viewer with an ironic smile, while a man, whose face is hidden by a large hat, hugs her from behind (Figure 4.4). As the parenthetical title indicates, all the elements of the narrative are already here: the mirror, indicating self-reflection, introversion, and vanity, and the man, representing romance, extroversion, relation. A whiskey bottle and two glasses mark the sociality of the moment, just as the brush and comb on the table indicate the man's intrusion on the woman's space. "Man and mirror" are equivalent, both functioning as props—his hat like the mirror faces us and offers a space of reflection. The woman has to "make her self up" for him and for the mirror as both occupy the position of the gaze. But the camera, into which the woman looks directly, is a space of both reflection and self-reflection because, in looking at the photographer, the woman is also looking at herself.

In subsequent images the relationship continues as the couple play cards, hug, eat, smoke, read, seek each other's attention. Soon, however, we see the woman alone hugging her knees by the telephone, or with women friends talking, laughing, brushing each other's hair. With her daughter, they put on makeup together and, in the next images, work through their different needs as the woman wants to read and the daughter demands attention. The last images show the woman alone again, standing defiantly under the lamp looking out, feeding the bird in its cage, lying on her back on the table

**4.4**

thinking, and, finally, contentedly smoking, eating chocolates, and playing solitaire. The images alone reveal a narrative of relationships engaged and abandoned as the woman develops personal strength and self-reliance. But the camera frames the figures and the room so closely and squarely as to create a feeling of claustrophobia in the viewer: we desperately want to see more of the room, not just the image but what is around it—the space-off. The camera, however, is static and unrelenting, just like the overhead lamp with its small illuminated circle which leaves the rest of the room in shadow.

If there is a space-off, it is in the verbal texts facing and supplementing these images. Here we can read more about the romance and its breakup, more about the child and the woman's decisions and adjustments: "She felt monogamy had a place but invested it with little value . . . He was grateful for such generosity . . . In their daily life together trouble lurked. He said she was much too domineering . . . She insisted that what he called domineering was a jacket being forced on her because he couldn't stand the thought of the inevitable shift in the balance of power." Image and text are often radically divergent from each other. For example, a number of panels after the man has entirely disappeared from the visual images, he keeps appearing in the text, filling it with his presence while the pictures show the woman with her friends or alone: "No really, she fussed, fussed all day long; he was worthless, not a man but a chump, couldn't fight his way out of a wet paper bag . . . Before she could collect her wit or make a dash for the door, he seized her and hung her upside down out of their seven-story apartment window and said, 'Talk shit now, godamnit.'" Text and image would seem to be complementary rather than parallel, as each seems to fill in the other's omissions. The man may be "out of the picture" but the relationship is still alive in her thoughts and stories. This incongruity between image and text can perhaps describe the unconscious optics defining this woman's familial story.

The people and the objects in the pictures create a layered domestic space in which looks and gazes circulate to shape the characters' interactions. In the first image, for example, the woman is looking at the viewer while both the mirror and the man look at her. The viewer is invited into the scene to comment on the embrace. This is a gesture of defiance, directed, as Weems herself insists, not only at the individual viewer but at a hegemonic representational system: "All the pieces in the *Kitchen Table* series highlight 'the gaze,' particularly the piece where the woman is sitting with a man leaning against her, his head buried in her neck, a mirror placed directly in front of her but she looks beyond that . . . at the audience . . . You know, just using that as the beginning and the turning point to flip all that shit around, and to start creating a space in which black women are looking back, right?" (hooks, 85).

But, in the second image the man and woman have eyes only for each other. Their gestures and looks exclude outside scrutiny, though Malcolm X on the wall does monitor their seemingly private interaction, ironically raising a V for victory (Figure 4.5). Even the woman's totally private moments are interrupted by the camera and the viewer's look, leading her to turn her back or to look away so as to maintain that solitude. "Untitled (woman and daughter with makeup)" most clearly inscribes this unwillingness to look back (Figure 4.6). The woman and the girl look into the mirrors facing them; they do not face one another or the viewer. Their relationship

**4.5**

is based on mirroring one another's activities, but without looking. The mirror is the cultural gaze imposing the need for makeup and the transmission of femininity from mother to daughter—though Weems never identifies herself as "mother," always as "woman"—and the two figures act out the imperatives of the gaze in a spirit that remains unreadable to the viewer.

Just as the woman refuses to return our look in the last images, so the images and the texts themselves are ultimately closed to our probing scrutiny. Our spectatorial curiosity is frustrated by the perfectly static quality of the images, the firmly square visual borders around the written text, its symmetrical typographical arrangement, the clichés it contains that resist rather than satisfy our curiosity. Although text and image partially supplement each other, they work together as much to conceal as to expose the

**4.6**

woman's story. The static camera maintains an even distance, refusing to engage the photographic techniques—"its lowerings and liftings, its interruptions and isolations, its extensions and accelerations, its enlargements and reductions"—that Benjamin compares to the psychoanalytic processes that provide access to the unconscious. These images, like their textual counterparts, describe surfaces that cover depths they will not reveal. The mirror occasionally placed on the table is a figure for that hermeticism: an analogue for the camera's lens, the side facing us reflects only the surface of the table, while the other side, we know, reflects the woman's face—but only to herself.

Weems's is less an individual than a collective narrative, assembled out of stereotyped and archetypal moments, divulging not so much psychological as social and cultural concerns. Neither camera nor text here has the power to expose the unseen and unacknowledged. Weems is more interested in displaying the smooth and impenetrable surfaces of photographic images and cultural myths. Her two-part titles show how image and text conspire in closing off the work and excluding the viewer. The entire series and each individual image is "Untitled," perhaps suggesting that pictures are all just that, visual and not verbal. "Untitled" announces, as well, the discrepancy between image and text. But titles do appear in parentheses after all, promising to satisfy the curiosity and frustration aroused by the uniformly "untitled" images. These parenthetical titles, however, are the most general anti-narrative descriptions. Generic rather than autobiographical, they tell us no more than what we can see: "Kitchen Table Series," "Woman with daughter," "Woman standing alone."

With the frustrated promise to show and to tell, Weems insistently protects her characters from the camera's external gaze. The door at the back of the room remains closed. Where the notion of unconscious optics disrupts the surface of the visible, inviting us to probe the unseen, Weems is intent on reestablishing the smoothness of that surface, showing instead just what, personally and culturally, may have to remain hidden. African-American family and domesticity have to be closed off from a social gaze that still invests them with stereotypes and clichés, even if that spectatorial gaze coincides with that of the African-American photographer herself. For looking over her shoulder are other eyes whose motivations may well be more suspect.

Weems's restraint and her effort to direct our eyes to the surface of her images—to keep the door closed—is another form of masking the subject. The masks assumed by her characters are figures for the photograph's continual determination to conceal rather than reveal. They are also analogs for the screens through which we see. When I open the door to my house to describe the pictures on my dresser and the objects on my walls, I do not remove the masks. Autobiography is not necessarily self-revelation. Still, as I reflect back on my own personal exploration of the unconscious optical relations shaping family life, I am aware of the difficulty of keeping the tension between revelation and concealment that I would have liked to illuminate with my narrative. As I write about my own family pictures and as I get caught up in the power they hold over me, I find that I need them to counterbalance my critical voice. But in the personal mode, the balance between nostalgia and critique is not easily achieved. Often exposure seems unseemly, excessive, charged with a familial ideology I would like to but cannot always resist. I find myself inside the family's unconscious optics, struggling to regain the distance of Spence's and Weems's performative and resistant aesthetics.

# $\mathcal{M}$ATERNAL EXPOSURES

What I am really saying is that she put a border around my life,
as if we lived in a photograph.

ANN BEATTIE

A sort of umbilical cord links the body of the photographed
thing to my gaze.

ROLAND BARTHES

Photographing them in those quirky, often emotionally charged
moments has helped me to acknowledge and resolve some of
the inherent contradictions between the image of motherhood
and the reality.

SALLY MANN

## *immediate family*

In its December 27, 1992, assessment of "The Year in the Arts," the *New York Times* cited an event in the world of photography: "Sally Mann's show at Houk Friedman sold a record 300 photographs, bringing in better than $900,000 and consigning Mann to her darkroom for six to nine months to fill orders" (35). In spite of this remarkable commercial success, Mann's exhibit and resulting book *Immediate Family* has met with critical resistance.[1] The three hundred pictures Mann so successfully sold are all photographs of her three children, Emmett, Jessie, and Virginia, many of them nude shots taken during the four to five years preceding their adolescence. The "six to nine months" she spent in the darkroom "to fill orders," the critics imply, are months she presumably did not spend caring for her children, but instead remaking them into flat surfaces, reinventing them for public consumption, in a time frame which, ironically, approximates gestation.

Mann's pictures raise a number of issues that go beyond the circulation of her children's images in the economy of the art market and their display in more than three hundred living rooms. Reviewers have interrogated, with intense interest, the nature of Mann's relationship with her children, the effect on them of their mother's publicity and their own notoriety, and the peculiar way in which they work for her. Invariably reviewers have been moved by the children's beauty. But they have also scrutinized the properties of the childhood world Mann reveals, and its disturbing suggestions of violence, abuse, and eroticism: they have asked again and again about the nudity.

The fictions Mann creates with her children's collaboration, enhanced by the archaic-looking quality of her prints and the old-fashioned large-format camera she uses, evoke profound cultural fantasies of an innocent, "natural" childhood. At the same time, the images touch dangerously on the currently pervasive eroticization of children's, particularly little girls', bodies in American advertising and movies, and they engage, although not directly, current debates about child pornography laws. Boldly defying the taboo of childhood nudity, Mann presents beautiful children whose bodies are submerged in water, asleep on beds, covered with caked flour, bruised, swollen, hanging from hooks, dead-looking, surrounded by ominous presences, threatened, touched. Other scenarios are equally provocative: Jessie, her hair down to her shoulders, holds what the caption tells us is a "candy cigarette," in a remarkably adult and seductive pose. Jessie and Virginia as "The New Mothers," wheeling doll strollers, holding cigarettes, wearing sunglasses, pretending to flirt. "Jessie at five" looks twelve in her makeup, earrings, and pearls; at six, nude in eerie bright lighting, she looks ageless and otherworldly.

The children seem completely self-absorbed in childhood fantasy and a play-world to which viewers have only limited access, and, at the same time, they appear overly self-conscious and knowledgeable, available as mediators of unsettling and sensational cultural representations, fears, and fantasies. What we have before us is not a childhood glimpsed but a childhood invented—one that is performed and theatricalized with makeup, costumes, and props. And it is a childhood represented within a particularly charged cultural context that pits the rights of children against the rights of mothers, that represents the family as potentially abusive, that sexualizes nudity and takes it as the measure of violence and transgression. This is the culture in which Sally Mann produces her pictures, and her pictures reveal this context to us.

In his glowing afterword to *Immediate Family* Reynolds Price asks: "To

what significant extent are a viewer's feelings about the artist and her subjects altered by a knowledge or an ignorance of the fact that, behind the
lens, stands the children's own mother?" Notwithstanding Price's sense that
"these loving, fearful, trustworthy and profound pictures explore the nature
of family love, *maternal* love and child response," Sally Mann's photography
is, in the terms of *The New York Times*, "disturbing" precisely because it
brings together two equally intense cultural obsessions: the vulnerability of
childhood, on the one hand, and the idealization and fear of maternity, the
fantasy of maternal omnipotence, on the other.

As a photographer who is also a mother, and who chooses her own children as the subjects of her art, Mann echoes the preoccupations of several
contemporary novelists and filmmakers who have used mothers who are
photographers as their subjects. Rosellen Brown, Ann Beattie, and Camille
Billops, among others, thereby explore cultural attitudes toward maternity
and the shapes of maternal subjectivity, while at the same time commenting
on the role of photography in contemporary American family life. Their
works are disturbing counterparts to fictional representations of the paternal
photographic gaze, invariably represented as objectifying and invasive, if
not abusive, especially to daughters. The most traumatic memory of Marie
Cardinal's protagonist in *The Words to Say It* (1975), for example, a memory
uncovered after years of psychoanalysis, is the childhood scene in the woods
where her father takes her picture as she hides among the trees to urinate.[2]
The "click, click" sound of the shutter follows her in her nightmares into
her adulthood. The young male photographer in Agnes Varda's 1978 film
*One Sings, the Other Doesn't* seems to kill the women and children on his
prints. The women's task is to get themselves and their children out of his
frames, and, when they try to, he commits suicide. The film juxtaposes the
vitality of song, coded as feminine, to the murderous quality of the image,
coded as masculine. Kathryn Harrison's 1993 novel *Exposure* goes further
by representing the father, a famous photographer, as incestuous and abusive, exposed by his victimized daughter, after severe repression, on the
occasion of an important museum retrospective on his work.[3]

Surprisingly, the maternal photographers in the texts of Brown, Beattie,
and Billops have equally damaging potential as these paternal photographers, even though they are characters in the works of women artists. It is
as though the position behind the camera had the capacity to erase vast
differences in gender, power, and familial role. As Joanne Leonard, herself
a mother and a photographer, has said: "Is it photography's inherent intru-
siveness that brings charges of exploitation and intrusion against mother-

photographers? Even without a camera, many people regularly experience their mothers as intrusive."[4] More is at stake here than simply a representation of the mother as phallic or monstrous, however. Invariably these fictional mother/photographers are extremely problematic figures, dangerous to their children's welfare. Mothers who place themselves behind a camera, more than mothers who are writers, tend to be represented in their capacity to wound, scar, or kill their children, but they do not do so in the same ways as the father/photographers in the works of Cardinal, Varda, or Harrison.

The exchange of looks within the family and the child's acquisition of subjectivity through the process of looking and being looked at place very specific demands on mothers. If there is a hegemonic familial gaze, imposing rigid familial ideologies, then mothers are most cruelly subjected to its scrutiny. As Naomi Scheman reminds us, "Mothers are the objects of the social-scientific gaze, which judges the adequacy of their mothering from behind the one-way mirror in the psychologist's playroom. The maternal gaze is not unobserved and, although it can certainly be felt as powerful by those who are its objects, it is itself closely watched to ensure that actual empowerment flows from and not to it."[5] The representations of the familial gaze and the maternal look in fiction, in film, and in the work of maternal photographers reveal the gaze focused on mothers, as well as a range of maternal responses to it. They expose, in particular, the social pressures placed on mothers who want to be artists and the ways in which these pressures shape maternal creativity and subjectivity. They can thus help us see how mothers as opposed to daughters represent the family's unconscious optics.

In this light we can read Sally Mann's photographs as studies of the figure of the mother/photographer, as Mann's own "allo-portraits," rather than as representations of childhood and of her children. Reading Mann's work as her own self-representation, reading it in relation to fictional depictions of maternal photographers, makes her work, like theirs, a metaphotographic discourse, a commentary and critique of photographic conventions and, in particular, of dominant cultural myths about maternity, of the familial gaze. Such a reading might enable us to explore the confrontation between the familial gaze and the maternal look. But in a culture that values a maternity that casts an enabling and mirroring look at the child, supporting the child's subject-formation and serving as a mediating force to the familial gaze, the mother with a camera is bound to challenge these expectations.

The intervention of the camera and the dominant cultural fantasy of maternal omnipotence bestows on the maternal look some of the disturbing characteristics and qualities of an all-seeing dominating gaze. The maternal gaze I will discuss in this chapter is the maternal look, filtered through the camera and the power of development and exposition, in a culture that invests maternity with omnipotence. As we will see, Sally Mann both deploys and resists the power of this threatening maternal gaze.

## shooting back[6]

If the notion of a maternal *gaze* is unsettling within the logic of familiality, it has to do with the importance psychoanalytic and psychological theories attribute to the maternal *look* in the process of the child's subject-formation and within the unconscious optics that structure familial interaction.[7] We need only remember Roland Barthes's evocation of the clarity of his mother's eyes and his fantasy of being seen and recognized, reflected in those eyes. What sense of self do children acquire if, instead of finding such confirmation in their mother's eyes, they see themselves reflected in the lens of her camera, reversed in her negatives, reduced to small squares on her contact sheets, exposed on the flat surfaces of her prints, the objects of commercial transaction? Mothers may frequently take their children's pictures, but are professional photographers in a different relation to their subjects? What are the implications—for child and maternal subjectivity—of this unconventional form of visual maternal/child interaction? We might address these questions, raised in Sally Mann's photographic practice, by placing theories of subject formation into dialogue with theoretical reflections on the gaze. Since psychoanalytic approaches can obscure social factors, and since they tend to mystify childhood, it is important to remember, as well, the social pressures mothers who are artists face in contemporary culture.

In organizing her own and her children's lives around the photographs she takes of them, Mann literalizes and materializes the visual process through which, Jacques Lacan theorizes, subjectivity is installed. As early as the mirror stage, the child confronts herself as an image, however deceptive such a conception of wholeness and identification might turn out to be.[8] As the child faces the mirror, she is presumably held by her mother and thus also faces the mother's confirming and encouraging look (Lacan suggests, as well, the possibility of an artificial support, a "trotte-bébé," for example, but presumably the baby stroller would have to be wheeled to the mirror by someone). The journey from the imaginary wholeness and identification of the "I" to the state of being divided and subjected to the social "Umwelt," the journey from the "specular I" to the "social I," that is, must be facilitated and encouraged by the confirming look of another, maternal, figure who mediates the child's entrance into the social (*Ecrits,* 4, 5). When Lacan extends the process of the identification with images, the mirror stage, to the figure of the imaginary camera through which the gaze of the Other operates to install the subject visually in a system of representation, he constructs that camera as inherently alienating and constraining, based on Cartesian and Freudian conceptions of looking that separate subject from object. The mother, by implication, remains a mediating force in this negotiation between subjectivity and sociality.

But what if the mother herself operates the camera through which the child is appropriated by the "Umwelt"? What if it is she who, instead of mediating and facilitating, determines the child's interpellation into various social institutions and ideological systems, into visuality and familiality?

Lacanian film theory drawing on Laura Mulvey's classic essay "Visual Pleasure and Narrative Cinema" identifies the camera with the gaze.[9] In Mulvey's reading of Lacan, the gaze becomes necessarily masculine, while its object is coded as feminine. Active looking distances, objectifies, turns subject into object. The logic of Mulvey's theory of looking leaves no space for either a maternal look *or* gaze: the mother is the one who mediates the gaze of the other, she is the image to be looked at in the course of oedipal desire. In Mulvey's unidirectional conception of looking, in which the look is rarely returned and in which only limited positions of identification can be conceived, the mother, as object and image, cannot be also in the position of the one who looks. If she did appropriate that position, she would do so only as the phallic mother, the monstrous, sadistic, voyeuristic, controlling, masculine mother who turns her child into her object, disallowing and displacing the process of the child's subject-formation.[10]

Yet, as we have seen in *Four Fundamental Concepts,* Lacan uncouples the look from the gaze.[11] Extending this distinction, we might differentiate a noninstrumental, embodied, situated, and mutual maternal look from the gaze-effect created by the conjunction of the mother and the camera, coextensive with the workings of ideology and with the ways in which society imagines authoritative vision.[12] While the look is returned, the gaze—the instrument of ideology—turns the subject into a spectacle. It is, in Kaja Silverman's terms, "exterior to the subject in its constitutive effects."[13] In what ways, then, we must ask, does a maternal gaze affect the child, and what, with the noninstrumental embodied mediating maternal look, is displaced from the child's development? The mother/photographers can help us to answer these questions.

D. W. Winnicott's reinterpretation of Lacan's "The Mirror Stage" makes these questions differently discomforting, for Winnicott conflates the mother with the mirror. The encounter Winnicott sees as constitutive of the "I" is the visual confrontation between mother and child, the child's look which the mother simply and fully returns: "What does the baby see when he or she looks into the mother's face? I am suggesting that, ordinarily, what the baby sees is himself or herself." The child's development depends on the mother's responsiveness: "if the mother's face is unresponsive, then a mirror is a thing to be looked at but not looked into," (and in this case the child will not thrive. Development depends on being seen, on being mirrored in such a way that growth can occur. Winnicott's reelaboration isolates mother and child and elides the space of the social and ideological other, so crucial to Lacan's conception. Although development is a process during which the "not me" gradually separates from the "me," the "not me" (or the mother) has the function of seeing, without needing to be seen or recognized in her own right. The child does not see *her* but, "ordinarily, what the baby sees is himself or herself." The mother does not mediate a process of accultura-tion, but, in this intensely dyadic structure of looking, reflects the child back to herself, so that the child might see herself as seen by the mother. Narcis-sism is never quite superseded, although separation and individuation are the primary developmental tasks: "When the average girl studies her face in the mirror she is reassuring herself that the mother's image is there and that the mother can see her and that the mother is en rapport with her." Psychotherapy is also, for Winnicott, a form of mirroring through which the analyst gives back to the patient what the patient brings. The mother, like the analyst, is a backgrounded figure against and in relation to which subjectivity and individuality are formed. Looking is unidirectional and specular: when the child looks she sees herself; when the mother looks she sees the child.[14]

The mother with a camera, this argument would imply, engages in a more active and controlling form of looking. The optical instrument interrupts the reflective process, fixing it, flattening it, making it static rather than dynamic, perhaps distorting the images, certainly complicating it. The child looking at the mother's camera sees herself reflected in a lens, an instrument, an apparatus, not an eye. That lens transfers the child's image to paper, and then, on the paper, the child can read the mother's reflecting work, a work which necessarily displays the mother's vision controlling the child's. What are the consequences of this shift in the mirroring process? How might the Mann children experience it, and how might it affect their self-perceptions and their developmental course? And how might a mother who is an artist cope with these restrictions on her own development?

More recent theoretical models of subject-formation, such as Daniel Stern's *The Interpersonal World of the Infant* and Jessica Benjamin's *Like Subjects, Love Objects,* developed in the face of the feminist movement and a fuller consciousness of female subjectivity, construct the dynamic inter-action between mother and child differently from Winnicott's object-rela-tions model, though the visual continues to be central. Unlike Lacan and Winnicott, Stern is interested in both subjectivities, the mother's and the child's, and Benjamin concentrates on an intersubjective model of subject-formation.

For Stern, the mother emanates from the holding background to act as an interlocutor in an intersubjective relationship with the child: if she sees, she must also be recognized. For the linear process of separation and indi-viduation Stern substitutes a more dynamic mutuality between self and other which is renegotiated at different developmental stages. Stern envisions the child as initially more separate and cohesive. Between two and six months of age the child begins to consolidate a sense of "core self," bounded, with a sense of agency, continuity, and affectivity. It is not the child's task to separate but to learn how to be "with another," to establish various forms of intersubjective union, to learn about sameness and difference. In her re-lational interactions, the very young child is already as active as the mother: "When watching the gazing patterns of mother and infant . . . one is watching two people with almost equal facility and control over the same social behavior . . . infants exert major control over the initiation, mainte-nance, termination, and avoidance of social contact with mother; in other words, they help to regulate engagement." And for infants, that engagement is often visual: "They can avert their gaze, shut their eyes, stare past, become glassy-eyed."[15]

Visual relatedness is subsequently supplemented by motor as well as by verbal interrelation, and eventually by a more complex process of symboli-zation, fantasy, image-formation. Stern posits two subjects in all of these forms of relationship: being is "being with another." Connection and sepa-ration are always in tension, and the child needs to recognize the mother's own subjectivity, her different view which, nevertheless, can be attuned to and shared with the child's.

This is not a process of mirroring because, as Jessica Benjamin suggests in her elaboration of Stern's argument, "the mother offers difference as well as sameness," and the child needs to recognize that difference.[16] Instead of reflecting the child's image back to the child, the mother introduces herself, her own feelings and preoccupations, and mother and child need to work together in negotiating that which connects and that which separates them. This mutuality does not harm the child; on the contrary, it is a key to the child's healthy development of a sense of self in relation to another. As Benjamin suggests: "In the elaboration of this play the mother can appear as the child's fantasy object and another subject without threatening the child's subjectivity" (*Like Subjects*, 44).

Mutual recognition, Stern speculates, allows for a dynamic process of identification/differentiation which, at its best, offers an alternative to the projections and fears that structure the intersecting fantasies of childhood vulnerability and maternal omnipotence. Unconscious fantasy scenarios and projections do inflect the formation of the subject, but they go beyond these narrow models. Resting on an intersubjective conception of familial relation, Stern's model seeks to reconceptualize familial roles and identities, thereby redefining familiality. Keeping both mother and child in view at the same time, Stern and Benjamin might enable us to demystify both childhood and maternity, seeing one as less fragile and the other as less omnipotent.

These varying conceptions of the role of the visual in the process of subject-formation enable different readings of the mother with a camera, different answers to the question of how the mother and the children negotiate with each other what they each see as they look at themselves, at each other, and at the photographs. Sally Mann's photographs are excellent examples, and, following Stern and Benjamin, I propose to try to read them from two perspectives: that of the mother and that of the child.

In terms of Lacan's photo session, Mann's children can see in her photographs the operation of the gaze: they can see how the maternal look can be displaced by a maternal gaze. The images show them how the culture sees children, what fears and fantasies structure childhood and therefore structure them. The click of the camera institutes certain scenes as prevalent: evanescent beauty, vulnerability, seduction, hurt and pain, the accoutrements of femininity and masculinity. Their bodies are available for exchange and appropriation by various fantasy scenarios. Their selves are multiplied, developed, reproduced, and disseminated. But, contrary to the construction of looking and being looked at in strict dualistic frames opposing subject/object, activity/passivity, sadism/masochism, Mann's children demonstrate some control over the perpetuation of their images. As they develop

5.1

some self-consciousness, and perhaps even unconsciously, they can manipu-late the images through their own play with costume and makeup; they can mimic and thus play with the childhood into which the maternal gaze—even if it is seen as disembodied, monstrous, phallic, and devitalizing—has fixed them.

On the cover of *Immediate Family* is the image of the three nude torsos, "Emmett, Jessie and Virginia, 1989" (Figure 5.1). Their arms are hugging themselves, they are looking straight at the viewer with a look of defiance or challenge, possibly anger, perhaps just annoyance and impatience. Al-though all three face the camera rather than each other, they are clearly a unit, their bodies touch slightly, they agree on their reaction to the click. They display an inscrutability which resists appropriation and positioning. They appear to be knowing, active, in control.

In contrast, "Emmett, Jessie and Virginia, 1990" (Figure 5.2) shows the three in a long shot at night, submerged in a river, only their brightly lit torsos showing, their arms hanging down, their facial expressions as tenta-tive and unfocused as their body language. Placed into this dark, perhaps

5.2

cold, river by their mother, they face the camera quite tentatively, unsure of their role in this photo session, unsure of what they are seeing as they look at the camera and at their imagined viewers. As she photographs them, their mother is hidden under the photographer's black cloth. Behind the bright car headlight that is illuminating them, she is most likely invisible in the nighttime scene. Even though we can imagine her talking to them, shouting instructions, they are out there, alone, unprotected. As the shutter clicks, what do we see in the children's eyes if not a reflection of the gaze of an unknown and unknowable Other? And what *visually* do they *see* when they look at the picture later?

Mann offers little mirroring in Winnicott's sense, and not only because the camera interrupts the crucial exchange of specular looks: "Photographing them in those quirky, often emotionally charged moments has helped me to acknowledge and resolve some of the inherent contradictions between the image of motherhood and the reality," she has said.[17] The "image of motherhood" may well be Winnicott's mirror role; the mother who merely reflects back to the child what the child offers, who does no more than to enhance it with her encouragement and delight, who is the object to the child's subject-formation: the mother constructed by the familial gaze. The "reality" may be what we see in Mann's photographs: her retort to the gaze, her own vision of her children, her own creation, her fears, fantasies, dreams, and desires. The pictures are her way of "shooting back," her own manipulation of the screen of familiality, a redefinition allowed by a self-conscious maternal subjectivity.

If there is mirroring in this reading of Mann's images, it is reversed, as the children reflect a maternal subjectivity, one she projects onto them, and one which is anxious for her children's safety, in awe of their beauty, identifies with their freedom, urgent and longing to capture something evanescent, fearful of her effect on them as she snaps shot after shot. "Perhaps it is my past I am photographing," Mann suggests, even as she asserts that she has virtually no memories of her own childhood and thus may be using her camera and her children to create a past and a childhood she never had.[18] With such a direct insertion of her own feelings and anxieties, Mann violates Winnicott's standards and becomes, in his terms, the kind of mother whose child will look, but see more than just her own image: it is possible, Winnicott suggests, "that the mother reflects her own mood or, worse still, the rigidity of her own defences" (*Playing and Reality*, 112).

What does Virginia see, for example, when she looks at "The Terrible Picture, 1989" (Figure 5.3)? Her eyes are closed, she almost seems to be floating, her naked body is covered with caked dirt, a stake seems to loom ominously above or just behind her head. Her eyes closed, Virginia does not engage the camera, but, when she looks at the picture later, she might read in it her mother's intense and complicated look, her mother's pleasure at her child's strange beauty, and her own discomfort with the position in which she has placed her young daughter. Would Virginia be better protected if the mother simply reflected safety and reassurance, if she knew how to erase herself, how to censor her anxieties and desires? Winnicott's affirmative answer is unequivocal.

Mann, however, describes her children as active participants in the photographs' creation, conforming much more to Stern's representation of familial intersubjectivity than to Winnicott's mirroring: "They have been involved in the creative process since infancy. At times, it is difficult to say exactly who makes the pictures. Some are gifts to me from my children . . . We are spinning a story of what it is to grow up. It is a complicated story

5.3

and sometimes we try to take on the grand themes: anger, love, death, sensuality and beauty" (*Immediate Family*, intro.). And in *Blood Ties* she adds: "We are spinning a story based on fact but embracing fiction." By performing childhood—and could we not see these pictures as another form of photo-theater?—the children can collaborate with their mother in demystifying the notion of childhood as natural, essential, or given, constructing these qualities as effects of the performance. The camera becomes an instrument of fantasy and play between parent and child, an occasion for "spinning a story" together. And play mediates the roles and relationships within the family, allowing each of us imaginatively to assume and thus to try to understand the other's position, to *be* both mother and child.

How can we imagine the compelling collaborative and creative process Mann outlines in these statements? Does it elucidate the images we find in her collection? Richard Woodward describes the photo session he witnessed when he interviewed Mann. Jessie and Virginia had just had an argument by the river, and Jessie ran off in tears. When she reemerged, she had "fashioned a skirt and bolero for herself out of green leaves, like a sprite of nature." As Mann set up the camera, the journalist sensed that Jessie was "taking visible pleasure that she, not her sister, has become the center of their mother's attention." This is a good example of intersubjective relation: Jessie was playing; her play included making a costume out of leaves; she thereby pleased her mother who is always looking for interesting photo opportunities, while at the same time pleasing herself because she managed to get the attention she needed. Her mother cooperated in her daughter's scenario by providing that attention and by reflecting back to the child the sense of importance and centrality that had been undermined by the argument with Virginia. Where Jessie had initially provided herself, body and costume, as subject, Mann directed the performance: "Raise your head. Look out the window. Point your toe. Bend your knee. Put your chin up. Make yourself veerrry uncomfortable."[19] Together they created images that tell the complex story of mother/child, sister/sister relationship, whether that story can be read in the images or not. Various forms of intersubjective negotiation of sameness and difference, mutuality and disidentification, mirroring and distortion create images that we as readers must surround with narratives drawn from our own experiences.

Yet even as we try to appreciate the collaborative character of Mann's images and see how each gives the other what she wants, we cannot forget the extreme differences in power, authority, and influence that separate parents from children. It is these differences that emerge in the finished images—static products of a complex interactive process. Mann has the camera, the audience, and the money; she has the capacity to develop and print; she offers her children images of themselves which, in turn, they can learn to duplicate, repeat, or transform. This process cannot be mutual: with the exception of the author photo taken by Jessie and Virginia, the children do not take any pictures, and Mann does not centrally include herself or her husband in any of her images. Usually behind the camera, under the black cloth, she is not a visible or bodily presence to them in the way that they are to her. Always the viewer, she cannot be the object of their look, at least not on paper. Unable or unwilling to share their vulnerability and exposure, Mann's look is not seen directly. Through the technology she manipulates she seems to be duplicating the alienating qualities of the gaze instead of mediating them for her children.

But, is she not also exposed in these photographs? If indeed we take into account the relationality and specular reflection of the look and the inter-connection of allo-portrait with self-portrait, then every one of the images of Emmett, Jessie, and Virginia Mann in *Immediate Family* is also, in some degree at least, a picture of Sally Mann. If the pictures reveal to the children how their mother sees them, they also show the mother how her children look to and at her. Every picture of a child is also, however indirectly, a picture of the mother. In that sense the maternal gaze is also always the maternal look: the intersubjectivity of maternity would refuse any clear-cut distinction between look and gaze. Mothers are always exposed by and through their children. Mothers' stories and children's stories are always intertwined: only theory can try to keep them comfortably separate.

This may well be what makes Mann's pictures so appealing, not the voyeuristic desire to look at beautiful nude bodies of children but the ambivalent urge to contemplate the look of mothers: what they see when they look at their children and what they have never openly talked about. These are indeed, as Mann emphasizes in relation to "The Wet Bed," scenes that occur in every household,[20] but we have not found the modes or the means to talk about the range of emotions, often transgressive or disallowed, that they evoke. Decidedly, they reveal the family's unconscious optical relationships.

"Hayhook, 1989" (Figure 5.4) offers a particularly troubling example of this "double exposure." It is an afternoon scene with friends and family on the porch. To the right and left sides of the picture, in the dark shade, clothed adults are standing or sitting in chairs, reading or talking with the naked Virginia, who is playing with a snorkel. No one seems to notice that at the center, just to the right of a large tree trunk, a nude Jessie, brightly lit, hangs from a large chain and hook suspended from the ceiling. Jessie's position, visually reminiscent of suicide or torture scenarios, may well be an innocent athletic exercise, but the picture disturbs profoundly because no one sees her, no one pays attention. What complicated unconscious optics are oper-ating here? Is Mann revealing the exposure and vulnerability of childhood in a world of uncaring and self-involved adults? Or is she revealing her own fears, projected onto Jessie's taut body, fears of her own exposure as her images hang, like her daughter, from hooks amid uninvolved spectators? If she displays her children to be seen, she also reveals herself, but always and only through them. But here is the difference: while their exposure is direct, hers is mediated, disguised. We may read "Hayhook" symbolically, emble-matically, or symptomatically, but I imagine that Jessie herself is likely to

5.4

read it literally. She will see that her mother, while herself remaining under her black cloth, has hung her child up for all to see.[21]

The fictional representations of maternal photographers show that her absorption in her work, combined with such a refusal to be seen, makes the mother/photographer appear uncaring, uninvolved, monstrous. But how could she appear in a different light, in view of the social and psychological gazes fixed on her, in view of the screens of familiality that systematically work against her—the pressures she faces as she balances the competing claims of her children and her own creative work? If we read her pictures from the perspective of mother and children and if we perceive mother/child relations as intersubjective, then we have to concede that Sally Mann herself is as vulnerable and as exposed in her children's images as they are. If we take this perspective then, though we do not see *her*, we do see her maternal *look*, what she sees—and what the culture sees—when looking at (her) children.

*sally bites*

The protagonist of Rosellen Brown's three-page story "Good Housekeeping" (1973)[22] begins her photo session with "the lens up so close to the baby's rear that she suddenly thought, what if he craps on the damn thing?" (151). Here is the refusal of mirroring, the disengagement from mutual recognition: the mother's camera faces the infant's rear, evoking not smiles or looks but "crap." If she is to take pictures, she must keep her child asleep, she cannot engage him. Her images of the house contain similar reversals of the story's ironic title: she takes pictures of dirty laundry, of accumulated sludge in the coffee pot, discarded skins of onions and carrots, rumpled bedclothes, dirty windows. Like her baby, seedlings are incubating in little pots on the window sill, but they are not yet visible; their future not yet assured. In the bathroom she focuses on a pile of bird feathers brought in by the cat: "are murdered birds a part of every household?" she asks ominously (152).[23] The story proceeds like a catalog of the images she takes, interspersed with a few parenthetical comments or thoughts.

Her photography not only records, it creates these images of failed nurturing and unsatisfactory domestic performance. As she takes off her underpants, puts her legs up into imaginary stirrups, aims without seeing through the viewfinder and clicks, she can feel the effect of her gaze herself: "ah, it was the shutter that came, that sound of passionless satisfaction, its cool little click sucking in the core of her . . . So long it had been her face, she might as well have its puckered features in good light, for posterity. Some faces gape more meanly, anyway. This was so very objective, it would transcend lewdness, anger, the memory of passion. The lens like a doctor saw only fact" (151). These facts are her physical material surroundings, whose particular beauty she can reveal. But they are also her own neglect: "Like a lecture from her husband the evidence piled up, orderly, inside the shutter, that she was wrong again. That she was right and wrong" (153).

In a beautiful irony reminiscent of Charlotte Perkins Gilman's famous story "The Yellow Wallpaper," Brown tells of a wife and mother of a young infant creating art out of the very domestic objects that entrap her and thus refocusing the familial gaze that defines her maternity.[24] As she makes her images, she reverses expectations, triumphantly asserting her freedom from convention and celebrating the mess and debris in her house, fixing it with the distant, objective medical gaze of the camera lens. But this is not a form of looking culturally available to the mother, and, in relation to the child, Brown presents it as harmful and violent.

The calm camera eye is deceptive: each image has a story to tell, and these stories hover disturbingly at the edge of violence, confirming the connection Laura Mulvey and Teresa de Lauretis have made between sadism and narrative (*Alice Doesn't*, ch. 5). Like the images described in Brown's story, Sally Mann's photographs suggest the violence simmering at every juncture of the life of the "immediate family," a violence visible to the maternal photographer—bites, burns, bruises, dead animals, stitches, swollen eyes, sibling rivalries, family battles. Sometimes the violence is not only recorded but also created by her. For example, Mann told an interviewer that the bite on the arm (her own) next to Jessie's angry war-painted face in "Jessie Bites, 1985" is hers and not Jessie's: the child's teeth marks had worn off by the time the photographer set up her camera, and to get the picture she had to bite her own arm herself. She creates these moments of violence precisely so she can record them: to have evidence, proof of complicated underlying familial feelings made visible in these pictures.

Narrative violence structures the images of Brown's fictional photographer: the feathers tell the story of the murderous cat, the bottom threatens "crap" and another diaper change, vegetable skins signal consumption, condoms suggest curiosity and sex, cigarette papers evoke marijuana, a spice bottle marked "Fenugreek" means that you will get high if you put it in your cooking. Brown conveys much more than photographic images of domestic objects: she shows us that each object tells a story of family and domesticity that barely contains a violence bordering on the murderous. The cool and alienating eye of the camera appears to provide distance, objectivity, unemotionality, but with the click of its shutter, and with its exposure, it reveals and encloses the sadistic tales, the unconscious optics of the "immediate family"—the struggle against the familial gaze.

In order to approach the baby with the lens, the mother/photographer first has to assume a great distance from herself: "she took the camera coolly into the little hall room, seeing herself from a great distance, doing an assignment on herself doing an assignment" (153). The confrontation between mother and infant that follows cannot possibly maintain this separation: it negotiates different looks and gazes, different shapes of recognition and differentiation; it is distorted by the intervention of the large black box in front of the mother's face. The viewfinder transforms the crying baby into a strangely endangered specimen: "So much light you could see the baby's uvula quivering like an icicle about to drop." As he looks at the camera, the baby calms down, becomes cool himself, offering the mother a specular space of recognition: "Eyes like cameras. His mother looked back at herself in them, a black box in her lap with a queer star of light in its middle." Yet, mediating between mother and child, the camera does not maintain the calm but becomes instead the instrument of passion, ambition, desire, and pain: "focusing as well as she could with one hand, the baby slapping at her through the bars, wheezing with laughter, she found one cool bare thigh, the rosy tightness of it, and pinched it with three fingers, kept pinching hard, till she got that angry uvula again, and a good bit of very wet tongue. Through the magnifier it was spiny as some plant, some sponge, maybe, under the sea" (153).

In order to get the picture the mother hurts her child. She makes the laughing baby cry. In her classic essay "Writing and Motherhood" Susan Suleiman reads this story as the fantasy of the writing mother who is afraid that her work will harm or kill her child.[25] Does the consciousness that this is a photographer/mother rather than a writing mother affect our reading? It has to, if we take into account the importance of the optical relation between mother and child and the ways in which the camera can shape and transform it. At one level, Brown's young mother seems to refuse recognition and mirroring to her baby; discouraging his curiosity and enterprise, his confidence in her, she frustrates his desire to look and play with the camera. As she takes her shot, she sees not the child but only his body parts, transformed into specimens—a bottom, a uvula, a rosy thigh. The child sees her angry cold face that is coextensive with the camera, "so objective, it would transcend lewdness, anger, the memory of passion" transcending all emotion, all maternal feeling or response. Even more than the writing mother, the photographer/mother seems to endanger her child by "sucking in the core of her" with the click of the shutter.

The homemaker going around the house snapping images of mess and debris offers an ironic critique of the demands placed on women. But, the story implies, the mother pinching her child's thigh to make him cry risks too high a price for her work. Instead of negotiating attunement to her child with the assertion of her own subjectivity, the mother affirms distance, through coldness, pain, the alienating click. But beneath that distance, barely contained by the shutter's cold click, is her rage, her violence, the pain she feels and inflicts, immortalized in the image of the crying child.

The writer writing the story of the mother/photographer splits her own voice and perspective between the child and the mother, between the child's fear of maternal omnipotence and the maternal frustration with the limitations placed on her by the cultural economy of the familial. In her image of the mother/photographer, Brown creates a contradiction between the needs of the child and the needs of the mother that is impossible to resolve within our present cultural constructions of childhood and maternity. Allowing herself to *see* means acknowledging and revealing something to which her child should not be allowed to have access. As she experiences it, to get her picture, the mother must deny her child what he needs. The picture of the child is also a picture of the mother: the picture of the spiny plant tongue, like that of the bird feathers, is a record of a crime committed.

Yet, we can also find irony and humor in the image of the baby's uvula—instruments for surviving maternity and domesticity and for confronting the familial gaze. Looking later at the image of his own tongue, "spiny as some plant, some sponge, maybe, under the sea," what will the baby see? Will he recognize, will he fear the mother's rage, or might he not also find in the mother's vision a playful, funny, perhaps even a healthy or a salutary form of acting out? And might they not be able to look at it together and laugh, especially if their relationship can accommodate conflict, reparation, and recognition? In the story's humor, however grim, we find the intimations of another plot—the possibility of fantasy and play between mother and child and thus, possibly, a space of subversion and a possible meeting ground.

### *every technology is a reproductive technology*[26]

In casting her mother/photographer as unnurturing, monstrous, and murderous, Rosellen Brown reflects a pervasive cultural anxiety about the connection between photography and maternity, an anxiety which, no doubt, has shaped the controversy over Sally Mann's *Immediate Family*. It is an anxiety fed by photography's life-giving powers, on the one hand, its distance, alienation, disembodiedness, objectivity, instrumentality—its ability to kill—on the other. In recent representations, however, these contradictory images of photography are unexpectedly gendered.

Roland Barthes's image of the umbilical cord linking the object photographed to his gaze reinforces a frightening connection between photography and maternity. In speaking of the photograph as a carnal medium, in emphasizing the "adherence" of the referent to the image and the photograph's power not just to call up but literally to "resurrect" the object represented, Barthes outlines photography's procreativity. When he finds the winter-garden image of his mother as a little girl, he is, in fact, able to resurrect her, to "give birth" to her, thus actually displacing her own maternity. Elissa Marder has argued provocatively that in Barthes's *Camera Lucida* photography assumes the role of Roland's "prosthetic mother."[27]

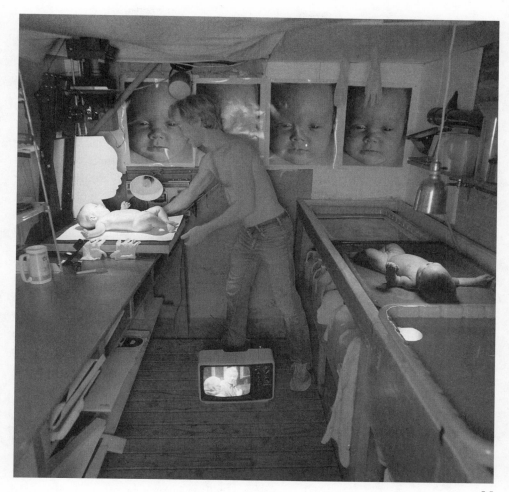

Usurping the maternal function, Barthes's camera technologizes and instru-
mentalizes the function of giving life, shaping a masculine maternity or a
paternal form of generativity, a techno-birth. In casting their cameras as
wombs, these examples of male techno-birth not only usurp maternal functions, they also attempt to recast the damaging representations of paternal
photographers we have seen in recent fiction and film. In Barthes's book the
mother is the object of the photographic gaze, not its subject. Her own look,
marked by her luminous eyes blinded by the sun, is unimpeded and, though
read in the pictures, seemingly unmediated by technology.

Vance Gellert's 1983 untitled image from his series "CarlVision" (Figure 5.5) offers a suggestive example of this masculine usurpation of birth through photography.[28] Gellert's biography at the end of *Flesh and Blood*, where his image is reprinted, reads: "Vance Gellert found himself a house-husband when his wife was completing medical school, just after their first child was born. Feeling 'trapped, bored, and hot,' he began to make images that reflect his anxieties, fears, and fascinations about fatherhood" (p. 185). The image itself is a picture of a darkroom, bathed in deep red light. There is a variety of darkroom equipment, and a number of pictures hang drying around the walls: all these are close-ups of the same infant face. In the center of the image, a young man wearing jeans and no shirt is at work printing, but facing him is not the print itself but a three-dimensional naked baby lying on the printing paper, illuminated by the white light of a large lamp in the shape of a baby's head. The father is smiling, ecstatically, at the surprised-looking child. Across the room, in the washing tray, a duplicate naked baby is illuminated by a yellow light emanating from a lamp shaped like an umbilical cord above him. Some plastic gloves are lying on the table and hanging from the ceiling, like hands ready to "deliver" this child. On the floor is a small old-fashioned portable television—a frequent intrusion in Gellert's images—on which are seen a grey-haired man looking at the camera and the back of a woman's head. On the wall behind them are a number of picture frames that echo the baby images on the darkroom wall.

Gellert's darkroom in which father and child are enclosed is red like a womb; but as he develops and reproduces the pictures of the material bodily baby in many copies ranging from flesh to paper to lamp, he usurps the maternity which has trapped him in this claustrophobic, uterine space. In a note to *CarlVision*, Gellert states: "My wife Sally did not get much exposure in these photographs, but she provided assistance in most of them and unwavering emotional support through all of *CarlVision*." Like the grand-fatherly figure on the television screen who has attracted our look at the expense of the woman whose back we see, the young male photographer has entirely erased and replaced the child's mother, using photography to redefine birth, paternity, and maternity, and radically to redefine as well the representational conventions—signaled by the television—in which the family is usually inscribed.

Gellert's picture in *Flesh and Blood* follows closely Patrick Zachmann's "Florence and Theo in the Bath, Paris, 1986," another image of paternal generativity (Figure 5.6). It is a closely cropped, black-and-white photograph of a pregnant woman in a bathtub, her hair submerged, her eyes unfocused,

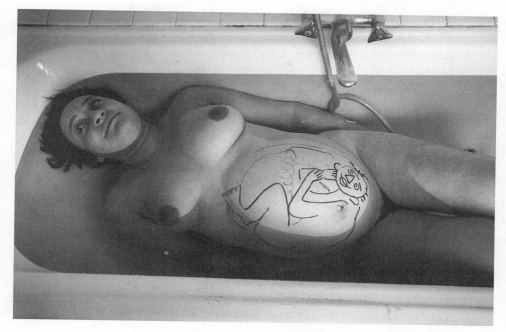

**5.6**

her body uncomfortably squeezed into the small tub. On her large pregnant abdomen, the fetus is schematically sketched in fetal position but with a cartoon face—triangle nose, big smile, large ears. Ann Beattie, in her introduction to the book, considers this picture:

> At first, the photograph seems strange and perhaps silly, and at the same time a little shocking . . . It seems to me that it is his vision: his wife in the bathwater, his son in the amniotic fluid . . . this photograph is remarkably analogous to the photographic process. Think of the way images rise to the surface when developed; that moment when, submerged in the developing fluid, what was invisible suddenly brightens into being: A real thing. A picture. A Theo. (8)

The photographic process is likened to a birth process which is now associated with men and with their ability to manipulate technology. The hidden competition that Beattie perceives between Patrick Zachmann and his wife, Florence, over the ability to bring the child out of the developing/amniotic fluid, she reflects in her own novel about photography *Picturing Will.*[29]

Feminist analysts observing the increasing medicalization and technologization of birth have proposed that male techno-birth is a symptom of masculine "womb-envy." Rosalind Pollack Petcheski's work on fetal images comes closest, perhaps, to connecting photography and medicine with reproduction and its politics.[30] Petcheski begins her analysis with the anti-abortion movement's "The Silent Scream" and the popular images in Lennart Nilssen's "The First Nine Months of Life." Both assume a positivistic position on photography and its tendency to "slice up reality into tiny bits wrenched out of real space and time" (268). Both portray the fetus as a detached and seemingly autonomous "space-man." Petcheski then discusses the representational practices of ultrasound imagery and their political implications. She emphasizes the predatory nature of the photographic consciousness, the militarization of ultrasound (one medical description compares it to submarine sightings), and the transformation of the mother into a "maternal environment" exposed to a "panoptics of the womb" (277) that transform the fetus into "evidence" and seek to control its behavior.

Petcheski insists that the success of fetal imagery derives from the fetishistic and mystical aspects of photography as well as the scientific, especially for the anti-abortion movement. The fetal image is supposed to appear convincing as a person and to encourage "bonding." Petcheski objects: "Indeed the very idea of 'bonding' based on a photographic image implies a fetish: the investment of erotic feeling in a fantasy" (277); fetal imagery, she insists, may well be a "manifestation of masculine desire to reproduce not only babies but also motherhood" (278). Yet, she also concedes that women who want a child do connect visually to ultrasound pictures, thinking of them as "my baby," and that, in fact, women often feel empowered by reproductive technologies, including fetal imagery. Fetal imagery disarticulates mother from child because, rather than "feeling" her fetus, the mother perceives it through what Petcheski describes as the alienating and objectifying, nonmaternal, sense of vision. The mother becomes the spectator of what goes on inside her own body.[31]

Petcheski is careful to make room for and respect every possible response that women might have to fetal imagery and to object only to the use of this imagery in anti-abortion propaganda. But even Petcheski's and Stabile's carefully balanced accounts of the sonogram participate in the "ocularphobia"—the connection of vision with distance, neutrality, and thus, traditionally, with scientific inquiry and masculinity—that shapes the negative representations of maternal photographers we have observed.[32]

Vision mediated by a technology appears especially to be antithetical to maternal relation, to what Sara Ruddick has called the "attentive love" associated with maternity.[33] The writer Hans Jonas cites three primary aspects of vision that would appear to be quite antithetical to maternal work: its "simultaneity of presence," or its spatial rather than temporal dimension; its "dynamic neutrality" or its lack of intercourse with its object; and its distance, which enables its perspective depth.[34] Mothers must see their children's temporal as well as spatial existence; mothers cannot refuse intercourse with their children; and an insistence on distance and objectivity would likely interfere with maternal work. To be congruent with the engagement of maternity, vision would have to be redefined.

Keller and Grontowski attempt such a redefinition when they return to an older, Platonic model of communion and connectedness within the visual, stressing the "meeting of like with like" (220), the kindred relation between seer and object seen (212). As long as the visual is equated with distance and objectivity, with disengagement and objectification, the maternal photographic look will always be inherently transgressive. But if we read the mother's look in conjunction with a more connected, mutual, and intersubjective conception of vision, then the fetal image and the work of the maternal photographer might provide the occasion for a feminine and even a maternal claim on technology. Parental photographs of children—connected not only with masculine womb-envy but also with a feminine reappropriation of reproduction—could thus signal a second birth, a maternal remaking of the construction of childhood and of maternal/child relations.

The cultural suspicion of the professional mother/photographer, however, is exacerbated by photography's intimate association with death. In the process of being photographed, Barthes says, he is "a subject who feels he is becoming an object: I then experience a micro-version of death . . . when I discover myself in the product of this operation, what I see is that I have become Total-Image, which is to say, Death in person."[35] From this point of view, the mother/photographer has the power to kill, to transform live children into one-dimensional figures, immobilized at a given instant, made into icons or fetishes, robbed of vitality. Rather than bestowing a second birth, the camera becomes a womb/tomb into which the child/object is reabsorbed or reincorporated by a frightening and deadly process of maternal vampirism.

Whether perceived as life-giving or murderous, representations of maternal photography feed fantasies of maternal omnipotence that isolate mother from child and highlight the mother's power in proportion to the child's perceived vulnerability. Yet, if looking can be seen as mutual and connective, does it not enable us to recognize, instead, the interconnected plots of mothers and children and the artificiality of pitting the interest of one against that of the other?

In her recent analysis of the fantasy of maternal omnipotence, Jessica Benjamin envisions this alternative intersubjectivity: "For it is not necessary that the fantasy of maternal omnipotence be dispelled, only that it be modified by the existence of another dimension—that of intersubjectivity" ("Omnipotent Mother," 141). She suggests that maternal/child intersubjectivity, and thus an affiliative conception of the subject, develops through the mutual recognition between mother and child defined in Daniel Stern's work. Fantasy and play, pretending, acting out, symbolization, also open up a necessary space between child and mother. Through play and symbolization mother and child can encounter each other as subjects. They can imagine each other's feelings and anxieties. The child can identify with the departing mother; the mother can identify with the separating child. They can modulate closeness with distance. Benjamin suggests that "omnipotence is transformed through use of symbolic processes" ("Omnipotent Mother," 141–142). Looking, we might add, provides the right stage for mutuality and intersubjectivity: when I look I am also seen. But the intersubjective encounter between mother and child has more than one dimension, Benjamin insists: "I suggest that the mother's face often comes to represent the primordial experience of beauty, and that it is an intersubjective experience: beauty belongs to the beloved who returns the gaze, in whose yes we see the sun. But in this first beauty, in the mutual gaze, also lies the beginning of terror—awe, idealization, overstimulation, violation, loss" (*Like Subjects*, 161–162).

Mann's images and the photograph described by Rosellen Brown suggest that the camera could become an instrument of play and symbolization, inserted between mother and child, and creating the necessary space between them, already possible in the ultrasound image as experienced by the woman who wants a child. The triangular field in which signifier, signified, and interpreting subject interact in the process of symbolization is much like the triangular field of the photograph, in which the photographer, the object, and the viewer interrelate through imaginary projections they more or less share. Power, in this structure of play, is not unidimensional or unidirectional: it circulates in multiple ways within the process of taking, developing, assembling, and reading pictures and within the social space and the historical moment in which photography operates. The present moment shaped by feminist consciousness, for example, has enabled us to reenvision mother/child relations and the valences of visual relations, and thereby to lay bare and to contest the cultural fantasy of maternal omnipotence.

Benjamin relates the structure of play to that of mourning, building on Eric Santner's definition of mourning in *Stranded Objects*.[36] Mourning, Santner maintains, opens a necessary space between self and other, an acknowledgment of the loss (and gain) that shapes all intersubjective relation. Benjamin suggests that "the real alternative to a defensive fantasy of omnipotence is the labor of mourning . . . And mourning gives rise to acts of reparation, which need not be perfect in order to restore the expressive space of connection to an understanding other" ("Omnipotent Mother," 144). This extended sense of mourning is perhaps especially applicable to the ever-shifting relation between mother and child which is based on loss and attempted reparation. The maternal photographer "picturing" her child initiates just such a process of mourning: the pictures she takes are pictures of a time lost, measuring change, separation, and reconnection. But in capturing a single moment of her child's life she places that life into a nostalgic and elegiac discourse that can never find consolation. And in placing the camera between herself and her child she introduces a distance that may enable mutual recognition, even as it focuses the pain of irrevocable distance.

Photography, revealing the family's unconscious optics, provides a medium for the exchange of the family's fantasies, and for the intersection of its looks, for the ambivalent processes of loss and mourning that structure family life. As such, it can offer both parent and child ways to acknowledge, to themselves and each other, some of their respective wishes, fears, and anxieties, even as it attempts to contain them within its frames.

### almost home

Camille Billops and James V. Hatch's 1991 film *Finding Christa* documents an attempted reparation, through the cinematic medium, of a mother/daughter relationship interrupted by adoption.[37] We can see in the film the camera's potential to act as a means of connection as well as disconnection in family dynamics. The film begins with a black-and-white still photograph of a 4-year-old African-American girl, dressed in white, her hair in braids and ribbons, followed by a brief color home movie sequence of the same child, tentatively facing the camera (Figure 5.7). A young woman's voice-over says, "My last memory of you was when you drove off and left me at the Children's Home Society. I didn't understand why you left me. Why did

**5.7**

you leave me?" A second home movie sequence shows a young woman changing a baby's diaper, and another voice-over says: "I wanted to offer her something else. I felt she needed a mother *and* a father."

After the credits, the scene shifts to Camille Billops's studio, where a photographer has been taking pictures of her sculptures and is preparing to take some pictures of her. Billops interrupts this photo session, to show the photographer a photograph of her daughter, Christa, whom , she says, she had given up for adoption in 1961 at age 4, and who had just found her birth mother and had sent her the picture and a cassette tape. "Isn't she beautiful?" Billops asks her photographer friend as she compares the photograph of a young woman in her twenties with the picture of the 4-year-old in the white dress. "She looks just like, just like me."

*Finding Christa* is Billops's reflection on her decision to give Christa up for adoption, and an account, as well, of her reunification with Christa nearly thirty years later, her reintegration of the young woman into her birth family and Billops's encounter with Christa's adoptive mother, Margaret Liebig. A mother/artist's film about "leaving" her child, *Finding Christa* explores a reluctant mother's confrontation with the familial gaze. Billops's film casts the maternal filmmaker as the abandoning mother, at the same time using photography and cinema to reassemble the pieces of the daughter's life. It is thus a useful text for consideration of the subversive possibilities of the mother with a camera within familial ideology, specifically located in the African-American family of the 1960s, 1970s, and 1980s.

The fifty-five-minute film is divided into four parts, announced by printed titles: 1. "Why did you leave me?" 2. "Christa, where were you?" 3. "Christa, now what?" 4. "Almost home." Through these titles, the film establishes itself as a dialogue and collaboration between Camille (whose nickname is Bootsie) and Christa, as an attempt to answer the daughter's initial question and, through the final chapter, "Almost Home," as an acknowledgment of the contingency and imperfection of this attempted reparation. This mother/daughter dialogue is filtered through several different media that connect the temporal levels of the film, the time before and after the adoption and the present. A wealth of documentary material includes family pictures and Christa's fashion model pictures, as well as home movies of Camille and her sisters as girls, of Camille's baby shower, Christa's babyhood, Camille's trip to Egypt, Christa's wedding and her singing performances, along with many interviews with members of Christa's birth family and her adoptive family, and recorded discussions between Camille and her friends. In addition, the film features some obviously staged theatrical sequences that challenge quite radically the truth claims of the documentary genre: a scene running over the beginning and end titles in which a group of Camille's family and friends light sparklers and yell "Welcome Home Christa"; some staged encounters between Christa and Camille, such as the "Mother/daughter recital," emceed by George C. Wolfe, in which Camille, dressed in a copy of the little girl's white dress that Christa is wearing in the childhood photograph, yodels, while Christa, dressed in a man's suit, accompanies her on the piano; the stylized scene in which the two women, in gypsy costume, exchange memories as though reading tarot cards. As Valerie Smith suggests, "viewers suspect that truths too deep for direct testimony reside in the hallucinatory interludes."[38]

These performative moments and the inclusion of several media relativize the documentary status of the intercalated photographs and home movies. The staged quality of the interviews is underscored by the props—teddy bears and Raggedy Ann dolls—that some of the relatives hold as they talk. The film's scenes are not documentary images but reenactments, at a later time, of crucial moments in Camille and Christa's reunion. As Billops has asserted, the filmmakers decided to wait several years after the initial reunion until the relationship had evolved and until Christa was older.[39] The film thus exposes cinema and photography for their constructedness and their dependence on convention, especially the conventions of the familial, even as it uses these media to challenge familiality and to narrate a break from those very conventions.

The documentary photographs and home movies inscribe the family into a scene of representation, a scene which Billops and Hatch's film perpetuates and also challenges. The documentary images depict the most conventional moments of black middle-class familial happiness, making it difficult for viewers to sympathize with Billops's account of her unhappiness and constraint as a single, "unwed" mother, her feelings that she "was not a good mother," that she "would have died" had she not given Christa up. We see the sisters and cousins growing up, the baby shower, family reunions that include the baby Christa, the picture of the little girl in white. We see a large extended middle-class family in various comfortable domestic settings, celebrating reunions, preparing food, eating, laughing, partying. Nothing *in* these images prepares us for Camille's desire to extricate herself from this familial scene, or for her decision to give up her child for adoption: the images counterpoint the narrative. Many of the interviews follow similar conventions celebrating familial relations: "Do you really want me to say this?" cousin Bertha repeatedly asks when she wants to criticize Camille, as though the conventions of the documentary could not contain any break in consensus.

Most of the home movies used in Billops and Hatch's films were taken by Walter Dotson, Camille's stepfather, and her previous films have been read as the daughter's responses to his objectifying patriarchal gaze, "the black feminist intervention within the family romance."[40] Camille's trip to join the white filmmaker James Hatch in Egypt and to work as an artist can be read as an attempt to escape from the stepfather's films and the familial ideology they promote into a different cinematic space in which she is freed from the rigid conventions of the extended African-American family that had cast her as an "unwed mother" and where instead she can become an adventurer in the company of interesting men. "Some women are not always nest-keepers," Billops says in *Finding Christa*. "Some men are nest-keepers." She continues to voice women's need for adventure and their exclusion from what she refers to as "the news." As Valerie Smith has said, *Finding Christa*, especially when read within the context of myths about powerful nurturing black mothers, "restores a much-needed sense of balance to representations of maternal love and power" (*"Finding Christa,"* 13).

Yet the very conventions that are seen to entrap the African-American woman and especially the aspiring woman artist in the scene of familiality are precious to and desperately needed by the adopted daughter Christa. As her adoptive mother insists, what Christa missed most was "somebody to identify with," and by that she means baby pictures and family photographs. That lack of pictures is a measure of the severity of her abandonment; she needed them so much that her adoptive father gave her a baby picture of one of his other children, saying it was hers. Photographs and films constitute a personal history from which Christa has been separated and which Billops's film reconstructs for her; thus all the adults who appear in the film hold up photographs of themselves dating from their youth, from the period when Christa was given up for adoption. The implication is that Christa will not recover until she, too, can read her history and constitute her self through such pictures, until, like Sally Mann's children, she can connect her present self to a past image of herself.

Herein lies the ambiguity of family photography, an institution undergirding the familial in Billops's film: the family photo is necessary for the self's constitution, and yet one could argue that for the female self, especially for the doubly oppressed black female self, it is detrimental to development and fulfillment. Practiced by the mother, moreover, the technologies of ideological interpellation can cause rupture, abandonment, and betrayal. In "leaving" Christa, and in allowing us to listen to Christa's feelings of abandonment, Billops supports the conjunction of maternal art and photography with the most extreme fantasies of maternal omnipotence: Camille, in entirely devoting herself to her art, in going to Egypt, in marrying Hatch, abandons her child, leaves her in an orphanage, and never returns. "Why did you leave me?"

Even Billops's stance in the film itself could be described as remarkably distant and uninvolved. She does not express remorse and she resolutely refuses to shed tears. She neither sentimentalizes nor romanticizes the maternal. Her questions to relatives about her own behavior are articulated in the objective tone of the documentarian: "How did you feel when I gave Christa up for adoption?" "Was I justified in giving her up?" "How did my mother feel about my giving Christa up for adoption?" In her questions and her tone, she sets herself apart from some of the other women, who act shocked, who assure her that they would have taken Christa, that they went out looking for her. A lot of people, as Camille's sister Josie says, acted "self-righteous and hypocritical." Billops calmly responds that when Christa was there, they did nothing to help: "we don't care enough, we love these rituals." "These rituals," the subject of photographs and home movies, only barely disguise alternate histories that call into question the image we receive of the happy extended clan. Thus Billops reveals that her sister and brother-in-law had offered to adopt Christa, but that she found him too unpredictable. Indeed, we know from Billops and Hatch's earlier film, *Suzanne, Suzanne* (1982), that her brother-in-law Brownie regularly beat his wife and his daughter Suzanne, who as a result became severely addicted to heroin. Camille's mother did not offer to raise Christa, various relatives suggest, because of "marital considerations." Confronted with her husband, Walter Dotson, and his home movies, and hearing him say that he never knew how his wife felt about Christa's adoption, we begin to gain some insight into these "marital considerations." Family is not as united and uncomplicated as the photographs and films might suggest.

Refusing sentimentality, Billops clearly asserts that she regrets the hurt she caused but she does not regret her act. She will not perform the role of the mother dictated by the familial gaze. When she and Christa are reunited and Christa wants to "hug her and touch her and look at her, she does not want to be touched" but acts like "the cactus" to Christa's "octopus." When Christa asks her mother for a specific photograph of herself, Camille refuses, "because it's mine." She actively resists tears, tells her sister a "funny story" to keep her from crying in the film. And, in part at least, she makes the film to show that "[Christa] did better and also I did better. I would have died and if I would have died, she would have died."

If *Finding Christa* supports this conclusion it is through the figure of Margaret Liebig, Christa's adoptive mother and herself a powerful black woman who has dealt differently with the familial ideologies that have so constrained Camille Billops. Margaret cries while telling the story of the adoption and while expressing her anger at being excluded from Christa and Camille's first reunion. In choosing to juxtapose Margaret and Camille, the filmmakers offer perhaps a more manageable resolution to the pressures of family in the African-American community: two mothers. "Somehow, when women want to change their lives, that's unacceptable, but when men want to leave, it's all right," Camille says, as she tries to explain her own choices.

Margaret accepted Christa, raised her, and integrated her into her own biological family although, as her children say to Christa "you were different": "I wanted my little girl to be dark, I envisioned her as about 3 years old, thick long braids of hair, but when we got there, that's not what I saw in the pictures." By the end of the film, Margaret and Camille have become co-mothers to Christa. Speaking to Christa, Margaret shows she can share: "Boy, am I glad Bootsie's here. She don't know what she's in for. I give it all to her, not you." And Camille, in her last line, explains the film's title. It is not the lie we at first suspect, it is not that she wants to pretend that she found Christa when, indeed, Christa found her. It is that she acknowledges that the film itself—as process and product—might enable Christa to find herself and that Christa is who she is because "Margaret found her. You did good Margaret."

If Billops's art, and her camera, have the potential of hurting or "killing" her child, then the credit she gives Margaret for "finding Christa," their co-mothering, and the resulting film celebrate Christa's rebirth. In making the film together, mother and daughter, perhaps belatedly, find the space of acting, fantasy, and play that allows them to meet on more equal ground, as adults. Of course, reparation can never be perfect. Assuming both the maternal and the child's perspective, the film attempts to understand and relieve the mother who made it, allowing her to share the work of mothering with others, even as it voices the child's cry of loss. Through the part Margaret Liebig plays in the film, Camille Billops can focus the camera gaze on herself, revealing her maternal feelings to the camera, in ways that Sally Mann and her fictional counterparts have not done.

Yet, as much as *Finding Christa* exposes familiality and attempts to find representational conventions that extend familial roles and relations, its very medium, the frames of cinema and photography, encourages concentration on physical likeness and on biological bonds that the film also wishes to contradict. Thus, surprisingly, blood connections and identifications are emphasized all through the film: "I look just like you," "you look just like me," "she sings like you." "Bootsie's a hippy. It's in the blood." "I look just like you, how could you deny me?" Christa asks her father. And she thanks her birth mother for accepting her back into her life, thus enabling her to "grow." This organic metaphor and biological bond strangely subvert Billops's desire to refocus the familial gaze, to multiply maternal positions, to refuse the bifurcation of the maternal look and the maternal gaze. One wonders, then, whether in making the film and thus remaking her daughter she does not risk falling back into a narcissistic and vampiristic form of self-reflection that would return us to the fears of the maternal gaze—fears that her film attempts to but does not quite succeed in dispelling.

In making herself visible Billops also makes herself vulnerable to the judgmental gazes focused on mothers, gazes that Sally Mann and Brown's protagonist might have tried to avoid but which they have only succeeded in even more fully attracting. The risks of maternal exposure are immeasurable—to mothers and to children. But only by becoming visible can mothers engage in a connected, a bodily form of seeing that relinquishes the distancing and objectifying effects of the gaze.

## a terrible picture

It arrived in a campus envelope in my departmental mailbox with a yellow sticker attached to the back: "Marianne—Matthew and I were looking at old photos and came across this, Matthew said 'Is that Oliver?!?' We had 2, so thought you might like this. Mary Jean" (Figure 5.8). No date, and no need for one: I can date it quite precisely by the baby's age and by the strange timetable of that year—it must have been late fall of 1977, Oliver is at most three months old. I don't in any way remember the occasion, but the picture reveals its own origin. It was taken in my friend Mary Jean's living room on a rocking chair I remember because, as assistant professors, we all had these cane chairs and hers had a brown wood frame, whereas mine, which I still have, is blond wood. The red Marimekko wall hanging and the plant locate the scene in Mary Jean's first house, one she has long since replaced by a more modern and elegant one.

It was in her collection of old pictures but I can find no such picture either in Oliver's baby albums, or in the many boxes of prints that were not quite "good enough" to be included in our albums. After I received it in my mailbox I briefly showed the picture to Oliver and then I put it away. I can hardly bear to look at it now. To Mary Jean it was just a picture of me and the baby Oliver, to Oliver, at 14 when I showed it to him, just another baby picture in which he had a funny expression. We laughed about it and I doubt he looked up above his head, to see my face.

I do focus on my face and, as I look at it now, from a distance of over fifteen years, I am frightened by what I see. On the surface, of course, there's

**5.8**

nothing unusual about it: it's just a picture of me as a new mother with my first baby. I'm visiting friends, they snap it with their automatic flash camera, to include in their collection, Marianne and baby Oliver, a new member of the community, a year younger than their son Matthew. I'm sitting on the brown rocker, wearing a drab brown turtleneck sweater that barely stretches across enlarged breasts: the sweater was short, just right for nursing. On my lap, on a blue fuzzy baby blanket, Oliver, wearing a blue-and-white terry infant suit, hangs, leaning into my left arm. He hangs because he isn't yet old enough to sit on a lap, though his left arm is stretched out quite feistily, his hand in a fist. The rest of his body also has some tension in it, as though he would like to sit up. His face certainly looks ready for something—the eyes huge, wide open, staring intently though not directly at the camera, into space—we used to joke about his surprised expression—his cheeks puffed, his mouth determined. He looks ready for action, curious. He looks big against my chest as my arms envelop him, my hands folded across his lower body. On my left ringfinger I am wearing a wedding ring, on my right a tiger's eye, brown again; on my wrists a watch and a thin gold bracelet.

It's hard for me to look at my face. My head is slightly tilted to the left. I am very pale, with no makeup or lipstick. My mouth is smiling painfully; there is no joy or pleasure in that ever so slight smile. My hair, parted at the side, has another section separated off; obviously, I didn't comb it for the picture. And my eyes—they are not focused: the right one looks at the camera, matching the pained smile. The left stares off into space. If I cover the left side of the image, I make the smile more genuine; if I cover the right, I bring out a terrible sadness and fear in the facial expression; the smile disappears. I try other combinations, as I look at the image. If I cover the top, I see a lap, an enterprising baby, comfortable and comforting maternal hands. If I cover the bottom, I see a young woman whose eyes don't focus, who is troubled, withdrawn, lost, and afraid, who looks out at the camera timidly, perhaps pleadingly, whose smile is pathetic. Putting the whole picture together, I see that she doesn't look ready for that curious, feisty child. Her arms can hold him, comfortably, but her face seems overwhelmed by a life and a task she cannot manage.

Why are there no such pictures in my collection? Looking at the picture brings back painful memories of a very difficult time of dealing with a sudden marital separation, a new baby, a job search. It is no wonder that, in the house of old friends, I was able to express the mixture of feelings I must have experienced—sadness and panic, as well as a strange joy and pride in this new baby. These are memories I have long since dealt with and laid to rest; why does this photograph bring them back with such force? Unlike the pictures in my own albums, this picture forces me to confront my own image not as I saw it, or wanted to see it, but as others did. Here is a picture that records those feelings that photographic conventions, especially the conventions of representing new mothers, usually censor—panic, reluctance, a plea for help. The picture is so hard for me to look at and to read, I think, because it violates so radically the conventions of the family album and of familial narrative. If I looked like this at the camera, how did I look at Oliver? What, in my eyes, did he see? And what did I see as I looked at him, reflecting me? Through what looks did we constitute each other as mother and son, as companions through a difficult time?

The "terrible picture" Mary Jean gave me forces me to revise the narrative I have constructed about that time, my story of courageous survival, righteous anger, and only slightly impaired maternal competence. It forces me to look at deeply suppressed feelings that must in some ways have affected my mothering and Oliver's development. Mostly, the picture seems composed of many parts, reflecting disparate needs, contradictory to one another, unassimilable under a common narrative. In keeping themselves out of their photographs, Sally Mann and her fictional counterparts may be trying to avoid directly seeing what I see when I look at this picture.

There is a complicated story embedded here, one that has kept this and other pictures like it out of family albums. The stories of maternal photographers on which I have focused in this chapter have revealed the pressures, both internal and external, mothers have to confront—pressures that inflect my story and this photograph. They have exposed the feelings mothers project into the images they create of themselves and their children, their fears of damaging their children by having feelings at all, the force of repression and distortion. They have represented acts of subtle and overt resistance to the conventional cultural narratives of motherhood.

Recent reproductive technologies divide fetus from mother, isolating each. Modern theories of vision exacerbate this isolation and separation between subject and object. In some of the representations we have looked at, ironically, fathers claim affiliation while mothers subject themselves to and perpetuate this isolation and invisibility. But, on another level, the photographs mothers take and write about assert a profound interconnection between subjects whose images are always images of self in relation to other: they expose seeing as connective rather than distancing.

In my picture, for example, there is a multiplicity of relationships: I look at the friend taking the picture, fifteen years later I look at myself, my hands hold Oliver and he holds on to me. Fifteen years later, we can look at it together and, even though each of us has a different perspective, we can meet in the picture's space and we can even laugh. There are broken relations implied in the picture too, such as the one to his father. Each of us has different memories, each would stress different views. If this picture, like all family photographs, tells a story, it is the complex, plural, contradictory, and interruptive story of familial relationships. If telling that story is the task maternal photographers take on, it is no wonder that they do so hesitatingly, and that they evoke such fearful response. For as much as they might wish to remain unseen, when they snap the shutter they inevitably expose themselves and their own ambivalences about maternity.

# 6

# *R*ESITING IMAGES

Family photographs may affect to show us our past, but what
we do with them—how we use them—is really about today, not
yesterday.

ANNETTE KUHN

## *a family album*

For my parents' fiftieth anniversary I make them an album. I make it for
myself as well, to assemble their lives and mine within the pages of the pretty
book I bought for the occasion. I begin with the few images I could find of
them as children (only one of my father, and he is already about 14) and
end with a triumphant, slightly mischievous picture my two sons took of
themselves in their messy room with a self-timer. I make sure to include all
the places in which my parents have lived, the people who have been most
important to them. I try to find images of their parents, but don't know
whether the young couple in turn-of-the-century clothing are really my
father's parents. I worry as I assemble and arrange the images, that looking
at them will make my parents sad, will emphasize the loss of homes, of
friends and relatives, of their own youth. Until the last moment I am not
sure I will really give it to them. It is this hesitation, no doubt, that causes
me to stress repetitions and continuities in my arrangement of these pictures.
I see how much my own feelings about this anniversary are projected into
the album, how much their album is actually mine.

In the album there are several series:

Me as a three-month-old held by my parents under the kitchen lamp,
   then me in the same spot held by my grandparents and then—in a
   double break from chronology—each of my children held by my
   parents in similar poses though in different domestic settings.

6.1

6.2

6.3

6.4

My parents and me hiking in the Carpathians (I am about 9) followed by the three of us hiking in the White Mountains of New Hampshire several years later. The quality of the second photo is better but the pose is the same, we are sitting on a large rock by a brook—it could be the same mountain (Figures 6.1, 6.2).

My father holding me on his shoulders on a Black Sea beach—I am already too old for him to hold me comfortably but we laugh as we act out an earlier pose; we laugh even harder in the next image as he holds me on his shoulders at age 18, on Cape Cod, my boyfriend running alongside and making sure I don't fall off. There are two more such images—my father holding each of my two boys on his shoulders; we are in Florida and in New Hampshire and he takes pleasure in the repetition, though in the last picture his face is strained, he is not smiling. Acting out this scenario has become an expected ritual (Figures 6.3, 6.4).

The old pictures, especially, are small, hard to read, precious. I place them carefully on the page, and I admire the series I create. This is an earnest album—it occurs to me that I could make it funny, that I could juxtapose the pictures to highlight the breaks, the ironies, the discontinuities, that I could come up with witty captions. But that would not be appropriate here. This album erases the ruptures of emigration and exile, of death and loss, of divorce, conflict and dislocation. Those realities are submerged between the pages, imperceptible to anyone who looks at the album, and, I hope, invisible to my parents, at least on the occasion of their anniversary.

This chapter is precisely about the discontinuities I banished from my own family album. It looks at four texts in which family photographs are used quite differently from the way I used mine on this particular occasion: to reveal the ruptures and dislocations in the autobiographical and familial narrative so as to find in those gaps spaces for daughterly resistance against familial ideologies. The four works are Jamaica Kincaid's autobiographical novel *Annie John* (1985); Marguerite Duras's autobiographical novel *The Lover* (1984); two autobiographical essays by the British psychologist Valerie Walkerdine, "Dreams from an Ordinary Childhood" (1985) and "Behind the Painted Smile" (1991); and a photograph by Lorie Novak entitled "Fragments" (1987). In each case, family photos play an important role in the narrator's self-definition as familial daughterly subject, and in each the photos are manipulated, transformed, mishandled, destroyed, and reinvented, so as to reveal what alternate stories may lie beneath their surfaces or beyond their frames.

Although they are all products of the late 1980s, these four texts emerge from four vastly different cultural contexts with different traditions of visual and verbal representation—the Caribbean, France, England, the United States. In spite of their significant cultural differences, however, they use remarkably similar strategies of self-presentation in pictures and words, strategies relating to the retrospective interpretation of female adolescence. The works themselves attribute varying importance to other social demarcations inflecting the influence of gender: thus gender is a more prominent social marker in *Annie John* than race, while class is as foregrounded as gender in Walkerdine's work and the colonial context importantly shapes the gender identity of Duras's protagonist.

The focus of my reading is their strategies of intervention into their familial and personal stories: going beyond the conventional techniques of photography, they invent ways to expose the unconscious optics of adult femininity and its relationship to female adolescence. Rather than rely on enlargement, reduction, or slow motion to create more revealing images, these writers and artists use or describe the manipulation of already existing images: they erase, invent, or reframe them so as to discover fissures and absences within them, contesting the plenitude promised by photographs. Getting beneath the surface or around the frame of conventional family photographs can make space for resistances or revisions of social roles and positions in vastly different cultural contexts—of conventions upheld through photographic practice. Locating resistance in adolescence, these texts occasion an adult rereading of girlhood as a foundational moment of (re)definition.

Why have conventional and ordinary snapshots that represent predictable daughterly roles and positions served as privileged sites of intervention into familial and social scripts, as useful sites of contestation? If the camera gaze of the family snapshot can be said to construct the girl as a social and familial category, then resisting the image—either at the time or later in the process of rereading—becomes a way of contesting that construction, of rewriting the present by way of revising the past. Reading, rereading, and misreading thus become forms of active intervention: they enable a revision of the screens through which the familial gaze is filtered and refracted and thus a contestation of the gaze itself. In focusing on family pictures and albums, these forms of resistance not only contest but actually reveal the power of photography as a technology of personal and familial memory.

## finding the space-off

*Annie John* is Kincaid's first novel. Composed of a number of stories originally published in the *New Yorker,* it tells the story of the narrator Annie's
childhood and adolescence on a small Caribbean island (perhaps the
author's native Antigua) which, at the end of the novel, she leaves for
England.[1] In her later works, especially in *Lucy,* as we have seen, Kincaid
writes about her own work as a photographer, which eventually leads her
to writing. The control of the camera enables Lucy to move from her
subordinate position as servant and immigrant to that of self-determining
subject who gains consciousness by analyzing, visually, the situation in
which she finds herself. In contrast to Lucy, Annie John is not a photographer but merely a reader of the conventional family snapshots on her night
table. Yet her manipulation of the photos endows her with some of the
control Lucy gains through taking, developing, and arranging photographs.
Whereas Lucy makes pictures, however, Annie erases them, to expose the
gaps that lie beneath and within them.

Photos in *Annie John* represent Annie's confinement within the institution
of family—everything that at the end of the novel she rejects for a new life
abroad. Thus, her mother's trunk contains, among the many objects collected since Annie's birth, a "photograph of me on my second birthday
wearing my pink dress and my first pair of earrings, a chain around my
neck, and a pair of bracelets, all specially made of gold from British Guiana"
(20). As a young girl Annie delighted in rediscovering all of the objects in
the trunk and hearing her mother's stories about them; in adolescence she
concentrates on the rings and chains and bracelets, the images of entrapment
in the script of daughterhood and femininity she eventually repudiates. The
golden rings and chains are also reminders of a slave history Annie tries to
leave behind when she goes to England. As she looks around her room in
preparation for leaving the island, knowing that she will never return, she
sees, for a moment only and without much regret, the "photographs of
people I was supposed to love forever no matter what" (131). Annie's change
in the course of the novel revolves around the figure of her mother, whom
she adores and with whom she feels symbiotically merged when a child. In
adolescence, however, she despises her, lies to her, tortures her, and rejects
her. The transition between a comfortable sense of home and the urgent
need to leave that home is told in a series of painful confrontations. A
strange encounter with her family photographs is crucial in focusing Annie's
shift from compliant, daughterly subject to resisting agent.

In the novel's penultimate chapter, Annie suffers from a protracted and inexplicable illness, mirrored globally in the three months of torrential rain that flood the island. Annie spends those months in bed in a retreat to childhood comfort in the constant care of her parents. Her illness follows the most serious fight she has ever had with her mother: immediately after, Annie asks her father to make her a new trunk. The fight is occasioned by Annie's first encounter with boys—a humiliating scene during which Annie chances to meet a boy she used to play with as a child, who subtly mocks her during the encounter. Later she remembers the last game they had ever played together as small children: the boy had asked Annie to take off all her clothes and wait for him under a tree in a spot that turned out to be a red ants' nest.

As she remembers this degrading and painful introduction to sexuality, Annie loses all sense of herself: "I began to feel alternately too big and too small. First, I grew so big that I took up the whole street; then I grew so small that nobody could see me—not even if I cried out" (101). This powerful image of alternately growing and shrinking—reminiscent of *Alice in Wonderland*—typifies the daughter's ambivalence about moving from childhood to adolescence; it describes the fractured and disrupted developmental progress of the female subject. Annie's first move into the world of adult sexuality—punished rather than supported by her mother who calls her a slut because she talked to the boys—sends her literally back to bed in a withdrawal that reads like a classic description of latency.

During her mysterious illness, Annie confronts the photographs that surround her bed. The photos suddenly protrude from the background of the room and "loomed up big in front of me" (118). Conventional family pictures, each illustrates one of the institutions into which Annie is in the process of being inducted as she becomes a social subject. In the first she is wearing her white school uniform. In the second, again wearing white, she is a bridesmaid at an aunt's wedding. The third is a picture of her parents, the father wearing a white baseball uniform, with a bat in one hand and the other hand around the mother's waist. The last photograph is the only one which elicits a memory and a narrative: Annie is wearing her white Communion dress and shoes with a decorative cut-out on the side, shoes her mother disapproved of as "not fit for a young lady and not fit for wearing on being received into church" (119). As Annie recalls the argument over the shoes—her wish that her mother were dead and the mother's terrible headache that made Annie fear she had indeed died—the photos begin to act very strange:

The photographs, as they stood on the table, now began to blow themselves up until they touched the ceiling and then shrink back down, but
to a size that I could not easily see. They did this with a special regularity,
keeping beat to a music I was not privy to. Up and down they went, up
and down. They did this for so long that they began to perspire quite a
bit, and when they finally stopped, falling back on the table limp with
exhaustion, the smell coming from them was unbearable to me. I got out
of bed, gathered them up in my arms, took them over to a basin of water
on the washstand, and gave them a good bath. I washed them thoroughly
with soap and water, digging into all the crevices, trying with not much
success, to straighten out the creases in Aunt Mary's veil, trying, with not
much success, to remove the dirt in front of my father's trousers. When I
finished, I dried them thoroughly, dusted them with talcum powder, and
then laid them down in a corner covered with a blanket, so that they would
be warm while they slept. (119–120)

The result of Annie's feverish manipulation of the photos is that they are
completely transformed: "None of the people in the wedding picture, except
for me, had any face left. In the picture of my mother and father, I had
erased them from the waist down. In the picture of me wearing my confirmation dress, I had erased all of myself except for the shoes" (120).

How are we to interpret Annie's strange intervention? The transformation
of the pictures occurs just at the point of her recovery—a symbolic rebirth,
a break from her girlhood past, after which she needs new clothes and shoes,
speaks with a different accent, develops great contempt for her classmates,
and eventually leaves home. Annie's encounter with the photographs is a
moment of resistance in which she attempts to erase the familial and social
script where she is positioned as daughter and social subject, shedding one
by one the institutions that have interpellated her.

Described as independent agents in the text, the photos enact the process
of growing and shrinking, the ambivalent confrontation with adolescent
development. They grow and shrink, they are exhausted, they perspire. In
Annie's narrative they play the role of dolls—inanimate objects endowed
with human characteristics, objects to be cared for and nurtured. Annie
reduces them, like herself, back to infancy, so as to have a chance at a
different start, one in which bodies, faces, and clothes interact differently
and acquire different dimensions. We could say that she acts out her fear of
adult sexuality as, synechdochically, she tries to remove the photos' bad
smell, erase her parents' bodies below the waist, and rub out the stain on

her father's pants and the wrinkles in the wedding veil. At the same time, however, she is more deliberate, motivated more by disgust than by fear, as she chooses to resist all the confining white dresses and the institutions they represent.

Annie stages resistance by means of a manipulation of photographs. Photography can further her act of opposition because the family pictures mark Annie's relation to her *past* and therefore to a *future she wants to choose*. In washing and changing the pictures and the relationships they depict, Annie can attempt to weaken the "this has been" of the photographic referent, Barthes's "ça a été"—the presence of the past moment. She can attempt to intervene in her past, to rewrite her memories in favor of representations that better fit with the new life she wants to explore. She can assume an adult role in relation to her own childhood poses as she bathes the pictures and powders them as though they were her babies. She can thus try to manage the confusing emotions of adolescence, figured by the powerful smell the photographs emit. When she finishes the feverish bath, she has erased the wedding party except for her own face, she has removed her parents' sexuality, and she has preserved the subversive shoes. Her face, her shoes, and her parents' torsos are all that remain, building blocks of new memories and new materials for adult life.

In addition, the photograph, especially a family photograph which depicts the subject interpellated by the familial gaze, embedded in relation and ensconced in institution, reinforces for the subject an imaginary sense of coherence and plenitude. The still picture freezes one moment and enshrines it as a timeless icon with determinative definitional power. Thus, the single still photo can be seen as a form of suture through which the subject closes herself off from the symbolic and the unconscious, from contradiction and lack. The subject gazing at her own image can find this coherence as she bridges the gap between herself as spectator and as object of representation. Annie contests this totalizing and rigidified sense of self—a girlhood self constructed according to social requirements—by creating open unmarked spaces in the pictures. Staring at the ruined images the next morning, she can find in them a more tentative, more fluid and permeable subjectivity— one that can include a desired imaginary wholeness even while opposing and rejecting it.

As Annie settles into her berth at the start of her transatlantic escape from a predetermined future, she repeats the erasures she performed on the photos: "I could hear the small waves lap-lapping around the ship. They made an unexpected sound, as if a vessel filled with liquid had been placed on its side and now was slowly emptying out" (148). This image of emptying reinforces Annie's rejection of an imagined plenitude. Annie's departure requires not continuity with past experience and the preservation of memory but empty open spaces on which new narratives can be inscribed. This is the opening she makes when she washes the photos.

To describe such a locus of ideological resistance, Teresa de Lauretis borrows a term from film theory, the "space-off," the "space not visible in the frame but inferable from what the frame makes visible."[2] De Lauretis describes a particular movement of resistance staged by "the subject of feminism," a movement I see Annie as charting:

> It is a movement between the (represented) discursive space of the positions made available by hegemonic discourses and the space-off, the elsewhere of those discourses: those other spaces both discursive and social that exist, since feminist practices have (re)constructed them, in the margins (or "between the lines" or "against the grain") of hegemonic discourses and in the interstices of institutions, in counterpractices and new forms of community. These two kinds of spaces . . . coexist concurrently and in contradiction. The movement between them, therefore, is not that of a dialectic, of integration, of a combinatory, or of *différance,* but is the tension of contradiction, multiplicity and heteronomy. (26)

In recasting her family pictures, Annie finds the space-off that was already inscribed in the incongruity between her confirmation dress and the cut-out shoes. Bringing the space-off to the surface and into the frame, Annie moves from interpellated subject to agent in her own story. She has replaced the old trunk, full of her mother's memories of her and her mother's memorabilia, with her own tabula rasa—a new trunk to contain the objects she herself will select. Thus Annie's resistance depends precisely on absence, discontinuity, and incongruity—a revision of the screens of a compliant girlhood. It depends on the negativity with which she has inscribed her adolescent break, her refusal to consent to a prescribed adult femininity.

But Annie's retrospective location of her resistance in a moment of adolescent rupture follows yet another ideologically predetermined script. From the perspective of Carol Gilligan's reading of girls' development, Annie rewrites her story of childhood connection in favor of what Gilligan calls the "canonical story of human development" in which breaks are mandated and childhood relationships must be devalued in adulthood.[3] Adulthood, in this script, demands a break from the powerful relationships of childhood, particularly from maternal attachments. Annie inscribes this break in her story as an act of erasure in which photographs play a central function. Photographs stand for one aspect of her childhood, the conventional, institutional side of girlhood leading to a consent to femininity as culturally constructed. And they allow her to forget, or to disavow, the other side of childhood, the world of ecstatic mother/daughter connection, the space of friendship and the feeling of being at home in the world that she presents in such lush detail throughout the novel's first part. That intricate world of intersubjective connection is not available to photographic representation: it remains in the rich texture of Kincaid's written narrative. Erasing the photographs creates spaces within them where such richness might be inscribed, but only by severely reinventing an available photographic medium.

## la photographie absolue

*The Lover,* like *Annie John,* is an autobiographical story of individual development and cultural displacement.[4] Like Annie, Duras's protagonist/narrator ends up leaving her family in French Indochina for a writing career in France. Family photographs are the pretexts of *The Lover,* which was originally entitled "La photographie absolue." According to an account notorious in the publishing world, the novel actually originated with a box of old photographs which Duras's son found among his mother's belongings and tried to publish. When the publisher asked that his mother add some captions, Marguerite Duras wrote *The Lover.* The text was too long for the first publisher and so *The Lover,* Duras's commercially most successful book, was published by the Editions de Minuit but without the pictures.[5]

This account of the novel's origin explains some of the incongruities in Duras's text and its loose structure. If we imagine the narrator leafing through a series of photos, returning to linger over some, building a narrative on the basis of images, we accept more easily the mention of Duras's friends from the period of the Occupation in Paris who mysteriously appear in the midst of a narrative that takes place in Indochina in the 1920s and 1930s. We also understand the point of the seemingly gratuitous reflections on image and photography included in the narrative of the family's life in Indochina.

Yet photographs are ambiguous for Duras; juxtaposed with written narratives they invariably represent the fixity and rigidity that the fluidity of writing aims to challenge. "I believe photographs promote forgetting,"

Duras says in *Practicalities*. "The fixed, flat, easily available countenance of a dead person or an infant in a photograph is only one image as against the million images that exist in the mind. And the sequence made up by the million images will never alter. It's a confirmation of death."[6] It must be this perception of photography that leads Duras to feature an absent picture, the "photographie absolue." In *The Lover* the "photograph" that was never taken becomes the medium of an alternate set of memories on which the rest of the novel is based. And this "photograph," retrospectively constructed, "records" the moment of adolescent rupture which alters the course of the narrator's subsequent development. It allows Duras to redefine the limits of still photographic representation.

Throughout the novel, the narrator needs to contest the formal family photographs her mother has taken of her children year after year:

> We don't look at each other but we do look at the photographs, each of us separately, without a word of comment, . . . we see ourselves . . . Once they've been looked at the photos are put away with the linen in the closets. My mother has us photographed so that she can see if we're growing normally. She studies us at length as other mothers do other children. She compares the photos, discusses how each one of us has grown. (94)

The formal portrait photographs the narrator grew up with equalize their objects, attenuate singular traits in favor of promoting, through similar pose, dress, and expression, what must have been considered a comforting resemblance—a generational and class belonging which erases particularity and self:

> All these photographs of different people, and I've seen many of them, gave practically identical results, the resemblance was stunning. It wasn't just because all old people look alike, but because the portraits themselves were invariably touched up in such a way that any facial peculiarities, if there were any left, were minimized. All the faces were prepared in the same way to confront eternity, all toned down, all uniformly rejuvenated . . . they all wore an expression I'd still recognize anywhere. (96–97)

Photographs can well promote this erasure of the particular as they reinforce the plenitude of the imaginary and the external signs of class and institutional allegiance. The touched-up picture her mother had taken before her own death is a good example: "In her photo her hair is done nicely, her clothes just so, a tableau" (96; my translation). Duras contests this rigid image-construction in the very form of her own imagetext: her verbal "photographie absolue" is composed in direct opposition to formal portraiture. As Duras verbally describes a picture that was not taken she bypasses the technical properties of photography and reappropriates the process of "touching-up," taking it to an extreme.

*The Lover* begins with the description of the narrator's ravaged old face—the opposite of the touched-up photo of her mother. Contemplating her own face leads her to consider the sudden break, between the ages of 17 and 18, that produced it: something happened to her appearance to give her the face she was to keep, which would then continue to age more gradually. The narrator emphatically describes this break between 17 and 18 and its ravaging effects, but she never directly motivates it in the long narrative that follows. Throughout the novel, we look for hints as to what happened between 17 and 18 to make her age so drastically. Duras, however, is more interested in the rupture itself than in an explanatory narrative that might have the undesirable effect of bridging it.

*The Lover* thrives on such discontinuities: "The story of my life doesn't exist. Does not exist. There's never any center to it. No path, no line" (8). Contrary to visual images, as Duras perceives them, writing can be made out of emptiness and rupture: "Sometimes I realize that if writing isn't, all things, all contraries confounded, a quest for vanity and void, it's nothing. That if it's not, each time, all things confounded into one through some inexpressible essence, then writing is nothing but advertisement" (8). Image and writing are opposed in Duras's text, one signaling fixity and cohesion, the other freedom and permeability.[7]

The "photographie absolue" is one of the text's multiple foundational images—the photograph that was never taken but could have been. This image of the girl crossing the river at age $15\frac{1}{2}$ is, in both senses of the word, a cliché of adolescent rupture and discontinuity: "It might have existed, a photograph might have been taken, just like any other, somewhere else, in other circumstances. But it wasn't. The subject was too slight . . . It never was detached or removed from all the rest. And it's to this, this failure to have been created, that the image owes its virtue: the virtue of representing, of being the creator of, an absolute" (10).

Why does this memory, as significant or insignificant as it may seem in the narrator's autobiographical musings, take the form of a photograph in particular? In what ways does photography enable Duras to construct the specific kind of subjectivity that emerges in *The Lover*? If Jamaica Kincaid's

Annie needs to weaken the "ça a été" of her photos' referent and thereby the fixity of memory and the past, Duras's narrator may need to do the opposite: to strengthen her memory and to solidify the lover's and her own tenuous earlier existence. If reference is, as Barthes says, the "founding order" of photography, a picture may be the optimal medium for such a process of consolidating the past and of bringing it into the present. When we look at a photo, or even when we read a description of one, we do assume that the referent is the "necessarily real thing that was placed before the camera." Even as the narrator tells us that the picture was never taken, we read its content and are able to imagine it in great detail. A picture described verbally is the same whether it "exists" or not: the referent of the picture itself seems more solid, but the referent of the description is more or less so according to what the narrator tells us. In this case she tells us that this picture is a construction, and we "see" it more clearly because the construction is described as a picture, but less so because she explains that it was never taken.

The details of the picture can begin to suggest the kind of intervention into her life story that the verbal composition of this nonexistent photograph constitutes for the narrator. It is a "picture" of herself at 15½ on a ferry crossing the Mekong river on her way from home to school. As a white girl, she is as striking a presence on the boat as the large black car belonging to the Chinese man who is to become her lover. Her description of her appearance begins with her silk dress, so old it is already transparent, hardly suitable for school. The leather belt she probably borrowed from one of her brothers and wears with it adds to her improper look. She is not sure about the shoes, and here the difference between photography and memory is clearest, for, if this had indeed been a photograph, the shoes would have been fixed in its image. Her assumption—that she was wearing gold lamé high-heeled sandals—soon becomes fixed in *our* vision, however.

But it is the hat which contains the picture's "determining ambiguity." It is a man's felt hat, flat-brimmed, pink, with a broad black ribbon, such as no one wore at the time. As clearly as she can still remember the hat, as unclear is her memory of its origin. She imagines that she might have tried it on as a joke and then talked her mother into buying it for her because wearing it transformed her appearance drastically: "Beneath the man's hat, the thin awkward shape, the inadequacy of childhood, has turned into something else. Has ceased to be a harsh, inescapable imposition of nature. Has become, on the contrary, a provoking choice of nature, a choice of the mind. Suddenly it's deliberate. Suddenly I see myself as another, as another would be seen" (12–13).

This shift from the given to the deliberate in her appearance is in itself an active intervention; the narrator wears the hat in a defiant gesture of self-definition—the self-definition of the adolescent in the process of breaking away from her family and her childhood. Yet the incongruities in her appearance are the "photo's" most important feature—not the hat but the ways in which the hat clashes with the rest of her clothes. In its contradictions the image can undo the suturing of the act of its construction: with its conflicting effects the picture acts out the opposing forces that define her subjectivity.

In constructing the photograph that was not taken, the narrator consistently underscores the otherness embedded in the self-portrait: her self-portrait needs to be an allo-portrait. Contrary to Annie's attempt to move from center to space-off, Duras's narrator creates an image in the space-off that then absorbs the focus as though it were centrally located within the frame. This ambiguity between the construction of memory as a photograph (an attempt at solidifying the "ça a été") and the chaotic aspects of the image itself (a reintroduction of fluidity and discontinuity) dramatizes the process of constituting the autobiographical subject out of different positions and within the framework of contradictory impulses and desires. In *The Lover* different subject-positions, the otherness of the self, emerge distinctly as the narrative switches, quite unpredictably and without clear motivation, from first to third person. "I" at times becomes "she" or "the girl"; she acts in the text and, especially in her encounters with the Chinese lover, she watches herself act and be acted upon. The narrator and the girl in the pictures are but two of the different positions Duras assumes in the text. In this sense, the photograph that was never taken would have been an allo-portrait.

Paul Smith, in *Discerning the Subject*, sees negativity—the space in between different subject positions, the space binding and unbinding them—as central to the subject's construction.[8] Photographs are perhaps best suited to demonstrating the ways in which we want to convince ourselves of our plenitude: the photo is, of course, literally developed from a negative. In *Annie John* negativity is nevertheless exposed as Annie wipes clean certain sections within her photos. Duras describes a more complicated process of negotiating between fullness and emptiness. The absolute she finds in the invented picture is negativity itself, the absence around which it takes shape in the narrator's and her readers' imaginations. By resisting the plenitude and fixity contained in conventional family pictures and finding a negative space, the familial subject returns to a break between life moments when subjectivity was less fixed, more fluid, more productive of different possible futures. That moment, for the narrator of *The Lover*, is the moment of adolescent rebellion—when she contests bourgeois colonial convention to take a Chinese lover, when she allows him to give her family money, when she identifies with him rather than with her mother or brothers, when, eventually, she leaves for France to become a writer.

But we might ask our earlier question again: in constructing the photograph as an "absolute" break, in stressing negativity and emptiness, what knowledges, what continuities, might she be denying? What affiliations emerge in the "photograph"—to her mother who bought her the clothes, her brother who lent her the belt, her lover who first sees her on that boat—that her own interpretation downplays in favor of its unique incongruity and thus the path to disaffiliation it can open? In the story of a girl's move from childhood to adulthood in a patriarchal and colonial social context, the line between adherence to convention and resistance can be difficult to locate.

## behind the painted smile

Unlike Kincaid and Duras, Valerie Walkerdine comes to family pictures not as a writer but as a professional reader of images, an analyst of film, photography, and other popular visual media. The two essays I would like to discuss here appear in two collections that feature photographs either as illustration *(Truth, Dare or Promise: Girls Growing Up in the Fifties)* or as subject *(Family Snaps: The Meanings of Domestic Photography).*[9] In her two companion essays, Walkerdine traces both her personal emergence from a small-town working-class British setting in the 1950s and her developing insights as a feminist theorist and activist in the late 1980s. Photographs of herself permit Walkerdine not only to interpret her childhood and family but to engage in a feminist class-conscious practice of reading. Her analysis evolves from an early Mulveyan perspective on women as objects of the male gaze to a more complex positioning of women as both objects and subjects, both creators and readers of their own images. In confronting radically different images with one another, Walkerdine focuses in depth on a break in her life story—a break she locates not in adolescence but earlier in her girlhood—and she finds in that break the possibility both for active resistance and for insight.

"Dreams from an Ordinary Childhood" appears in *Truth, Dare or Promise,* a collection of twelve personal testimonies by British feminists of the postwar generation. Each of the essays locates the author within the institution of the family and in relation to social changes introduced by the Education Act of 1944 and the founding of the welfare state in Britain. The stories the twelve authors tell are stories of upward mobility made possible by the sense of future possibility and sense of personal entitlement to which they attest in direct opposition to the myths that define femininity during the 1950s. As the editor insists: "There was a general confidence in the air, and the wartime image of women's independence and competence at work lingers on well into the decade in the popular literature and in girls' comics of the day" (6). By going back to childhood, the authors attempt to trace the sources of feminist consciousness in their family histories and class allegiances, in the course their lives took in contrast to the lives of their mothers and fathers: "All of these accounts contain an implicit avowal of how we see the world: all as feminists, though perhaps speaking with the voices of different feminisms, and all informed by other commitments—to socialism, anti-racism, or to other recognitions of ways in which the world needs to be changed" (8). The childhoods described in the book are the childhoods of future activists.

Each of the essays is illustrated by a photograph which shows the author at a young age, either alone or in the company of a sibling. Some are family snapshots, others more formal photos taken for specific occasions. The picture illustrating Walkerdine's "Dreams from an Ordinary Childhood" is typical of the volume in that it reinforces stereotyped images of girlhood: it is a picture of a little 3-year-old dressed as a bluebell fairy. Holding a star, little Valerie smiles tentatively but sweetly at a space that is off camera, beyond the picture's frame (Figure 6.5). The picture appeared in the *Derby Evening Telegraph* with the following caption: "Three-year-old Valerie Walkerdine, one of the 'fairies' in the fancy dress parade at Mickleover children's sports and field day last night" (66).

Walkerdine's analysis of the picture focuses on the little girl's off-camera look, on the picture's "space-off":

Whose gaze? In whose vision was I created to look like this, to display the winning charms, so that posing before the judges, they too, like the camera, would be won over? It is my first memory of what winning meant. But towards whom am I looking, who dressed me like this? Like all the fairy fantasies rolled into one? It was somebody's dream, their fantasy, my fantasy, meeting in the mutuality of the returned look; the gentle and uncertain smile created there too. (66–67)

6.5

That look, it turns out, belongs to her father, who called her Tinky and identified her with the fairy who might repair all his ills—his poverty, his sickness, and the threat of death.

Walkerdine's essay places the bluebell picture in contrast to her subsequent self—the fat, clumsy, frightened child who replaces the sickly and underweight but magical Tinky after she has her tonsils out. This is the break in her life story that the essay interrogates, but it is a break nowhere reflected in the illustration. But even in her new persona, one that fails to correspond to the "pre-adolescent feminist myth" of activity and athletic prowess, Valerie continued to please and to win—in school and in a variety of holiday competitions. Her strategy now is not the magic of Tinky but the plodding reliability and hard work that girls learn because it gets rewarded in school. This is the price of going from one victory to another, of being allowed to follow the dream of upward mobility: "They held out the knowledge, the position to me, and told me that I could claim it as mine, if I worked for it and had the ability" (75). But claiming the dream now, as she retells the story, is rejecting the good-girl image and asserting a dangerous power and knowledge: "We are beginning to speak of our histories, and as we do it will be to reveal the burden of pain and desire that formed us, and, in so doing expose the terrible fraudulence of our subjugation" (76).

Walkerdine's narrative takes her from the sickly bluebell fairy to the plodding reliable good girl to the rebellious Marxist-feminist who not only has followed the "dream of an ordinary childhood" but has turned that dream back on itself by exposing its fraudulence and its price. This is not a seamless linear tale. There is violence at the very center of it—the poison Tinkerbell drinks to save Peter Pan, the surgery Valerie undergoes which removes not only her tonsils but her magic and charm to be replaced by lumpiness and a disgust with her body. Femininity is defined either by frailty or by a "lumpen docility": "I find it almost unbearable to look at photographs of myself from that time on" (69). And yet Walkerdine emerges from the trap created by these two equally unacceptable subject positions as a feminist agent capable of claiming the power that comes with self-knowledge. How?

The gaps that remain in this narrative occasion a second essay, "Behind the Painted Smile," which appears in *Family Snaps*. In revising and supplementing "Dreams from an Ordinary Childhood," Walkerdine takes us beyond the space-off of the Tinkerbell photo and the father's gaze to the space-off of the essay itself, where she finds another, deeply suppressed and transgressive version of herself. In the first essay she described this other self, but here she allows us to *see* it as well; the first essay contained an illustration and an analysis of it, while the second takes us through the work of reframing and reconstructing images: "When I wrote that piece it was as though I had said all there was to say, but I knew at one level then, and I see more clearly now, that there are far more disturbing images to explore, which are hidden and covered over by the erotic allure of the bluebell fairy" (35). To expose those images—and their visual nature is crucial—Walkerdine must first tell the story of the first essay's publication:

> When I wrote the piece I sent the publishers two photographs: one of the bluebell fairy and another, a school photo of me aged about seven, looking puffed out, sickly and fat. They wanted to publish the latter. I, having sent it to them in the first place, adamantly refused to let *this* image be the object of public scrutiny . . . I continued to hide behind a wall of words, academic words, which kept me from exploring the traumatic effectivity of that and other reviled images of myself. (35)

In her subsequent analysis and, even more powerfully, in the essay's illustrations, Walkerdine exposes her own and her generation's subjection as well as her attempt to exonerate herself of any responsibility for it: "On one level, the idea that we are constructed in the male gaze is reassuring. We remain somehow not responsible for our actions, as though we were mere puppets to masculinity . . . It strikes me as easier to take apart a beautiful image, blame patriarchy, and yet hold on to that image (Yes, yes, I am that really) or to point to a void as its other side than to examine what else may lurk beneath" (36). To examine and ultimately to expose "what may lurk beneath," is the project of the second essay.

Getting to the space that lies beneath or behind the surface of the image is a complicated and painful, though ultimately powerful, process for Walkerdine—as deliberate an intervention as Annie's act of washing her photos or Duras's construction of a fictional picture. But Walkerdine goes beneath the absence and void central to the other two texts, in favor of the uncomfortable alternative of attempting to find, to touch, and to name what exactly lies outside the frame.

This involves work with images as well as work with words, and here Walkerdine's essay differs from Kincaid's and Duras's novels. Walkerdine expands the properties of photography beyond all convention, using every means at her disposal to expose through the photographs the family's unconscious optics, the gazes interpellating her, and the screens operative in her family album. She makes slides out of a number of family snapshots,

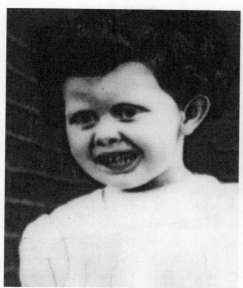

6.6

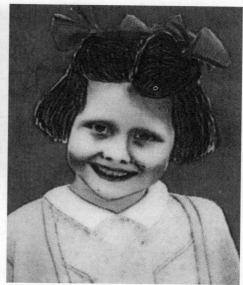

6.7

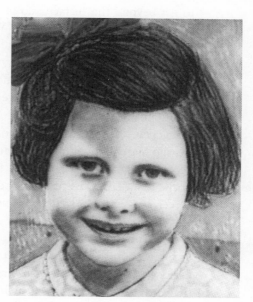

6.8

projects them on the wall, draws and colors all over the projected images, shades them in, writes on them, later makes pastel drawings from these new images, and exhibits them in an installation. She describes this as a shocking practice of self-mutilation which results in a series of extremely disturbing self-portraits—again, clearly in the form of allo-portraits, a number of which are reproduced with the essay (Figures 6.6, 6.7, 6.8). Two areas of the body are their main focus, the mouth and the abdomen, and the rest of Walkerdine's essay provides the analysis that explains their centrality—her obsession with food, her fear of speaking in public, and her fear of sexuality. Through her mutilation of the old images, Walkerdine finds what lies beneath their surface—"a terrible rage, depression and anger that have been entirely split off" (40) from her present self.

In her work with images Walkerdine negates the photograph's promotion of an imaginary plenitude, searching for its repressed unconscious content instead: "Like dreams, images are the manifest content which is only the surface cover for what lies latent beneath. Thus, although much radical work on photography has shown us how to read the semiotics of photographs it has not ventured much below the surface" (40). In finding a way to get beyond the surface and in reaching (doubly) outside the frame, and in naming what she finds there, Walkerdine can connect her present active intervention with the active impulses of her earlier self; she can find in the past not only frailty and docility, not only female impersonation and mimicry, but anger and rage, envy and greed.

Identifying her childhood anger and rage, envy and greed from the vantage point of her adult present constitutes a profoundly different definition of agency from what those emotions offered her in the suppressed past. During her childhood and even at the moment of the first essay Walkerdine perceived the break between the frail Tinky (identified with magic) and the docile schoolgirl (identified with compliance and plodding), but she did not perceive its violence. That violence, along with the anger it elicited in her, was hidden "behind the painted smile."

Both subject positions—the magical fairy and the docile schoolgirl—were dictated from the outside, projections of the familial and social gaze. The father constructs the fairy, the clapping hands keep Tinkerbell alive because they believe in her, the social institutions reward Valerie's diligence and award her the scholarships that allow her to leave home. Valerie fits into the images others project for her. And the only possibilities for her own active interventions are identified with unacceptable emotions and images: rage, greed, envy, eating too much, or saying something inappropriate.

"Covered over, I suggest, was the fantasy of the angry child, actively shouting out loud, crying and screaming; the all-consuming, rapacious woman with a large (sexual) appetite" (42). In her direct manipulation of images, Walkerdine can reach feelings—old and new—that she cannot reach through words, and eventually, as she reads the images, she can verbalize them. She can do this by reframing the images, by manipulating the screens that refract the institutional gazes. She rereads the images by substituting a feminist screen that can reveal hidden feelings and the possibility of appropriating them for positive intervention.

In her childhood the active girl was angry, the desiring girl greedy. In contrast, finding what lies behind the surface of the pictures and in the space-off of her first essay constitutes for the adult a redefined and politically meaningful form of resistance in the present. "I believe that investigating these issues takes us beyond a deconstructive examination of the feminine in representations. It takes us to an exploration of the powerful fantasies and anxieties which keep those representations circulating and provide us with the basis for other narratives of our histories and the claiming of our power" (45). Walkerdine can claim a power that has emerged through self-mutilation to acknowledge and revalue emotions deemed unacceptable. She finds these emotions on both sides of the break that constructs her story: leaving childhood and adolescence behind is not in itself a route to liberation. Adolescence, Walkerdine implies, is not the privileged moment of revision; that process needs to be repeated throughout adulthood. Power and knowledge can be found in the act of constructing and reconstructing, of reading and rereading, images both of compliance and of resistance.

## fragments

Lorie Novak's photograph "Fragments," exhibited in the 1991 Museum of Modern Art exhibition "Pleasures and Terrors of Domestic Comfort," also constructs the female subject as both creator and reader of her own self-representations (Figure 6.9).[10] Both Novak and Walkerdine engage in a kind of photographic self-creation which begins with the positioning of themselves as camera objects and then deliberately transforms that stance in an attempt to gain control through the reframing and manipulation of archival photographic materials. Novak presents a female subject who breaks with a past plenitude to embrace fragmentation, discontinuity, and absence. But what kind of agent is this fragmentary subject? How effectively can she intervene in the ideological script of family and society?

6.9

Throughout her career, Novak has worked with slide projections that embed archival images, both private and public, into new composite visual texts. Using interior spaces, living rooms, bedrooms, and kitchens, as the screens onto which she projects old and new images, Novak reenvisions and reappropriates the spaces of domesticity. The process of projection is both literal and metaphorical, both material and psychological for Novak; the layers in her work are the layers of memory, the competing claims of different family members, the interrelations between family members with public figures. Memory is both individual and collective as, in some of the work, private snapshots are superimposed onto images of public historical events. But, Novak cautions, "I feel that by projecting slides into any situation, I am raising questions as to what is real. In photographing a projected installation, I am, in a sense, documenting something that *is* but *isn't* there. I turn off the power and the subject no longer exists, but I have a photograph that shows that it once did."[11]

"Fragments" is indeed a collection of embedded images, the record of a series of superimposed projections: the large black-and-white family picture from the 1950s projected onto a corner wall where it fits uneasily into the space, a picture which itself has a portrait at its center, and a color photograph projected over white pieces of board onto the floor which occupies the bottom half of the work and cuts off the lower portion of the black-and-white photo. There are at least four female images in the work: two images of the photographer as a child, dressed in the identical round-collar dress, one in the embedded painting, the other in the black-and-white photograph; two adult women, the pregnant mother in the black-and-white photo and, in color, the photographer herself presumably, but barely identifiable, lying upside down on the floor on an orange float in a blue bathing suit. There are also at least two male images: in the 1950s photo, the father holding the little girl who is sitting on the mantelpiece next to her childhood portrait, and a headless upside-down male torso lying in fragments on the floor next to the woman in the bathing suit.

In her construction of "Fragments" Novak has created a composite image which illustrates the kinds of interventions we have seen in the written texts of Kincaid, Duras, and Walkerdine. She has challenged the plenitude that might come from gazing at an image of one's past or present self, multiplying the self-image to reveal the multiple subjectivities and relationships, the incongruities constructing a life story. She has broken through generational continuities signaled in the resemblance between the daughter and the pregnant mother in the 1950s photograph. She projected that picture onto a corner to make it look three-dimensional while deliberately cutting up its frame and cutting off its bottom half. The alternate history she proposes lies in fragments on the bottom and aggressively protrudes beyond the cut-up frame. Here lies the woman of a new generation, refusing continuity and reflection, finding herself in fragments. As our eyes try to reassemble the fragments we notice hints of irreverence: her closed eyes which refuse to gaze back at the viewer or to smile like the compliant women in the black-and-white photos, her hand reaching into her male companion's crotch. But the woman of the new generation is not just the collection of pieces of glossy paper on the floor, she is also the photographer who has so subversively disassembled herself in them.

Conventional family pictures provide Novak with the space of contestation. As photographer and subject, she can find herself both in the collection of contradictory, incongruous, and discontinuous images, spread across a table and tacked unto a wall, and in the act of reframing and rearranging them to trace a personal (and perhaps also a collective) history against their grain. But as she so deliberately attempts to reach beyond the constraining frame of the family snapshot, Novak also affirms its power in determining her personal identity and life story.

## rereading images

In constructing this unusual "family album" in a single image, Novak reveals something about the structure of the conventional family album—its stress on chronology, continuity, and repetition within and across generations, its predictable framings and messages. In literally cutting up the frame, she shows to what lengths one has to go to get out of the family frame. Certainly Novak's fragmentary aesthetic and the subject-in-pieces she depicts seem more irreverent and subversive than my own equally deliberate construction of familial and personal continuity. It turns out, as the next chapter will show, that I fostered continuity even during my adolescence and continue to find it there particularly because, for me, adolescence coincided with the intense upheaval of cultural displacement. In that experience, photographs were useful not because they could be fragmented or destroyed but because they allowed me to reassemble and reconnect—to find myself constant across tremendous geographical and cultural distances.

Kincaid, Duras, Novak, and Walkerdine privilege fragmentation, negativity, and rupture. It is the consciousness of a break, exposed in the radical and irreverent manipulation of images, that enables intervention, contestation, and change—whether personal or collective. For them, the break occurs in girlhood and adolescence, even if it is not "read" until adulthood.

In contrast, my own construction of familial continuity across continents and generations, and across an entire life story, is complicit with familial ideologies that position the daughter as future mother, that present the family unit as harmonious and free of conflict, that disguise the passions and rivalries, the anxieties and tensions of family relations, and that accept rather than resist the plenitude offered by photographic images. Yet in highlighting the break they support another set of cultural constructions of adolescence as the moment of revolt. In reunifying a fractured personal history, even as deliberately and consciously as I did, I may forgo the possibility of a radical break, but I resist a discontinuity that has also become coercive.

As I contrast my family album with the images in these four texts, however, I begin to perceive the discontinuities within my own story as illuminating and enabling. Reading these texts against one another and against the images embedded within them is in itself a form of agency, one which has occasioned for me a process of rereading my own adolescence as a space of many possible stories, with many possible interpretations. Making the album and reading it, placing it into this comparative perspective, reveals, moreover, the difficult and elaborate personal work involved in the analysis of family pictures—the autobiographical reading practice it seems inevitably to engage.

I have suggested here that writing, making pictures, and reading them can be seen as forms of feminist resistance. When we intervene in the ideological scripts determining our own lives, I would like to maintain, we are also intervening politically. What kind of feminist agent is the maker and reader of images? She can, it seems to me, combine two necessary elements enabling her to transform hegemonic constructions. She can perceive familial ideologies and see herself both reflected by them and opposed or adjacent to them. She can understand her determinations and interpellations and attempt to confront and resist them. At best, therefore, she can be an empowered actor who can speak and act on behalf of women, for by going from the center of the image into the space-off, by refracting the familial gaze through different screens, by attempting to reveal the family's unconscious optics, she can make a space for "see[ing] differently."[12] Thus she can reclaim repressed and censored emotions that can perhaps free her to act. But, by reading and remaking familial images, she can also reveal, through splits and contradictions, through incomplete suturings, the complicated and painful process of identity.

She uses available technologies in the practices of her everyday life, reclaiming them from the oppressive spaces to which they have been relegated by cultural critics. She uses these technologies to reread and redefine coercive ideologies. But she goes beyond this deconstructive process to define a new aesthetic—one which assembles and reconstructs personal and domestic images that are individual yet collective, fragmentary yet continuous, revealing both breaks and interconnections. And she can use her anger and her rage, as well as her love, as motivating forces in her creation, defining an aesthetics of love and anger and pointing to its distinctive beauty.

# 7

# Pictures of a Displaced Girlhood

Displacement is an exile from older certitudes of meaning and selfhood, a possibly permanent sojourn in the wilderness.

MARK KRUPNICK

Borderlands are physically present wherever two or more cultures edge each other . . . Living on borders and in margins, keeping intact one's shifting multiple identity and integrity, is like trying to swim in a new element, an "alien" element . . . not comfortable but home.

GLORIA ANZALDÚA

This clumsy looking creature, with legs oddly turned in their high-heeled pumps, shoulders bent with the strain of resentment and ingratiation, is not myself. Alienation is beginning to be inscribed in my flesh and face.

EVA HOFFMAN

## *two displaced girls*

I am sitting on an airplane crossing the Atlantic. It is September 1991, a few days before my birthday, and I am returning to the United States from a study trip through Kenya and Tanzania. It is the second leg of a long journey and I am tired though happy to be going home after visiting so many unfamiliar places and feeling so much like an outsider, a tourist. I spend my time reading: it's what I most enjoy about airplane travel—reading in a state of suspension, a no-place between home and away which gives me the possibility of immersing myself entirely in the space of the book I have selected for the occasion. Only this time I am not prepared for what happens. I am reading Eva Hoffman's *Lost in Translation,* a book I have owned since it was first published in 1987, but which I have resisted even though friends urged me to read it right away.[1] Actually, I had intended to read it on a previous vacation but lost it along the way and had to purchase it again when I came home. Now this trip is almost over and I have finally settled into the book. I come to the end of the first part of Hoffman's narrative, the end of her sea journey from Poland to Canada at age 13. *I discern the outlines of massive gray shapes against the cloudy sky,* I read. *Closer still, the shapes resolve into buildings, tall and monolithic to my eyes. Montreal. It actually exists, more powerful than any figment of the imagination. We look at the approaching city wordlessly. The brief Batory interlude is over and so is the narrative of my childhood* (95). But now I can no longer see the page. Tears are flowing down my face, I realize I am sobbing. These sentences have released a loss whose depths I had never, until that moment, allowed myself to feel or remember.

It is July 1962. I am almost 13 and I am crossing the Atlantic, from Brussels to New York, on only the second airplane journey I have ever taken. But I am not sitting by the window. I do not want to see the expanse of ocean that will separate me from the familiar world I am leaving behind forever and, indeed, from my childhood. I do not want to see the shapes of the cities, rivers, and mountains that are to be my new home, the spaces of my adolescence and adulthood. Am I reading a book on this trip? I don't remember—all I remember is crying through what feels like the entire fourteen-hour flight, crying with abandon, in public, so that everyone can see that I do not want to go. I take some small pleasure in the tears and the attention they are attracting, especially from the handsome young Lufthansa steward who keeps bringing me snacks and drinks to console me. My parents have given up trying to make the move seem acceptable, they are just letting me cry as they deal with their own excitements and anxieties. But I know I am miserably unhappy and I am determined to remain so.

I continue to cry as we land in New York, and as we go through the endless bureaucracies of immigration at Idlewild Airport. I cry on the plane to Providence, Rhode Island, where from a window seat, I see an empty expanse that seems totally unpopulated to the European eye. I cry as we are picked up at the airport by Mrs. Hoffmann (no relative of Eva's I'm sure) from the Jewish Family Service, and I cry as I enter the South Providence flat—the upper floor of a brown wooden house on what looks like a desolate street—she has rented for our adjustment period. My mother waits for Mrs. Hoffmann to leave. And then she, too, starts to cry.

Eva Hoffman's story is my story, and the only lens through which I can read it is an utterly unreconstructed form of identification—a response quite disconcerting to someone who has been studying and teaching literature for twenty-five years, and one which makes me uneasy.[2] Yet I recognize so many of the scenes she evokes. I too *come from the war,* from that generation of the immediate postwar in Eastern Europe which grew up hearing stories of hiding, persecution, extermination, and miraculous survival every day and dreaming of them every night. *This—the pain of this—is where I come from, and . . . it's useless to try to get away* (25). I recognize myself in her portrait of *children too overshadowed by our parents' stories, and without enough sympathy for ourselves, for the serious dilemmas of our own lives* (230).

Her Cracow is so much like my Bucharest, her parents' urban middle-class respectability and relative material comfort and their simultaneous marginality, and discomfort as Jews, so much like those of my parents. Also similar are our parents' far-reaching ambitions for their children's happiness and success, ambitions which do not offset the attitudes of *modernist nihilism* and deep skepticism with which they raised us. So many details match, down to the remedy for a cold made from milk, egg yolk, and sugar (but my mother, unlike Eva's, never added chocolate, perhaps because cocoa was so rarely available). I, too, remember vividly the day of Stalin's death and the somber funerary marches through the city under enormous images of Lenin and Stalin and "the two grandfathers" (as I called Marx and Engels). I can still conjure the *cognitive disjunction* in which my friends and I grew up, hearing at home that we are to disregard most of what we are told at school. Around the same time, in the late 1950s, her parents and mine made the enormous decision to get out—to leave the place that was both *home* and *hostile territory*—and at roughly the same age Hoffman and I left behind the only world we knew.

It is with smiling recognition that I read Hoffman's first impressions of Vancouver; I nod through her bafflement at the shaggy bathroom rugs, at the toilet paper that comes in different colors, at her paralysis when it comes to choosing among brands of toothpaste. I recognize her inability to understand American humor, her incompetence at telling a joke. I empathize with the loss she experiences when her name is changed from Ewa to Eva—a slighter change than mine, who had to switch from Marianne to a Mary Ann whose "r" I could not pronounce, making it "Mady Ann." *These new appellations which we ourselves can't yet pronounce, are not us. They are identification tags, disembodied signs pointing to objects that happen to be my sister and myself. We walk to our seats, into a roomful of unknown faces, with names that make us strangers to ourselves* (105).


*The relentless rhythm of the wheels is like scissors cutting a three-thousand-mile rip through my life. From now on, my life will be divided into two parts with the line drawn by that train* (100). The flight across the Atlantic is for me what the train ride through Canada is for Hoffman. That is why it is so hard for me to write about the period of transition—my adolescence. My childhood remained in Rumania. It is in Vienna that I have my first period, my first crush, wear my first stockings, first try on lipstick. My first date, my first kiss, my first dances, and parties, are all in Providence. That's where I lose my pudginess, grow another two inches (or is it two centimeters?), have my teeth straightened, become a teenager. But which of those changes are due to chronology, which to geography? I have never been able to sort them out. During my year in Vienna I am unable to find a single comfortable item of clothing—everything itches and scratches, everything feels wrong against my skin, everything makes me miserable. Is it because I have just turned 12, gotten my period, and am going through puberty, or is it because everything I wear is too childish and totally "square" by Viennese standards and I go through each day feeling wrong, ashamed, out of place? In the space of a few weeks I try to make the transition from ankle socks to nylon stockings, from soap and water to face creams, makeup, and cologne, from sandals to heels, from childish freedom to flirting and an obsessive interest in boys—but at what cost? What gets silenced and censored in the process? And how do I manage, in the space of another few weeks of adjustment, to make a second transition to small-town American teenagerhood—another set of rules and standards, for me only another set of faux-pas and embarrassments? Like Hoffman, I feel *less agile and self-confident with every transformation. I hold my head rigidly, so that my precarious bouffant doesn't fall down, and I smile often, the way I see other girls do, though I'm careful not to open my lips too wide or bite them, so my lipstick won't get smudged . . . Inside its elaborate packaging, my body is stiff, sulky, wary. When I'm with my peers, who come by crinolines, lipstick, cars, and self-confidence naturally, my gestures show that I'm here provisionally, by their grace, that I don't rightfully belong* (109–110).

But does any girl "come by crinolines, lipstick, cars, and self-confidence naturally"? Were my discomfort and Hoffman's the result of our cultural displacement, or were they due to a chronological transition that teenage culture and the demands of adult femininity have made inherently and deeply unnatural for even the most comfortably indigenous American girl?

In their research into female adolescence, Carol Gilligan and her colleagues find that girls use images of violent rupture, death, and drowning in describing the transition between childhood and adolescence, a transition they locate between the ages of 12 and 13.[3] Gilligan's reading of Margaret Atwood's poem "This Is a Photograph of Me" allows her to characterize this transition topographically as a form of displacement. When she moves out of childhood and into adolescence, Atwood's persona simply disappears by drowning. As she describes the lake, the poet locates herself at the center, beneath its surface:

> It is difficult to say where
> precisely, or to say
> how large or small I am
> . . . but if you look long enough,
> eventually
> you will be able to see me.

Around the age of 13, Gilligan suggests, girls lose their place: without their voice and their certainty, they become "divided from their own knowledge, regularly prefacing their observations by saying 'I don't know'" (*Making Connections,* 14). Whatever knowledge they preserve from their earlier selves must go underground; if they want to conserve or to perpetuate it they must "join the resistance." Gilligan describes this underground world as a "remote island," implying that every transition into female adulthood is a process of acculturation to an alien realm—or, could one say, an experience of emigration? The lessons of femininity acquired during adolescence require a move into a different culture and language. Girls must unlearn what they know as they gain, sometimes through gestures of mimicry and impersonation, new skills and new selves.

But if for American girls the move into adolescence feels like emigrating to a foreign culture and learning the new language of femininity under patriarchy, what additional pressures confront girls like Hoffman and me who, in addition to learning the language of patriarchy, literally had to learn the English language and American culture? Reading Gilligan's work has been a discovery for me because, like Eva Hoffman, I had attributed my awkwardness and alienation to my status as a "newcomer" and was, therefore, unable to perceive the similar discomfort and alienation of my female peers. At my twenty-fifth high school reunion, classmates confessed their own insecurities, but remembered me as completely "together" even as early as tenth grade—only a year after I came. I can only marvel at my own powers of impersonation, but I realize now what I could not see then: that my contemporaries also had to exercise a form of mimicry in their performance of feminine behavior. Yet unlike theirs, my own and Hoffman's process of unlearning and learning, of resisting and assimilating, was a double one which must have been doubly difficult to negotiate. It must have left us doubly displaced, doubly dispossessed, doubly at risk, perhaps doubly resistant to assimilation.

If most girls leave their "home" as they move into adolescence, Hoffman and I left two homes—our girlhood and our Europe. If this double displacement made our girlhoods less rebellious, more compliant, than those described by Kincaid, Duras, or Walkerdine, pictures still served as important elements in our adjustments. Photographs can be the symbols of constraint and imprisonment in an unacceptable past, or the blocks for rebuilding a lost world. They typically mediate the losses of cultural displacement as well as the dislocations of adolescence: Hoffman and I rely on them for both.

Still, despite the common structure, despite the uncanny similarities, Hoffman and I ultimately developed different strategies of relocation to deal with the effects of our double displacement.

## pictures

On the cover of my copy of *Lost in Translation* there is a picture of a photo album, set at an angle, facing a pink flower. A small black-and-white photograph, mounted with old-fashioned black triangular photo mounts, shows two little girls in a bleak-looking forest or park. It is late autumn, the leaves are on the ground, and the two little girls in the photo are wearing winter coats and hats. Presumably the older girl (she seems to be 6 or 7) is Eva and the younger (who looks to be about 4) is her sister Alina. Eva is smiling self-confidently as she protectively puts her arm around her sister in her plaid coat, white tights, and high top boots. Alina looks more tentative, less comfortable. This is Eva (or Ewa) in the Polish surroundings she inhabits with such effortlessness, the home which in her book is cast as *paradise* and *the safe enclosures of Eden.*

Later Hoffman describes another photo, one she did not select for the cover of her book: *About a year after our arrival in Vancouver, someone takes a photograph of my family in their backyard, and looking at it, I reject the image it gives of myself categorically. This clumsy looking creature, with legs oddly turned in their high-heeled pumps, shoulders bent with the strain of resentment and ingratiation, is not myself* (110). In the American photograph as an adolescent, she is not herself: she is only herself in the old pictures taken in Poland.

A third photograph described toward the end of *Lost in Translation* mediates Hoffman's astonished reunion in New York with a childhood friend from Cracow. *In this picture three little girls are standing on a riverbank holding hands and showing off the daisy wreaths on their heads. I remember the day when this picture was taken quite distinctly—the excursion on the Vistula during which we disembarked on a picnic, and how the three of us looked for flowers to weave those wreaths, something little girls in Poland did during those days. But as Zofia and I look back and forth from the photograph to each other, we feel the Madeleine's sweet cheat: "Oh my God," Zofia keeps saying in mixed delight and befuddlement. We can't jump over such a large time canyon. The image won't quite come together with this moment* (222). The two women are unable to recapture their past. The photograph does not enable them to find their past connection: it measures the depth of their disconnection. It evokes a world and a friendship they lost and cannot recapture. I understand this failure but, nevertheless, I begin to wonder about Hoffman's obsession with the canyon, with a disjunction that defines her life and her book: I begin to notice the pervasive nostalgia that clings to everything Polish. Suddenly alienated by the way she has constructed her story, I resist identification, start shaking my head in disagreement, resent her for breaking the ease with which I had been making my way through her book. These feelings, within the autobiographical mode of reading in which I am engaging, are in themselves strongly personal. Autobiographical reading has become for me a desire for dialogue.

The three photographs trace Hoffman's journey from *paradise* into *exile* and to the *new world*. In paradise she is at home with herself, smiling self-confidently; in *exile,* she has become not herself, someone she is forced to reject, denegate. *The new world* is defined by the unbridgeable canyon at the center of her life. Eva and Zofia can find themselves in the past but not the present—for Eva locates herself more in that childhood image than in her adulthood, and the photograph is a false madeleine which cannot bring that past into the present. An adult American writer in New York with a Harvard Ph.D., Hoffman still describes herself as a newcomer, an immigrant, unable to read her husband's emotions, still uncomfortable in English. Her friends are always either *Polish or American;* to them she remains throughout her over thirty years on this side of the Atlantic a foreigner, a *silly little Polish person.* When she describes relationships with friends and lovers, it is to point out how different her view of the world is from theirs, it is to analyze their consensus and her own exclusion. Even when she feels that she is in her world *(I fit, and my surroundings fit me),* her consciousness splits off, and there is *an awareness that there is another place—another point at the base of the triangle, which renders this place relative, which locates me within that relativity itself* (170). I understand this doubleness and relativity but I cannot identify with Hoffman's nostalgic attempt to overcome it by returning to her Polish childhood. Her discomfort with her present double vision is clearly motivated by her unequivocal construction of Poland (or is it childhood?) as *paradise,* home of *the first things, the incomparable things, the only things. It's by adhering to the contours of a few childhood objects that the substance of our selves—the molten force we're made of—molds and shapes itself. We are not yet divided* (74). The photographs only reinforce her feelings of a lost unity and plenitude: gazing into the childhood photos she sees herself. Looking at them with Zofia, she recognizes the loss of that self. Looking at the adolescent photo, she does not recognize herself. Thinking about my own experience, I want her to see that in Poland, as a child, she was already divided, already, in some ways, not uniquely, not fully, herself.

As I continue to read I am increasingly bothered by the contradictions between the Edenic construction of Cracow, figured by her smile in the cover photo, and the prehistory of her parents' hiding in a *branch-covered forest bunker during the war:* could it be the same forest where the two little girls' picture is taken, I wonder? What repressions make possible the feeling that Cracow is *both home and the universe* when only a few years before her birth all of her parents' relatives and many friends had died there, including her aunt who *was among those who had to dig their own graves, and . . . her hair turned gray the day before her death* (7). What does it take for Hoffman to consider this place *paradise?* Why would she want to recapture a childhood that rests on such a legacy? What I can only see as Hoffman's denial is painful to read, yet it is basic to her construction of her narrative and her world, of her self: *this is real,* she says about an eyewitness's account of her aunt's death. *But is it? It doesn't have the same palpable reality as the Cracow tramway. May be it didn't happen after all, may be it's only a story, and a story can be told differently, it can be changed.* In her vivid and generous evocation of childhood plenitude, Hoffman has displaced the reality of the war, of the anti-Semitism she admits she still experiences, but which she dismisses by calling it *primitive.* Canada to her own Polish self was *an enormous cold blankness,* but to her parents, during their wartime forest confinement, it spoke *of majestic wilderness, of animals roaming without being pursued, of freedom.* Conceived out of this prison-house imagination, Canada is freedom, but, in spite of so many assurances to the contrary, Hoffman, in what may well be an understandable childish strategy of survival, has displaced her parents' suffering with her own happiness, and for her Canada is only *exile.*[4]

I identify neither with Hoffman's nostalgically Edenic representation of Poland nor with her later sense of utter dispossession, nor do I share her desperate desire to displace the relativity, the fracturing, the double-con-sciousness of immigrant experience. For me displacement and bilingualism preceded emigration; they are the conditions into which I was born. Even as a child, in the midst of those first affections so eloquently celebrated in *Lost in Translation,* I was indeed already divided. If displacement is indeed an "exile from older certitudes of meaning" as Mark Krupnick suggests, then I was already born in "the wilderness."[5]

As I recognize these differences between us, I see that I can read Hoffman only as a pre-text for my own narrative of cultural displacement, a narrative which, like hers, centers on language even as it relies on the mediating force of photographs. This is after all what autobiographical reading is: Hoff-mann's book can serve as my allo-portrait. The resemblances we share, the differences that divide us allow me to look at her pictures and stories affiliatively if not familially and thus to place my story alongside hers. In this shared mode, autobiography becomes autohistory—our personal story as the story of our generation.[6] Photographs mediate this story, but in the intragenerational narrative of female friendship I will tell—a story pre-figured by my identification with Eva Hoffman—they can divert the familial gaze in favor of an affiliative form of looking that takes us outside the strictly familial.

\*      \*      \*

The legendary place of origin I invest with nostalgia is not, like Hoffman's, a place I remember or have even ever seen. My parents' Czernowitz, my cultural home, is the space of my postmemory. Throughout my childhood, my parents and all their friends spoke of this city, where they continued to speak German through years of Rumanian and Russian rule, where they studied French and poetry, went to concerts, swam in the Prut River and climbed the Tsetsina mountain, strolled down the Herrengasse on Sundays, ate delicious Torten at each other's houses and cheese dumplings at Friedmann's restaurant. My maternal grandfather was a lawyer, and my mother grew up in a comfortable apartment with Persian carpets and a set of brown leather furniture in their "Herrenzimmer," a room whose uses I have trouble imagining. My father's family was struggling, his mother a widow with four children, but he told other, glamorous stories of socialist and Zionist youth movements, of hard work and its rewards, and of youthful camaraderie with friends who continued to be close throughout his life. Here too is where my mother could not study medicine because Jews were permitted to enroll only in a few subjects and where my parents could not leave the house without wearing the yellow star.

These scenes and objects are in many ways more real to me than the scenes of my own childhood, especially when it comes to the narrative of my parents' survival during the war: certain moments from my parents' history easily displace my own narrative. Later, when I learn that "our" Czernowitz is the home of Paul Celan, Aharon Apelfeld, Josef Schmidt, Rose Ausländer, and other well-known "German" artists, I merely nod—that is in fact the image I always had of it. I know many details of the two years of Russian occupation and the two years of the Antonescu collaborationist regime. For years I have located myself in the courage of their survival, of my parents' unique marriage in the ghetto the day before they thought they might be deported, the two times they evaded deportation, the night my father got out of bed to answer a knock by the Gestapo. Their subsequent escape, after the war, from what had become a Soviet republic to Rumania and the three years preceding my birth—the pain of leaving everything they knew behind, the hardships of their migration, my mother's two miscarriages—in my mind displace my own losses and dislocations.

The pictures that supplement my parents' detailed narratives are mostly tiny snapshots of groups of family and friends, a few school and movement photos, some studio images such as the one of my grandmother and aunt, a few vacation shots on beaches, mountain hikes, riverfronts. Not much to feed my eager imagination. There are no pictures of my parents' unusual wedding in the ghetto, none in which they are wearing the yellow star. One image of the smiling newlyweds, their arms interlaced, walking on the Herrengasse, taken by a street photographer, betrays nothing about the hardships of that time: "Here we are during the war," they tell me with amazement and some amount of defiance. Why is there no yellow star?

Throughout her thirteen Polish years, Hoffman lives in the same house, sleeps in the same bed, speaks one language. I am born in Timişoara, a city with a sizable German and Hungarian population, but move to Bucharest before I can remember. Timişoara remains a second home, this is where my grandparents stay, but the building where I spent the first two years of my life is only a façade to me. In Bucharest we switch apartments when I am 8. In Timişoara I grow to the age of 2 speaking only German—my grandmother knows only enough Rumanian to buy eggs and vegetables at the market. In Bucharest I learn Rumanian but speak it with an accent. I go to a German school and am more fluent than my classmates, many of whom are Rumanian and speak a strongly accented and grammatically incorrect German. But in third grade my best friend is Marianne Döhring from East Berlin and I quickly realize that my German, of which I had been quite proud, is literally a Balkanization of the real thing. I learn to imitate "Berlinerisch" and to be embarrassed about the way I speak my native language. This gets worse when I move to Vienna and my German is no longer recognized as native—at this point, although I express myself with ease and am proud of my writing, I also don't have a language any more. Thus I cannot share Eva Hoffman's shock at her linguistic dislocation: *But mostly, the problem is that the signifier has become severed from the signified. The words I learn now don't stand for things in the same unquestioned way as they did in my native tongue. "River" in Polish was a vital sound, energized with the essence of riverhood, of my rivers, of my being immersed in rivers. "River" in English is cold—a word without an aura . . . I am becoming a living avatar of structuralist wisdom; I cannot help knowing that words are just themselves. But it's a terrible knowledge, without any of the consolations that wisdom usually brings . . . It is the loss of a living connection* (106–107). For me, this is a connection I never knew, since I was never located in one single language as was Hoffman.

Like Hoffman, I am conscious of my Jewish identity throughout my childhood in Rumania. We don't ever go to synagogue—my father has been secular since his teens and I will always wonder how a rabbi could have refused to marry my parents in the ghetto on a Friday afternoon—so being Jewish is the history and the reality of anti-Semitism and persecution, it is the cultural legacy of Czernowitz, it is, just as for Hoffman, a sense of cultural superiority. It is also my difference from my Rumanian friends ("How do you cross yourself, with two fingers or three?" they ask to determine whether I am Catholic or Orthodox. My shameful reply that I don't cross myself reveals that I am nothing). And being Jewish is also the fear of repetition, the nightly dreams of the war. It is what makes us leave and what allows us to leave. When we get to Vienna my parents decide it might be easier not to be Jewish any longer, and they truthfully fill out "atheist" on our forms. But that is a lie I have to defend in front of Sabine, the only other Jewish girl in my class. She eventually guesses, of course, and I confess. But when I join the Hashomer Hatzair to which she belongs, I only feel more left out because I don't know any of the songs and stories about Israel, even though my father belonged to the same group thirty years earlier. Jewishness is an ambiguous and complicated location: one in which I both am and am not at home depending on how it is construed.

For us Vienna is just a way station to our future home. We consider Israel, Canada, Australia, the United States, and then spend eight months waiting for our American visa. I desperately want to stay in Vienna: in spite of the lie about our Jewishness, in spite of the fact that my German sounds wrong and that I am much more childish than my classmates, in spite of the two damp, dark rooms without kitchen privileges we rent, I begin to feel at home here.

My cousin Brigitte, who is five years older, introduces me to the mysteries of Western consumerism ("there's this drink called Coca Cola and it is so amazing that once you taste it you will never be able to stop drinking it"). I spend the summer at an international camp where I use the little bit of French I learned in Rumania to interpret between the Austrian and the French girls. By the end of the summer I can actually speak French. In the neighborhood Gymnasium I attend for the year, I have a best friend, Angelika, who also feels like an outsider—her mother is an actress, her parents don't live together, she has less money than the other children. Through Angelika I want to become Austrian, but when there is a chance to act in a television commercial with her, I am rejected because of my "foreign" accent.

Looking at pictures from that year I see the sadness and discomfort I displaced by fighting not to emigrate further. In most of the photos I anxiously hold on to Klementine, the brown-and-white guinea pig I acquire to consolidate my friendship with Angelika, who has a black guinea pig named Vladimir—we want them to play together and marry (Figures 7.1, 7.2). In

7.1

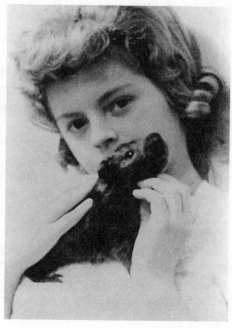

7.2

the pictures Klementine and I both look rather forlorn—she is the repository of my loneliness and desire for love and acceptance. But I smile in the picture Angelika takes—the guinea pigs bring us closer together. I have often come back to this girlhood fantasy of relocation through a friendship which, by way of the guinea pigs, becomes a fantasy of marriage, home, and lasting togetherness. ("Your son-in-law Vladimir" Angelika writes on the back of the photograph which shows her with the black guinea pig.) It works, because by the end of the year I look happier. My hair is wavy, I am wearing a petticoat, I pose in front of various Viennese monuments, I look a little more like the other girls in the photos: I have to prove that this has become home. I don't want to leave and, when I do, Angelika keeps Klementine—now, indeed, wedded to Vladimir, but not quite as we had imagined.

My history of displacements—linguistic, national, relational—makes displacement (and relocation) a strategy of survival. When I get to Providence, I don't know English—I have resisted learning it so as to have some control over my fate. Eventually I have to learn, but I continue to raid the public library for all the French and German books they have. A girl named Jennifer is the only one who expresses an interest in my story, but even she finds me hard to take on. I know so little, I am younger, I do everything wrong.

In the pictures from our first summer, I wear a sailor dress that is much too small for me and I look grotesque: a chubby child infantilized by my linguistic paralysis, I look much younger than in the Vienna photos taken a month earlier. *This clumsy looking creature . . . is not myself.* I try to repeat the comfort Klementine gave me, but my hamster dies two months later. Other hamsters follow but it never works; they are single hamsters, not the instruments of relationship like Klementine. The cages they live in show my distance from them and stand as emblems of my own confinement in this lonely new, American, teenage identity I reject.

I stop crying when Mona arrives with her family from Egypt. She's a year older but she's in my class, we can speak French, together we can try to read the cultural signs. The French we speak is our own private language: we both roll our r's and there are many words I don't know, so we mix it with the English we are both acquiring. To her I am not "Mady Ann," but "Marianne" pronounced in French. I become comfortable with the Arabic sounds I hear at her house and I learn some Arabic words. Her family is also Jewish but it means something entirely different to them. I prefer the Middle Eastern dishes they serve to the tuna fish sandwiches on sponge-like white bread I get at American homes. I become involved in her brothers' and parents' adjustment problems. We try to teach her mother enough English to do the shopping, and we explain to her that American girls are allowed to go out. I'm better in school, but Mona is much better at learning the styles, the songs, the gestures that will make us American—something we both want and do not want to be. She's better at flirting and more attractive to boys, but I join in the talk, I have crushes on the best friends of the boys she has crushes on, we go to dances at the Jewish community center where I have to lie about my age to join, and we have our first boyfriends.

Mona is the mediating figure who allows me both to acculturate and not to. Together we create a space at the border, a space that is neither Rumanian nor Egyptian nor American, with an idiolect that is neither German nor Arabic nor English, but some mixture of all of these, translated into the French that is "our" language. When I go to France for a summer and learn a more authentic accent, I cannot use it when speaking with Mona. My pride in my good accent is mixed with regret at losing the French of the borderland home I shared with her. And later in life when I meet Mona and we both have children nearly of the age we were then, we speak English and I know we cannot be close in this "foreign" tongue in which, after all, we have come to lead our lives.

At the end of ninth grade I know enough English to write a composition about what it is like to lose one's country—to be located nowhere, and have no cultural identity. I express the pain and nostalgia of homelessness so eloquently and describe so feelingly patriotic feelings that have no *patria* to which to attach themselves that I am asked to read it at a school assembly. Some people weep, and I get much praise, but I am a bit embarrassed by the nostalgia I have been able to evoke and which I cultivate so as to remain on the border. I also want Mona to participate in the glory and urge her to write her own version of this story; our origins could not be more different, but the feelings of displacement are so much the same. They are me, communicated to the whole school in English, but they are also an acting job, an impersonation of what I think it all should sound and feel like.

But in our graduation picture from Nathan Bishop Junior High School, Mona and I sit in the front row, our hair is teased just the right amount, we smile just like the other girls, and we fold our hands on our laps with just the right modesty: we pass (Figure 7.3). Only some of the inscriptions on the back give me away. Most are generic: "To Marianne, a great kid whom I'll never forget, Love ya, Nancy Weisman." "To Marianne, A real sweet kid, AFA, Mary Beth." But some note the difference: "To 'Maddy Ann,' a wonderful kid with the cute accente, Karen Powell." "À Marianne

7.3

(Mady Ann), The Silent One, It's been great knowing you and since we live so close, I'll see you dans l'avenir, Good luck, ne jamais, Mike Dickens." And Mona, of course, grew up with a different style of dedication: "À ma soeur Marianne, Tombe du 1er étage, Tombe du 2ème étage, Tombe d'où tu veux, Mais ne tombe pas amoureuse, Mona Chamuel," she writes, and places an elegant squiggle under her signature. This formulaic verse actually says a great deal about our struggles with adjustment to American teenage girlhood: our sense of falling and the ways in which we caught ourselves and literally held on to each other in our friendship.

For a time, Mona is in every picture taken of me: she comes to all our family trips and outings, as I go to hers. I am blond, she is brunette; my hair is thin and straight, hers is thick and wavy; yet we have the same outfit, the same posture, the same hairstyle, in every photo (Figure 7.4). To locate our friendship, I make a photo album in a small red book entitled "MY GANG" in gold letters. It starts, in the front two pockets, with pictures of Angelika and Mona, and it assembles most of my best friends from all the different periods and places of my life: childhood birthday party pictures in Bucharest, class photos from my first three grades, photos with the children of family friends with whom we went on vacation, photos with neighbor

**7.4**

children, of pen pals I never met, with vacation friends, with my close friends in Rumania saying goodbye before I leave, with Mona and another new friend in America. Most of the pictures are group photos or images of me posing with each of these friends, some are of me with several friends who met through me. The album brings them all together, allowing me to surround myself with a multitude of friends, displacing their dispersal and my loss.

The initial picture of Mona is a baby picture in which she wears an adorable tulle dress and bracelets: on the back, she writes in the hybrid idiom we have adopted: "A ma très chère amie et soeur, Marianne, There are golden ships, There are silver ships, but, the best ships are, FRIENDSHIPS, Love always, Mona '63.' Je te donne cette photo pour me voir quand j'étais petite et mignonne." I give you this picture so you can see me when I was little and cute. Did I ask her for the photo so I could make our lives more parallel, extending our friendship backward into the early childhood we spent on different continents? Like the album I made for my parents, this one stresses continuities and repetitions, erasing breaks and dislocations. The album of "my gang" is an expanded family album, or the album of an expanded family: school, camp, graduations, get-togethers with friends are the subjects of the affiliative looks of the elective family of friends, mutually constitutive, vital for survival during a displaced girlhood. Unlike Walkerdine, or Kincaid, or Novak, I treat them with reverence. I try to recognize an essential element of my relational self in each, for they are the mirrors of plenitude, found not in an isolated self but in friendship and relationship, and in their photographic records, which make the ruptures of the borderland bearable. Affiliative looks displace and familiarize the alienating gazes of unfamiliar cultural institutions. But the familial screen is displaced by the centrality of friendship.

After Mona goes to a different high school and we begin to spend less time together, I do not attach myself to an American friend but choose Marta, who came from Brazil to live in Providence for several years. This time I can initiate her into the ways of American teenagerhood. Her experience is different from mine, for she has already spent one year in the United States and is determined to go back home as soon as she can. Still, we share both a basic alienation and a pervasive cultural relativism through which we observe the practices of our peers. Now I hear a lot of Portuguese, learn how things are done in Brazil, and my borderland existence continues. I don't have the right "r" but I know how to pronounce the "t" in her name, avoiding the more common "Marda" or even "Martha" she has become. We even speak some French together, and for years people comment on the Eastern European accent Marta acquires in English. In all our pictures we wear the same outfits and hairstyles, our postures and gestures are identical, and through high school and later college we are inseparable (Figure 7.5).

We need each other to mediate our acculturation, and I identify with Marta's desire to go back home although I don't have a place to which to return. I am homeless and, in a different way, so is she, since she has recently lost her mother. We understand each other's pain. We tentatively join the group of outcasts in our high school. They all smoke and wear black and

**7.5**

act out their rebellion, but for us it is more reasonable to watch and only join in the conversations about Dostoevsky as we safely continue our mostly good-girl existence. We cannot afford to alienate our parents quite as much as they can; we have to be more cautious, more measured in our rebellions. Our families, after all, are on the border with us: my mother is especially unhappy about everything "American" and needs, demands, protection and support, not adolescent rage and rejection. I get annoyed by her unhappiness but in retrospect I realize that my own strategies of displacement act out her ambivalence about assimilating, that my feeling perfectly acculturated would be a betrayal of my connection to her. Again relationship becomes the place of relocation, the substitute for assimilation. Thus cultural displacement requires different negotiations in the process of separation and individuation than those theorized by psychoanalytic models. Marta and I negotiate together the contradictions between 1960s adolescent rebellion and the strong familial bonds, the need for continuity, forged by the experience of emigration.

As it turns out, Marta stays in the States and we both go to Brown, take the same courses, and major in Comparative Literature, the academic counterpart of the borderland. We share emotional and intellectual passions. Our English gets good enough to love T. S. Eliot and Yeats and our French to read Baudelaire. We study for exams together, read each other's papers, share each other's anxieties, and reassure each other. We live with our parents and study together in the snack bar and the reserve room of the library. We provide for each other the peer experience others find in the dorms, or in clubs and sororities. She continues to date her high school boyfriend and I quickly find a steady boyfriend in college. We always go out together—both boys are American—and we marry within a week of each other. Eventually we are both divorced.

The late 1960s offer many opportunities for group identity, but even as I protest the Vietnam war and become involved in curricular restructuring at Brown, I do so always from the margins. The women's movement changes all that. I join a consciousness-raising group in 1970 and experience a feeling of group allegiance for the very first time in my life. The recognition of commonality, the feelings of connection and mutual understanding are exhilarating, and I become addicted to them. Not only do I see my own experiences validated and mirrored in those of my peers but we find a mission in common, we create a politics based on those experiences. Feminism offers the life-sustaining re-locating friendships I had with Mona and with Marta, but now practiced on what feels like a global scale. Things really come together when I am able to incorporate female/feminist bonding into my work as well as my life. I have described my personal and professional "coming to feminism" as a "story of affiliations and collaborations":

> It was through several collaborative writing projects and through repeated dialogic encounters with other feminist critics that I was able to develop a feminist reading practice and a feminist critical voice of my own. To see

7.6

my ideas mirrored in those of others, to develop together a politics and a practice of mutual support, was not only to acquire professional confidence, but also to experience thinking as powerful and radical. I see now (and I appreciate the irony) that I learned in those years to fear conflict and disagreement. Was it my personal history that made consensus so precious? Or was it that our commonalities were made precarious by institutional pressures?[7]

In 1979 seven women from my department at Dartmouth College decide to edit a special issue of a journal together, featuring the latest work in feminist literary scholarship. During the last stages of our editing work, as we are revising our introduction for the umpteenth time, we ask a photographer to come and record this unusual collaboration (Figure 7.6). Even with a wide-angle lens, she finds it virtually impossible to fit the seven of us into one frame as we are sitting, in an oval, in one of our living rooms during a midsummer afternoon: in each print, those of us at the edges are distorted, with wide arms and twisted faces. We look very earnest in this posed photograph, poring over the typed pages of our manuscript. We don't smile or engage the photographer, nor do we look at one another. Although some of the tensions in the group may already be visible in this picture, I have kept it in my office, always. Much has evolved for the individuals depicted in the photograph and for the group as a whole: departures, tenure denials, personal rivalries, continuing friendships. But for me, seeing myself embedded, visually, in this oval-shaped group, working together on a project of great urgency, has remained, in spite of the difficulties, an idealized moment in my professional career, as tenuous and fleeting as the click of the shutter would indicate.

Feminism is an enlarged borderland space for me, one which has changed, reshaped and transformed itself over the years. At first cultural differences seem to fade into the background, suddenly unimportant in the face of female bonding which had replaced culture, had become a location. Later I begin to look at differences again. From a polar geography dividing the feminine from the masculine world, and studying the specificity of each, I have moved to a multiple topography that sees differences within masculine and feminine locations. Again, my history of multiple displacements has prepared me to conceive of identity as fractured and self-contradictory, as inflected by nationality, ethnicity, class, race, and history. But it has also made me appreciate those moments of commonality which allow for the adoption of a voice on behalf of women and for the commitment to social change. I am now beginning to understand how my feminist work is inflected by my girlhood adjustments. During adolescence, friendship provided a form of displacement and resistance: to cultural assimilation as well as to femininity. It was a place on the border between cultures, between girlhood and womanhood. Like those early friendships, feminism itself became a space of relation and relocation, a place from which I could think and speak and write, a home on the border. Its affiliative mode of looking could at least attempt to refocus the alienating gazes of professional competition; it could offer an alternative, based in the friendships of female adolescence, to the constraining gazes of familiality and their images of a traditional adult femininity.

*Everything comes together, everything I love, as in the fantasies of my childhood; I am the sum of my parts* (226). Yes, there are such moments but I am suspicious of them as, ultimately, is Hoffman. The difference is that she once believed in a center while I never did. *I have been dislocated from my own center of the world, and that world has been shifted away from my center. There is no longer a straight axis anchoring my imagination; it begins to oscillate, and I rotate around it unsteadily* (132).[8] Displacement, or "Verschiebung," is the transfer, Freud says in *The Interpretation of Dreams,* of psychic energy from one idea to another, one which originally had little intensity but which, in the process, gains centrality and importance. As a strategy of defense and survival, it offers a way to appease the censor. As an aesthetic it favors metonymy over metaphor. It corresponds to the structure of the photo album. The albums that I tend to construct, based on repetition and continuity, where recognition is never simple, locations and relationships are never singular, sequences are never linear, follow the associative structures of displacement.

As I finish reading Hoffman through the lens of my own experiences, I see the differences between us in terms of displacement. Both of us were culturally displaced. Yet displacement for Hoffman was the removal from one mythic place of origin and plenitude to another space of exile. Except for her passionate involvement with music, which she abandons in the third part of the book, there was no visible reinvestment of energy, no relief in the Freudian sense of displacement as "Verschiebung." This direct, unmediated confrontation of cultures accounts for what Hoffman calls her "immigrant rage" and the "trained serenity" with which she has learned to disguise it.

I chose a different strategy, that of the border, which may be seen as a kind of "Verschiebung." In fundamental ways I remain in this shifting space. Often longing for a more singular and more straightforward sense of identity and identification, whether past or present, I nevertheless embrace multiple displacement as a strategy of both assimilation and resistance. The issue of my name, for example, is never resolved—it's Marianne [Märiäne] in German and Marianne [Märiän] in French, Mariana [Märiänä] in Rumanian, but in English I accept many versions, from Mary Anne to Maryanna [Maryanä] to Mary Anna [Märyänä] to Marian [Marien]. I sometimes find it hard to remember which I am to which friends, and I do wonder what this multiplicity means, but it simply doesn't bother me as much as it does some of my friends who have to get used to using different signifiers when referring to the same person. Is it significant that I will not tolerate a misspelling of my name, that my identification with it seems to be visual—easier to transpose between languages than the aural?

Instead of engaging directly the America I was placed in, I came to it through a chain of displacements and attempts at relocation—through Vienna, through my involvement with French, through my friendships with

Mona and with Marta. As I look through old pictures, I find myself multiply connected and thus forever relocated in familial relationships and, beyond the familial, in friendships and in professional affiliations. I find myself embraced by an affiliative gaze that displaces, however tenuously, conventional institutional gazes—including the familial. Thus, I do not shuttle between the surface control and the internal rage that define the sides of Hoffman's Archimedean triangle. Instead, I invest my psychic energies in a series of (dis) and (re) locations that allow me to live in this "permanent sojourn in the wilderness," this "alien element," which is, and always has been, "not comfortable but home."

# 8

# Past Lives

I neither emigrated nor was deported. The world that was
destroyed was not mine. I never knew it.

**HENRI RACZYMOW**

*exile*

In the summer of 1991, in the aftermath of the Gulf War, I was very moved
by the Israeli writer Yoram Kaniuk's article in the German newspaper *Die
Zeit*.[1] The article, entitled "Three and a half hours and fifty years with
Günter Grass in Berlin," reported on an open discussion in Berlin a few
months earlier between the two writers, and addressed German intellectuals'
opposition to the war in view of Germany's massive sales of arms and poisoned gas to Iraq during the preceding years. Kaniuk, up until that moment
an active member of the "Peace Now" movement, tried to explain how
different things looked to him in Tel Aviv than they did to German intellectuals in Munich, Frankfurt, or Berlin. Kaniuk invited Grass, an outspoken
opponent of the war, to contemplate the enormous distance separating these
two men, otherwise friendly and of very similar yet fatally different backgrounds. For as they were sitting on stage in March 1991, talking about
Israel and Germany, Kaniuk said he could feel the spiritual presence of their
two fathers and their four grandfathers.

In the article Kaniuk claimed his right to speak out and to address Grass
so aggressively as a birthright. Conceived in Germany, like Grass, yet born
in his parents' exile in Palestine in 1939, Kaniuk grew up in Tel Aviv. But,
he explained, walking down Ben Yehuda Street as a child, he experienced
as more real and more present the streets of his parents' prewar German
world named in the German children's book *Emil and the Detectives*. His
parents' German reality, transmitted through daily stories and references,
yet as a Jewish culture irrevocably destroyed, nevertheless had the power to
displace and derealize his own immediate childhood world in the Middle

East. "I hereby decide that we lived here in a small Berlin that we called Tel
Aviv, and from which we would have wanted to return again or blend in"
(18).[2] This "memory" of a Germany in which he had never lived, on whose
streets he had never walked, whose air he had never breathed, and whose
language he eventually abandoned, remained, until the day of his dispute
with Grass fifty years later, the place of identity, however ambivalent.
Through words and images, this lost world acquired a materiality in his
memory that determined his adult discourse and self-definition as an Israeli
writer.

My reading of Kaniuk's article was so overwhelmingly autobiographical
that it filters many of my recollections of the Gulf War. Unlike Kaniuk, I
was not conceived in my parents' native Czernowitz but was born in
Rumania four years after their exile. Still, the streets, buildings, and natural
surroundings—the theater, restaurants, parks, rivers, and domestic settings
of Czernowitz—none of which I have ever seen, heard or smelled myself,
occupy a monumental place in my own childhood memories. All the while,
as I was growing up hearing my parents' stories, I knew that I would never
see that place and that my parents would never return there. I knew it not
only because Czernowitz now belonged to the Soviet Union and travel there
from Rumania was difficult: I knew it from my parents' voices and de-
meanor, from the sense they projected that this world, their world, no longer
existed, had been destroyed. That left a rift in their lives, and in mine, similar
to the rift between Günter Grass and Yoram Kaniuk, one writer living at
home, one forever homeless. I realize that, literally, Grass also does not live
at home: as a result of the same war, his German home city, Danzig, became
the Polish Gdansk, and Grass was also displaced from his place of origin.
Still, I believe that the violent destruction of the Jewish communities and
the Jewish cultures of Eastern, Central, and Western Europe—the destruction not only of the people but of the records and memories of their
existence—is of a different order than the displacements other Europeans
had to suffer because of the two wars, painful though they must have been
for many. In our own familial discourse, Czernowitz embodied the idea of
home, of place, but to me it was, and would remain, out of reach. Kaniuk
and I share with many European Jews of our generation this sense of exile
from a world we have never seen and which, because it was irreparably
changed or destroyed not by natural or historical evolution over time but
by the sudden violent annihilation of the Holocaust, we will never see.

None of us ever knows the world of our parents. We can say that the
motor of the fictional imagination is fueled in great part by the desire to

know the world as it looked and felt before our birth. How much more ambivalent is this curiosity for children of Holocaust survivors, exiled from a world that has ceased to exist, that has been violently erased. Theirs is a different desire, at once more powerful and more conflicted: the need not just to feel and to know, but also to re-member, to re-build, to re-incarnate, to replace, and to repair.

For survivors who have been separated and exiled from a ravaged world, memory is necessarily an act not only of recall but also of mourning, mourning often tempered by anger, rage, and despair. As Nadine Fresco writes: "The destruction was such that not an image was left from the Jewish life before the war that was not in some way encumbered, tainted, marked by death."[3] But Holocaust postmemory, the memory of the children of survivors, similarly determinative, may be less ambivalent and conflicted. The children of exiled survivors, although they have not themselves lived through the trauma of banishment and forcible separation from home and the destruction of that home, remain marked by their parents' experiences: always marginal or exiled, always in the diaspora. "Home" is always elsewhere, even for those who return to the Vienna, the Berlin, the Paris, or the Cracow their families had to leave, because the cities to which they can return are no longer the cities in which their parents lived as Jews before the genocide, but the cities where the genocide happened and from which they and their memory have been expelled. As Fresco suggests, "Born after the war, sometimes in place of a child killed in the war, the Jews I am describing here experience their lives as a sort of exile, not from a present or future place, but from a completed time which would have been that of identity itself" (211). This condition of exile from the space of identity, this diasporic experience, is a characteristic aspect of postmemory. It brings with it its own narrative genres and aesthetic shapes and thus it permits us to return, from a somewhat different angle, to the photographic aesthetics of postmemory—the photograph's capacity to signal absence and loss and, at the same time, to make present, rebuild, reconnect, bring back to life.

Postmemory—even that of a circumscribed population like the children of exiled Holocaust survivors—can take many forms. Based on a series of interviews with others of her generation whose parents never spoke of their abandoned world or of their wartime experiences and who thus had almost no access to the repressed stories that shaped them, Nadine Fresco speaks of "absent memory." In her terms, the postwar generation's diasporic life is a *diaspora des cendres*—the place of origin has gone up in ashes. There is no return.[4] Her contemporary, the French writer Henri Raczymow, insists that this absence, this void, is a condition that must be preserved and should never be bridged. The memory he describes is a *mémoire trouée,* a "memory shot through with holes": "In my work, such a void is created by the empty memory I spoke of, which propels my writing forward. My books do not attempt to fill in empty memory. They are not simply part of the struggle against forgetfulness. Rather, I try to present memory *as* empty. I try to restore a non-memory, which by definition cannot be filled in or recovered."[5]

In his evocation of the absent memory that serves for him as the motor for writing, Raczymow adopts Kafka's spatial conception of time, articulated in the 1920s: "If the earth is turning to the right . . . I must turn left in order to catch up with the past." European Jews of the postwar generation are forever turning left, but we can never catch up with the past; inasmuch as we remember, we remain in a perpetual temporal and spatial exile. Our past is literally a foreign country we can never hope to visit. And our postmemory is shaped by our sense of belatedness and disconnection: "I neither emigrated nor was deported," says Raczymow. "The world that was destroyed was not mine. I never knew it. But I am, so many of us are, the orphans of that world" (103). Fresco's and Raczymow's reflections echo Alain Finkielkraut's definitions, in *The Imaginary Jew,* of postwar Jewish identity as a form of absence: "What makes me a Jew is the acute consciousness of a lack, of a continuous absence: my exile from a civilization which, 'for my own good,' my parents did not wish me to keep in trust."[6]

This "absent memory" does not correspond to my own experience as a Jewish child of exile, nor do I experience my Jewish identity as empty. On the contrary, many Jews have acquired or built an identity as Jews precisely through the shared traumatic memory and postmemory of the Shoah. For me, having grown up with daily accounts of a lost world, the links between past and present, between the prewar world of origin and the postwar space of destination are more than visible. The Czernowitz of my postmemory is an imaginary city, but that makes it no less present, no less vivid, and perhaps because of the constructed and deeply invested nature of memory itself, no less accurate. The deep sense of displacement suffered by the children of exile, the elegiac aura of the memory of a place to which one cannot return, do not create, in my experience, a feeling of absence: I've sometimes felt that there were too many stories, too much affect, even as at other times I've been unable to fill in the gaps and absences. "We cannot even say that we were *almost* deported," says Raczymow (104). Does he wish he had been? What relationship can one have to the traumatic events of one's parents' lives—horror? ambivalence? envy? a negative nostalgia?[7]

8.1

In perpetual exile, this/my generation's practice of mourning is as determinative as it is interminable and ultimately impossible.

The aesthetics of postmemory, I would like to suggest, is a diasporic aesthetics of temporal and spatial exile that needs simultaneously to (re)build and to mourn. In the terms of Nadine Fresco: "[It is] as though those who were born after could do nothing but wander, prey to a longing forever disenfranchised" (211). In attempting to relocate themselves they forge an aesthetics of postmemory with photographs as the icons of their ambivalent longing.

I choose as my chapter title and emblem "Past Lives," a 1987 photograph by the Jewish American artist Lorie Novak (Figure 8.1). "Past Lives" is a photograph of a composite projection onto an interior wall. Novak populates this domestic space with a picture of the Jewish children hidden in Izieu and eventually deported by Klaus Barbie, superimposed on a picture of Ethel Rosenberg's face, superimposed on a childhood image, from the 1950s, of Novak herself held by her mother. Consisting of many ghosts, "Past Lives" visually connects personal with public memory, allowing the U.S. domestic interior to be invaded by the painful aspects of its history. As her childhood image is merged with these pictures of murdered children, as the picture of her own mother merges with the image of the mother who was executed, Novak begins to define the aesthetic strategies of mourning and reconstruction of her generation of postmemory. In her image, as in the other projections, memorials, and installations that I discuss in this chapter, space and time are conflated to reveal memory's material presence.

## memorial books

During the first waves of refugee emigrations from Eastern Europe to the West, following the pogroms in the early part of this century, a Jewish memorial tradition developed among diasporic communities, a tradition based on ancient and medieval Jewish practices of commemoration which may well serve as a resource and a model for children of survivors. The *yizker bikher,* or memorial books, prepared in exile by survivors of the pogroms were meant to preserve the memory of their destroyed cultures. The survivors of Nazi genocide built on this memorial tradition and prepared for subsequent generations similar memorial books devoted to the memory of individual destroyed communities. (Over four hundred memorial books have been written by survivors of Polish communities alone). They contain historical accounts of community life before the destruction as well as detailed records of the genocide that annihilated those communities. They contain photographs as well as texts, individual and group portraits evoking life as it was *before.* They contain accounts of survivors' efforts to locate the remains of their family members in order to give them a proper burial, and they detail the acts of commemoration devoted to the dead.

The memorial books are acts of witness and sites of memory. Because they evoke and try to re-create the life that was and not only its destruction, they are acts of public mourning, forms of a collective Kaddish. But they are also sites where subsequent generations can find a lost origin, where they can learn about the time and place they will never see. In the words of Jonathan Boyarin and Jack Kugelmass, who collected translated selections from the Polish memorial books, "The memorial books are the fruit of the impulse to write a testament for future generations. They constitute an unprecedented, truly popular labor to record in writing as much as possible of a destroyed world."[8] *Yizker* books, with their stories and images, are documents to be invested with life: they are spaces of connection between memory and postmemory. Many communal organizations think of them as their memorials or monuments or, as Raczymow says, they "take the place of graves for those who had no graves" ("Memory Shot Through," 101). As such they can serve as inspirations for other acts of memorialization by children of exiled survivors. They provide the paradigms for a diasporic aesthetics of postmemory.

Henri Raczymow's *Tales of Exile and Forgetting* is a kind of memorial book, but its radically different form can illustrate the difference between memory and postmemory.[9] While the *yizker* books contain testimonies and reminiscences, Raczymow's tales are reconstructions that do not disguise their exploratory and probing relation to an unknown past. "I know nothing about Konsk," insists the protagonist and historian Matthieu Schriftlich (19). "Who can speak to me about Konsk, shadow of shadows and without a grave?" (37). Why does he want to know? He is intrigued by a few names and a few stories he heard, particularly by Matl Oksenberg, a grandmother who frequently appears in the tales of his sometimes reluctant informant Simon Gorbatch: "I am the old man and you are the one who questions the past" (51). But can Matthieu ever know Matl Oksenberg and her world? He insists that he can't and that, in fact, a certain distance must be maintained. Even as he writes the stories of Konsk, Schriftlich must inscribe the impossibility of knowing or understanding them. He must preserve the shadows surrounding Konsk and his grandmother, even as he tries to lift the veil of mystery that attracts him to them in the first place. As his name indicates, he can be no more than a medium; as "schriftlich" he is not a writer, but "written" or "in writing." He is a qualifier, an adjective and not a noun.

His point of access is a network of names; the narrative emerges from the names, slowly becoming coextensive with them. As Simon tells the stories, Matthieu abandons himself to the absence of memory. The names are available and they are richly interrelated. As one name evokes another we find ourselves in an intricately woven social fabric of words that no longer refer to specific people but become separated from their content, generalized and interchangeable, empty vehicles of an absent memory. "The names of the dead, aren't they available to our fantasies, Simon?" (103).[10] Matthieu, with the help of the ever more tentative Simon, reinvests them with a narrative, but in the process he loses his individuality: he comes to embody his function of scribe and historian, "Schriftlich."

Just as the authors of the *yizker* books are agents of memory, so Matthieu Schriftlich is the agent of postmemory, someone who gives narrative shape to the surviving fragments of an irretrievable past. But the stories do not add up; the names continue to resist Matthieu's curiosity, Konsk never emerges from the fog that surrounds it. This resistance is as necessary to the practice of postmemory as is the elegiac tone of Raczymow's tales. But the mourning Matthieu practices is anything but sentimental: as Raczymow plays on the double meaning of the French word "larme" (both tear and drop), the tear *(larme)* with which the last tale ends is not a tear at all but a *drop* of vodka, "une *larme.*" Nostalgia and sentimentality are always undercut both by the knowledge of what occurred in Konsk and by the impossibility, finally, of understanding it. With his *Contes d'exil et d'oubli,* Raczymow has developed an aesthetic that emerges from the absences of his earlier *nouveaux romans* and from his personal need to re-member the forgotten places of his ancestors' exile. His book becomes itself a site of postmemory, a reconstructed village in which, however, no one can live. Too many questions remain. Raczymow's tales evoke not so much Konsk as its absence—the condition of exile from Konsk.

### memorial constructions

*Yizker* books contain texts and images, but the book of Matthieu Schriftlich is limited to oral and written stories. There are no pictures of Matl or Noïoch Oksenberg, no photographs of Szlama Davidowicz or the streets of Konsk. Do pictures provide the second- and third-generation questioner with a more concrete, a better access to the abandoned parental world than stories can? Or, as indexical traces, do they perhaps provide too direct and material a connection to the past?[11] Photographic images, as we have seen, shape the work of postmemory in important ways.

When I visited the United States Holocaust Memorial Museum in Washington, D.C., I thought a great deal about these questions, for the museum,

I realized, is also dedicated to bridging the distance between memory and postmemory, and between postmemory and oblivion. The museum was created not primarily for survivors and deeply engaged children of survivors like me, but for an American public with little knowledge of the event. At its best, the museum needs to elicit in its visitors an imaginary identification—the desire to know and to feel, the curiosity and passion that shape the postmemory of survivor children. At its best, it would include all of its visitors in the generation of postmemory. The museum's architecture and exhibits aim at just that effect: to get us close to the affect of the event, to convey knowledge and information, without, however, attempting any facile sense of recreation or reenactment.

The proper mode of representation is hotly debated in Holocaust studies, and Art Spiegelman's *Maus* has already provided the occasion for some reflections about this question here. The Holocaust museum is a text addressed to the largest possible audience with the greatest range of knowledge and relationship to this history and thus with many possible points of entry into its exhibits. It thus faces an even greater dilemma than most narrative, photographic, or cinematic representations whose addressees might already be more initiated. The museum's challenge is to effect an interest based on a form of identification that does not promote the straightforward universality and familiality of *The Family of Man* or the sense, evident in Steven Spielberg's *Schindler's List,* that every form of human experience can indeed be represented, re-created, and understood. Raczymow's particular tone seems appropriate for the representation of the Holocaust—an attempt both to represent and in some instances to re-create a traumatic past even while acknowledging the difficulty of access, the resistance to knowledge. In many of its exhibits the museum's speech act is performative—it enacts the past rather than representing it, and it engages the visitor's emotional as well as intellectual and critical responses. But that enactment is always qualified, distanced, displaced.[12]

How could the museum give some small sense of the world that was destroyed, beyond concentrating on the destruction alone? Is it possible to show visitors passing through its edifice in Washington that Jewish experience was more than only that of victims, to convey the richness and diversity of Jewish cultures before their destruction? How could the museum reconstruct the world that had been destroyed?

As with most of its exhibits, the museum has chosen to attempt that representation of life "before" through photographic images, allowing us to consider specifically the power of images as agents of postmemory. Thus

8.2

there are a number of portraits of famous Jewish artists and intellectuals banned by the Nazis, killed or forced into exile. There are portraits of the writers whose books are being burned in the films of the book burnings. There is a small room devoted to a few of Roman Vishniac's images of the lost world of the Polish shtetl: some faces, some lonely street scenes, a dance. And, in its photographic archive, the museum collects as many photo albums of survivors as it can get, carefully cataloguing and dating the prewar birthdays, anniversaries, family outings, and school pictures of random Jewish families. Filling the shelves of the photographic archives, along with notebooks full of images of horror—ghetto scenes, shootings by Einsatztruppen, arrivals at concentration camps, selections, bodies, personal belongings surviving the destruction of their owners—these conventional family pictures testify to the full range of Holocaust photography. They attempt to reverse, as well, the Nazi destruction not only of people and their communities but of the very records—pictures and documents—that might have testified to their former existence.

Many survivors, in fact, have no photographs that precede the war years:[13] it is as though the museum collection were trying to repair this irreparable loss. The family and community pictures, particularly, provide a part of a record and a narrative about the Jewish world lost in the Holocaust and thus place the images of destruction into a needed contextual framework. More than that: they re-create something of what has been destroyed, even as they elicit and facilitate the viewer's mourning of the destruction. The conventionality of the family photo provides a space of identification for any viewer participating in the conventions of familial representation; thus the photos can bridge the gap between viewers who are personally connected to the event and those who are not. They can expand the postmemorial circle. Photographs of the world lost to genocide and to exile can contain, perhaps more obviously than the names and narrative fragments handed down to Matthieu Schriftlich, the particular mixture of mourning and re-creation that characterizes the work of postmemory.

This is nowhere more visible than in the "Tower of Faces" situated at the very center of the Holocaust Memorial Museum (Figure 8.2). Chronological in conception, the museum's permanent exhibition begins on the fourth floor with the rise of Nazism, leading to the prewar "terror in Poland" and the Nazi euthanasia program. Next we pass over a glass bridge whose walls are inscribed with hundreds of names, each representing a town or a community destroyed in the genocide. In a radical break in chronology, we then enter a room shaped like a tower and constructed entirely of sepia-toned photographic images that hover all around us. An introductory panel explains that what we are seeing are several hundred photographs of the Lithuanian shtetl of Ejszyzski collected by a child survivor of the town, Yaffa Eliach, the granddaughter of the town's Jewish photographers, Yitzak Uri Katz and Alte Katz.

Some of the photos are at eye level, others are out of reach, hard to see. We are separated from them by the bridge on which we are standing, which keeps us in the middle of the room, removed from direct contact with the images. The Ejszyzski photographs are ordinary portraits of individuals and groups, of family and group rituals, of candid moments (Figures 8.3, 8.4). They are, as the museum's director, Michael Berenbaum, insists, the pictures by which we mark life's transitions, the pictures we would send to friends and relatives abroad. In the context of the museum, they are meant to "personalize the story of the Holocaust."[14]

If the Ejszyszki photographs represent the typical Jewish prewar life of the town, they prove the diversity and range of that life. These pictures do not emerge from a narrow historical moment but span what must be a thirty-year period. We see observant as well as assimilated Jews. We see young and old. We see a great range of class and economic backgrounds— laborers and scholars, farmers and professionals. We see an even greater range of activities: bicycling, eating, boating, mourning, reading, walking, posing with friends or alone. Many types of work and many types of leisure appear.

My first reaction, similar to that of many others, was to marvel at how rich and varied a life was destroyed. The pictures gain by their diversity and their multiplicity: after looking at them for a while, it becomes less important to see individual images than to take in a sense of the whole, and of its relation to one's own family albums. "Look, look, look," I hear people saying all around me, "we have a picture just like this one in our album." Or: "Look, that looks just like Grandma!" Interestingly, in the minutes I spend in the room, I find that this identification easily transcends ethnic identity and family history.

The conventional nature of family photography makes the space for this identification, this erasure of time and space. We might leaf through any of our own family albums and find similar photos. But if the tower is a family album, then we are situated right inside it. Like all family albums, the tower preserves and creates memory: it is a site of remembrance and commemoration. The people depicted diverge from one another in historical moment, occupation, class, and style, and they are separated from us as viewers by

**8.3**

**8.4**

at least a half-century and by the radical break the Holocaust introduced into this century. Nevertheless, the conventional and familial nature of the images themselves manages to transcend these distances, figured spatially by the bridge that separates us from the pictures, and to foster an affiliative look that binds the photographs to one another and us to them. Most of the photographs remain anonymous, but some have names and dates inscribed on them; some have arrows leading from a name to a face. Even these names, however, serve less to individualize then to generalize: in the photographs' multiplicity, the names become anonymous and generic, like Raczymow's Matl, Simon, Schlomo, and Chaim.

When we enter the Tower of Faces, we leave the historical account of the museum and enter a domestic space of a family album that shapes a different form of looking and knowing, a different style of recognition, one that is available to any viewer and that can connect viewers of different backgrounds to one another. This is a collective and not an individual story, yet the process of affiliative familial looking fosters and shapes the individual viewer's relationship to this collective memory: they can adopt these memories as their own postmemories. The Tower provides for visitors a space in which they can become a community: descendants of those killed decades ago in a small shtetl thousands of miles away.[15] We have seen that familial looking can be and has been used both compellingly and problematically to produce broader extrafamilial affiliations based on the very loaded notion of family. If the Tower of Faces is to succeed it must promote such affiliation even while avoiding the false universality of *The Family of Man*. The tower's architecture and its particular location inside the museum are instrumental in enabling this exhibit to avoid some of the traps of familial looking. The museum carefully and meticulously contextualizes the family pictures in the tower. Carefully guided and shaped, the act of familial looking is located in the gap between the 1940s in Europe and the present in the United States, a gap that is underscored by the museum's architecture and exhibits.

Visitors descending through the museum encounter the Tower of Faces twice, first on the fourth floor, at the end of the exhibits pertaining to the rise of Nazism, and again, on the third floor, as a culmination of the exhibits detailing the Final Solution. After walking through a railroad car used in the Polish deportations, seeing a model of the gas chambers and crematoria in Auschwitz, walking by a pile of shoes brought from Auschwitz and seeing an actual oven from Mauthausen, we cross another glass bridge, right below the one that listed the names of lost communities. This bridge is covered with hundreds of first names—I find mine, my mother's and father's, that of each of my grandparents, those of my sons. After a few other memorial exhibits this bridge leads to the Tower of Faces on a level below the bridge on which we initially stood. This exhibit is introduced by a panel narrating the town of Ejszyski's destruction by a mobile killing unit in September 1941. We are told that there were virtually no survivors of that action, though we assume that some people, like Yaffa Eliach and her parents, had gone into hiding beforehand.

This is a radically different encounter with the images. The lower room is much darker since the light comes from a distant skylight obscured by the opaque glass bridge on which other visitors are standing on the floor above. This room is square, and we can go right up to the images—we are no longer separated from them. We see the faces more closely, we look into the eyes of people who were alive, full of joy, confidence, and hope. The images are at once more accessible, because we are closer to them, and less so because there is so little light. I notice, for the first time, the black borders surrounding the sepia images, and I wonder whether the intent is aesthetic or funereal. And, as I look up toward the next floor and the distant ceiling light source way above that, as I see the images rush down toward me, so many much too distant to recognize, I realize, with a shudder, that this tower is in fact a chimney, that this album is also a tomb, that commemoration is also mourning. I realize that these are not merely pictures of the dead, but that a violent murder has been committed. And I am reminded of Paul Celan's famous evocation of the "grave in the air" in his "Todesfuge."

The Tower of Faces brings out most forcefully photography's connection to death, and thus the power of photographs as media of mourning. The pictures in the Tower of Faces tell us the immediacy of life at the moment photographed, transformed in the instant of this recognition into the death we know that soon followed. They evoke both the anger and the disbelief accompanying this temporal jolt. With death as the photographs' latent content, commemoration becomes rememoration—a collective act of resistance against forgetting.[16]

By using the most conventional of photographic genres, family pictures, with its characteristically affiliative look, the tower preserves the power of commemoration into the generations of postmemory. The architecture itself figures the nature of postmemory. As Andrea Liss has said, the double encounter with the tower "functions more in harmony with the layered way in which memories overlap and cross the mental time zones of the past and the present, especially involving circumstances of extreme traumatic dislocation."[17] We reanimate the pictures with our own knowledge of daily life, and we experience, emotionally, the death that took those lives so violently. But, in its historical specificity, the tower has also been able to attribute guilt and responsibility, to define agency.

*traces*

Yaffa Eliach and her family were able to escape the town's extermination and to survive in hiding. Yet in 1944, when they returned to Ejzyski, they were subject to a local pogrom in which many of the twenty-nine surviving Jews, including Yaffa's mother, were killed. Yaffa escaped with photos hidden in her shoes and strapped to her brother's body. Later she assembled the 6,000-picture archive from which the tower is composed by collecting the pictures that her compatriots had sent to relatives around the world or had saved in many unbelievable ways.[18] Yaffa Eliach is a child survivor with memories of Ejzyski; the Tower of Faces is her memorial book addressed to the subsequent generations that will visit the museum. With the help of the architect, she has constructed a site of postmemory and mourning that is at the same time a reconstruction of the town itself.

The Tower's memorial form reflects specifically the investment of a survivor and her effort to create and to reach as inclusive a postmemorial generation as possible. A different investment shapes the interest of the second generation, for example the postmemorial work of the French artist Christian Boltanski.

Unlike Eliach, Christian Boltanski, whose middle name is Liberté, grew up after the Holocaust; he was born on the very day that Paris was liberated from Nazi occupation. Boltanski's father was born a Polish Jew and, though he had converted to Catholicism, he spent the entire occupation years in hiding under the floorboards of his home in Paris. Although Christian's mother was Catholic, and although he repeatedly speaks of his "Jewish culture, non-culture," his paternal history has no doubt determined the shape of his avant-garde photographic career. But Boltanski's work defines a different aesthetic of postmemory than Eliach's Tower of Faces, one closer to the opaque distance claimed by Raczymow, to Fresco's and Finkielkraut's absence. Also attempting both to re-create and to mourn a lost world of parental origin, Boltanski signals more clearly the gap between memory and postmemory, the difficult access to that world, and the complex suspicion that surrounds photography's documentary claims in a postmodern and post-Holocaust world.

Boltanski's early work, marked by this suspicion, is devoted to uncoupling any uncomplicated connection between photography and "truth." Most of his work consists of images that are rephotographed, altered, and replaced with others, thus losing their purported credibility. Boltanski uses this myth of credibility, in fact, to establish as "true" situations he invents, such as his elaborate "record" of a bicycle accident he never had, or the use of images of anonymous children to "document" his own childhood. In Boltanski's work the indexical nature of the photograph is in itself a trace as he succeeds in disguising the arbitrary connection between image and referent. Many of his images are, in fact, icons masquerading as indices, or, more radically, symbols masquerading as icons and indices.

The detective function of photograph—forever questioned and parodied—runs through Boltanski's many images of objects through which he traces the lives of individuals and families, images reminiscent both of the cases full of objects in traditional ethnographic museums and of the belongings collected by the Nazis before they gassed their victims—the so-called Canada storehouses. Each of his works aims not toward particularity but toward anonymity, not toward an individual but toward a collective identity, or non-identity. He often speaks of the effort to erase himself, so as to be able to reach a communal memorial layer, unconscious reminiscences and archetypes through which viewers can supply their own stories as they look at his images.

But that deeper layer is not just psychological: it invites a historical and political reading as well. The critic Lynn Gumpert, for example, has situated installations such as "The Clothes of François C.," "The Inventory of Objects Belonging to a Woman in Bois-Colombe," and the rearranged photo album of the D. family, 1939–1964, within the history of France and Europe during these years.[19] Boltanski uses objects as clues to a communal history that raises troubling questions: what did the D. family or the woman from Bois-Colombe do during the occupation? What world did they construct for themselves? Is it a normal everyday world that disguises the presence of the war, or do their objects allow us to confront the problematic history of French collaboration and resistance?

Not until the mid-1980s, when he undertook a series of installations grouped under the general title of "Lessons of Darkness," did Boltanski confront directly his own postmemory of Holocaust, exile, and survival. "There were all sorts of things about my own childhood that I suppressed in my work because they were too special. For example, in my first works I never mention that I was from a Jewish family, I described it as a normal French family" (quoted in Gumpert, 97). His new series of installations begins with "Monuments: The Children of Dijon" and "Odessa Monument" (1985 and following)—large structures built out of many rephotographed faces of his own school picture and a school picture from Dijon, mounted on walls with individual lights or sitting on tin boxes within tin frames, connected by electrical cords that provide the lighting (Figure 8.5). Boltanski did a number of these installations in Paris, Dijon, Venice, New York, and elsewhere.

Although the actual children depicted may well still be alive, their images form altarpieces, reminiscent of Byzantine icons, commemorating the dead. Through iconic and symbolic but not directly indexical implication, Boltanski connects these images of children to the mass murders of the Holocaust: the pictures themselves evoke and represent the actual victims, but neither we nor the artist has a way of knowing whether the individuals in the photos are Holocaust victims or enlarged faces of random schoolchildren. Through their lack of specificity they represent even more forcefully Boltanski's search for a post-Holocaust aesthetic that would contain his generation's absent

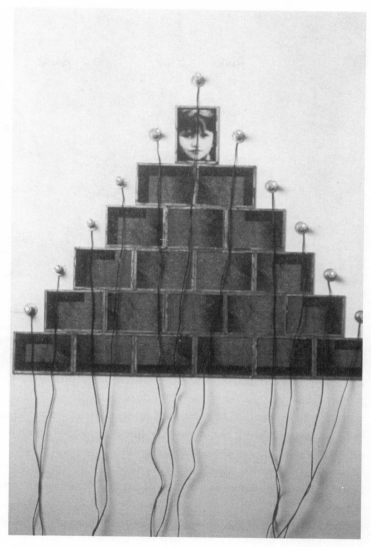

8.5

memory shaped by loss, mourning, and ambivalence. "I have never used images from the camps," Boltanski says in an interview. "My work is not about, it is after."[20]

"Lessons of Darkness" culminates in a series of installations that use photographs of actual Jewish children, in particular a 1931 class picture from a Jewish high school in Vienna, the Chajes Realgymnasium, that

8.6

Boltanski found in *Die Mazzesinsel,* a book on Vienna's predominantly Jewish second district (Figure 8.6), and the photograph of a Purim celebration from a French Jewish school in 1939. Again, Boltanski rephotographs and enlarges individual faces, installs them on top of tin biscuit boxes or mounts them on the wall, illuminating each with a black desk lamp that creates a large circle of light at the center of each picture (Figure 8.7). The biscuit boxes, empty containers of a life story and of individual memory, are stripped of their possessions, just as the faces themselves are stripped of individuality. Even though their indexical, referential function reemerges through the use of the class photo of a population the majority of which certainly ended up in Hitler's death camps, the images, blown up to enormous proportions and thus depersonalized, become icons of untimely death, icons of mourning. Stripped of their connection to an actual abandoned and destroyed community, stripped of the narrative the actual class picture tells, the faces from the Chajes school, like the children of Dijon, and "Monuments" made of Christian's own elementary class picture, echo a collective act of destruction and evoke the post-Holocaust viewer's fears and sorrows, without conveying any specific informational content.

The sculptural installations allow Boltanski to (re)build a lost world, but one that looks anonymous, requiring both a certain contextualization (the fact that the high school was Jewish) and a certain investment by the

8.7

viewer—the viewer's own memories and fears—to carry any meaning and power. This is equally true of the subsequent installation "Canada": here we don't know the identity of the faces depicted or the source of the objects on the floor; we know only the title "Canada," which evokes, for those who *know,* Hitler's storehouses.

The gaze that connects us to these images and installations is affiliative only in the most general sense: we recognize not the people or the world rebuilt but the forms of memorialization, the technological shapes of Holocaust persecution and extermination, the names of a destroyed world and

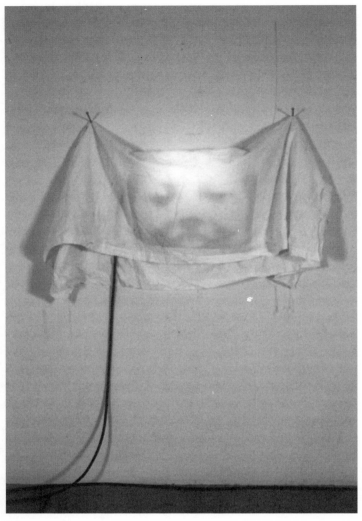

**8.8**

of the means of its destruction.[21] "For me it's very important to start with a real image," Boltanski insists. "Then I blow it up to make it universal."[22] In these new installations, using ghostly sheets and black mesh, visibility is severely impaired. They highlight, more and more forcefully and brutally, the violence of photographic exposure and revelation. The pictures suggest a truth, but they remain blurry, unforgiving and unyielding (Figure 8.8).

Like Raczymow's, Boltanski's connection to the world he reconstructs is shaped primarily by his own need to remember and to know and by a profound ambivalence about that need. "I think," he says in an interview, "that my work is bound to a certain world that is bordered by the White Sea and the Black, a mythic world that doesn't exist, that I never knew, a sort of great plain where armies clashed and where Jews of my culture lived" (Marsh, 5). "Anyway, this is all very fuzzy in my own mind; I have no Jewish culture. I am like the Indians who, in westerns, serve as guides to the soldiers: they forgot everything, but when they drank, Indian dances came back to them" (quoted in Gumpert, 96).

For Boltanski postmemory is indeed empty, shaped by deep and residual cultural knowledges, overlaid with more present practices. Thus the lessons of darkness bring together Jewish and Christian modes of memorialization (the Jahrzeit or Chanukah candle with the altarpiece and the icon), made more poignant by the transcendently painful figure of the dead child. The objectification inherent in the still photographic image is reinforced by the fact that the faces on the walls are children's faces, looking forward to a life they were never to have, faces reproduced and rephotographed to the point of third- and fourth-generation fuzziness, made hollow and empty by enlargement. Darkness is death, absence of light, the dark room: photography can re-create this darkness dependent as it is on light. Family and school photography have lost all sense of comfort and safety, revealing an irreparable darkness and a danger from which our familiar social institutions cannot shield us.

As an aesthetic of postmemory, Boltanski's works reach an extreme. The empty content of the boxes and the generality of the pictures allow us both to believe and to suspect the documentary aspect of the photograph. But to call the truth of pictures into question in view of current Holocaust denial is risky indeed. Yet to reconstruct a destroyed world in the shape of a memorial and a site of mourning extends the need to remember even as it acknowledges the loss of knowledge and specificity. Boltanski's lessons are not history lessons: they are lessons about mass destruction and the need to recall an irrecoverable past in the absence of precise knowledge about it. They are lessons about a form of disconnection and loss that is the condition of exile without the hope of return. And, with their unforgiving electric lights, they are lessons about the violence of knowledge, the brutality of exposure, the ultimate incapacities of our technologies of revelation.

Boltanski's images are thus particularly compelling at a moment when survivors of the Holocaust are rapidly disappearing from within our midst, taking with them the possibility of direct memorial access to the event, however mediated by the present of recollection. Although they are broadly accessible and disturbingly evocative, I wonder whether the "Lessons of Darkness" nevertheless risk too radical a disconnection from their source and thus the possibility of further manipulation and appropriation, too decontextualized and ungrounded a form of looking. If we look at the original image of the Chajes school graduating class, we recognize an historical moment, with its distinctive clothing, body language, and representational styles. Boltanski's recreations leave only eerily empty faces and enormous eye sockets waiting to be filled with the viewer's own affective responses.

When Boltanski says that he starts with a "real" image and that he then blows it up to "make it universal," he highlights what is troubling about his installations: if the appeal is too general, if the specificity of reference is lost, if the images evoke loss, death, and mourning without the anchors of agency and responsibility, then the Holocaust risks becoming a general trope for the postmodern condition. As a third generation grows to maturity and postmemory becomes increasingly disassociated from memory, we are left to speculate on how and what these images can communicate in the different contexts into which they will be inserted.

### ghosts

A different form of remembrance based on a closer connection between image and referent is exemplified in the work of the American photographer Shimon Attie. By fully exploiting photography's capacity to evoke absence as well as presence, Attie may provide Yoram Kaniuk with a more satisfying way to "return" to the Berlin into which he might have been born. Visiting Berlin in 1991, Attie began to ask: "Where are all the missing people? What has become of the Jewish culture and community which had once been at home here?"[23]

A concerted search led Attie to a number of historical photographs of Berlin's Scheunenviertel, its Jewish quarter during the 1920s and 1930s. Making slides of them and using several powerful projectors, he projected these old images onto the precise locations where they were originally taken, thus "rebuilding" the ruined world on the very site of its ruin. Then rephotographing the projections, Attie created layered images which have become moveable memorial sites, sites each of us can invest with our own nostalgic and elegiac needs (Figures 8.9, 8.10). In his work, the site of destruction has

been reconnected to the site of commemoration, icon merged with index, context and referent restored. But is it? Attie admits that he "made every effort to project the image onto its original site" (11), but it was only possible in about 25 percent of the installations. Sometimes he had to use an adjacent building, sometimes another site altogether. In five of the seventy installations, moreover, he used images from other Jewish quarters and ghettos in Eastern Europe. "When it was necessary to choose between being a good historian and—hopefully—a good artist, I always chose the latter," he admits.

I can identify with Attie's impulse to (re)build Jewish Berlin through his shadow play. The ghosts in Novak's, Attie's, and Boltanski's images also haunt my imagination. Looking at the children's faces in Novak's photograph and in Boltanski's installations, at the shadow figures haunting Attie's

8.10

projections, I see the children in my mother's and father's school classes who did not survive, I see the buildings of Czernowitz now inhabited by young people who don't remember their parents' neighbors. I see the child I could have been and the child I was in my own childhood nightmares.

As postmodern subjects is our generation not constructed, collectively, in relation to these ghosts and shadows, are we not shaped by their loss and by our own ambivalence about mourning them? As we look at them, they look back at us, constituting, as Dominick LaCapra has recently argued, the return of the repressed that identifies the postmodern with the post-Holocaust.[24] This mutual look is the optical unconscious determining our postmodern subjectivity, which, as Fran Bartkowski suggests, is shaped "in relation to an elsewhere"—in a temporal/spatial diaspora.[25] Photographs can suggest what that elsewhere is or was, they can provide a visual content for our ambivalent longings. In the spatial aesthetic of the United States Holocaust Memorial Museum, and in the work of Novak, Boltanski, and Attie, they can become building blocks of postmemory. As such, they can also remind us of the distance, the absence, the unbridgeable gap that, in postmodernity, makes us who we are. In this "we" I do not include only Jews or those whose families were directly affected by the Holocaust either as victims, as perpetrators, or as bystanders: I include the much vaster community of postmemory that will, ideally, be forged by the aesthetics of the Tower of Faces, or of Boltanski's and Attie's installations. This aesthetics is based on the identifications forged by familial looking.

In the photographs that form the bases of these very different installations, we see faces looking ahead toward a future they were never to have. The photograph's temporal irony elicits mourning and empathy. We mourn the people in the photographs because we recognize them, but this identification remains at a distance marked by incomprehension, anger, and rage. They may be like us, but they are not us: they are visibly ghosts and shadows. They are and remain other, emanations from another time and space. They are clearly in another world from ours, and yet they are uncannily familiar. Our entry into the circle of postmemory through the act of familial looking enlarges the notion of family without dislodging it from a historical and geographical specificity that signals its difficult accessibility.

For years I thought I would never be able to go to Czernowitz, and I shared my parents' sense that their world is simply gone, surviving only in their stories, memories, and friendships. But after 1989, at the same time that East Berlin became available to Attie, Czernowitz, now in the Ukraine, began to admit some visitors from the West. Several German television, radio, and newspaper stories were produced there to capture some of the flavor of the city of Paul Celan, and some tours were organized in Israel so that former residents might return for a few days. I read some of these stories and suggested to Leo and to my parents that we take a trip to Czernowitz in the summer of 1994. After some research I knew the travel conditions would be harsh whether we chose to go by car or train and was a bit discouraged by a photo exhibit on the Bukowina which showed a dismal landscape. But I thought that as experienced travelers we could all handle it and that the visit would be well worth the trouble.

My fantasy was that we would spend several days walking around the city, whose prewar buildings are still standing. We would visit my father's cousin Rosa, now in her eighties, one of the very few remaining Jews of the prewar population, and we would meet her son Felix, who grew up in the Soviet Czernowitz. We would have our still camera and our video camera along and we would record our walks and talks. "Remember, so and so used to live here," I imagined my parents saying to one another; "No, you're wrong, it was over there." Somewhat like Christa Wolf and her family in *Patterns of Childhood,* we would discuss our impressions and share our reminiscences. My parents would show us their old apartments, the schools they attended, the houses of many friends and neighbors. They would retrace their steps, tell us where they met and where they used to spend time together. They would relive the years before the war and also the war, and they would relive their departure. Together, we would try to make the place come alive, investing it with memories of old, and memories created in the present, memories transmitted across generations. Together we would populate the empty streets in Attie's images, making family pictures where he is limited to urban landscape photographs.

The trip never happened. Every time I called about making reservations, or to discuss our itinerary, my mother asked was I really so interested in going, and why? It dawned on me that Leo's and my desire, not theirs, was driving this plan. They were ambivalent and finally dissuaded by the practical difficulties of the trip and, I'm sure, by the fear of seeing only ghosts, like Attie. The summer passed and we have mentioned it again, only regretfully to decide again not to go. Will I ever go there without them, like many friends who have gone to trace their roots in Poland, Czechoslovakia, and Hungary during the last five years? I doubt it. Instead I will have to search for other, less direct means of access to this lost world, means that inscribe its unbridgeable distance as well as my own curiosity and desire. This search will be inspired by Kaniuk's rage and by the aesthetics of Spiegelman, Raczymow, Novak, Boltanski, and Attie. And it will certainly include the many old pictures of people and places, the albums and shoe boxes, the ghosts that, like Novak's projections, populate the domestic spaces of my imagination.

# notes

## introduction

1. *Camera Lucida: Reflections on Photography*, trans. Richard Howard (New York: Hill and Wang, 1981), p. 64.

2. The "verbal picture"—the description of (usually) an imaginary visual object—is a very old and well-studied artistic genre, known as *ekphrasis*. At the very least, it dates back to Homer's description of the shield of Achilles. For a recent full discussion of the contradictions inherent in the attempt to translate between image and word, word and image, and of the incommensurability of the two artistic forms, see Murray Krieger, *Ekphrasis: The Illusion of the Natural Sign* (Baltimore: Johns Hopkins University Press, 1992). W. J. T. Mitchell in *Picture Theory: Essays on Visual and Verbal Interpretation* (Chicago: University of Chicago Press, 1994), and Mieke Bal in *Reading "Rembrandt": Beyond the Word-Image Opposition* (Cambridge: Cambridge University Press, 1991), have enabled us to bypass a lengthy discussion of the word-image opposition and to see the collaboration and the interdependence of the visual and the verbal in most visual and verbal texts, even those which appear to be "purely" one or the other. It is my argument in this book that all family photographs are composite, heterogeneous media, "imagetexts": visual texts, that is, whose readings are narrative and contextual but which also, in some ways, resist and circumvent narration. See also Mitchell's reflections on "Photography and Language," pp. 281–285, where he prefers to see the relationship of photography and language as a site of resistance.

3. "The signifying system of photography, like that of classical painting, at once depicts a scene *and the gaze of the spectator,* an object *and* a viewing subject." Victor Burgin, "Looking at Photographs," in *Thinking Photography* (London: Macmillan, 1982), p. 146.

4. "The winter-garden photograph must be read *as writing* and not seen *as image.*" Richard Stamelman, *Lost Beyond Telling: Representations of Death and Absence in Modern French Poetry* (Ithaca: Cornell University Press, 1990), p. 265.

5. I have found W. J. T. Mitchell's terms "textual pictures" and "pictorial texts" most useful in relation to my own conceptualization of the hybrid texts consti-

tuted by and around family photographs. In my work on this project in the years preceding the publication of *Picture Theory,* I referred to verbally described photographs as "prose pictures," and to photographs that constitute narratives as "visual fictions" or "visual narratives."

6. See Jacques Derrida's moving reading of *Camera Lucida* in "The Deaths of Roland Barthes," in Hugh J. Silberman, ed., *Philosophy and Non-Philosophy since Merleau-Ponty* (New York: Routledge, 1988), where he expands on this idea in relation to his own mourning of Barthes.

7. John Tagg writes of the "burden of representation" in *The Burden of Representation: Essays on Photographies and Histories* (Minneapolis: University of Minnesota Press, 1988).

8. Throughout this book I use the term "ideology" in the Althusserian sense of "the system of representations by which we imagine the world as it is." Louis Althusser, *For Marx,* trans. Ben Brewster (London: New Left Books, 1977), p. 233.

9. In identifying photography as an "art moyen," a middle-brow art, Pierre Bourdieu makes this connection between "photographic practice" and "its *family function.*" *Photography: A Middle-Brow Art,* trans. Shaun Whiteside (Stanford: Stanford University Press, 1990).

10. Burgin, "Looking at Photographs," p. 146. I use the term "screen" in the Lacanian sense further theorized by Kaja Silverman. Jacques Lacan, *Four Fundamental Concepts of Psychoanalysis,* trans. Alan Sheridan (New York: Norton, 1978); Kaja Silverman, *Male Subjectivity at the Margins* (New York: Routledge, 1992) and *The Threshold of the Visible World* (New York: Routledge, 1996). See Chapter 3 for a more detailed discussion and application of these terms to family photography. Regrettably, Silverman's *The Threshold of the Visible World* was published when this book was in its final stages of revision and thus I do not fully consider the implications of her further theorization of notions that are extremely resonant for my argument throughout my book.

11. Cited in bell hooks, *Black Looks: Race and Representation* (Boston: South End Press, 1992), p. 5. Silverman, in *Threshold,* theorizes these implications of the screen, esp. in ch. 6: "The screen or cultural image-repertoire inhabits each of us, much as language does. What this means is that when we apprehend another person or an object, we necessarily do so via that large, diverse, but ultimately finite range of representational coordinates which determine what and how the members of our culture see—how they process visual detail, and what meaning they give it" (p. 221).

12. Walter Benjamin, "The Work of Art in the Age of Mechanical Reproduction," *Illuminations* (New York: Schocken, 1969), p. 237. See Chapter 4 for a fuller discussion of this notion.

13. Julia Hirsch, in *Family Photographs: Content, Meaning and Effect* (New York: Oxford, 1981), reminds us that this scrutiny has a long representational history starting with the Renaissance family portrait. Hirsch usefully and movingly

traces the continuities between the conventions of family portraiture and those of family photography.

14. For this distinction between the look and the gaze, I rely on Jacques Lacan's differentiation between "oeil" and "regard" in *Four Fundamental Concepts of Psychoanalysis*. See Chapter 3 for a fuller discussion of these notions.

15. Jo Spence, *Putting Myself in the Picture: A Political, Personal and Photographic Autobiography* (Seattle: Real Comet Press, 1988), p. 208. The notion of interpellation is Louis Althusser's and describes the ways in which, as social subjects, we are addressed by dominant ideologies and how, often unconsciously, we subscribe to them.

16. Jo Spence and Patricia Holland, eds., *Family Snaps: The Meanings of Domestic Photography* (London: Virago, 1991), pp. 13–14.

17. Linda Hutcheon, *The Politics of Postmodernism* (New York: Routledge, 1989), p. 22.

18. W. J. T. Mitchell's title "Picture Theory" illustrates this interactive relationship between picture and theory as well as seeing theory itself as the act of picturing.

19. Hal Foster, *The Anti-Aesthetic: Essays in Postmodern Culture* (Port Townsend, Wash.: Bay Press, 1983), pp. xiv, xv.

## *1. mourning and postmemory*

1. Susan Sontag, *On Photography* (New York: Anchor Doubleday, 1989), p. 70.

2. *Practicalities: Marguerite Duras Speaks to Michel Beaujour,* trans. Barbara Bray (New York: Grove Weidenfeld, 1990), p. 89.

3. Helen Epstein, *Children of the Holocaust: Conversations with Sons and Daughters of Survivors* (New York: Penguin, 1979), p. 11.

4. Pierre Nora, "Between Memory and History: Les Lieux de Mémoire," *Representations* 26 (Spring 1989): 19.

5. W. J. T. Mitchell, *Picture Theory: Essays on Verbal and Visual Representation* (Chicago: University of Chicago Press, 1994), p. 192.

6. "Postmemory" is usefully connected to Kaja Silverman's notion of "heteropathic recollection"—her elaborate psychoanalytic theorization of the self's ability to take on the memory of others, even culturally devalued others, through a process of heteropathic identification. Silverman's argument also relies on the visual and considers the role of photography, though not the notion of family. See *The Threshold of the Visible World*, esp. ch. 5.

7. Nadine Fresco, "Remembering the Unknown," *International Review of Psychoanalysis* 11 (1984): 417–427.

8. Henri Raczymow, "Memory Shot Through with Holes," *Yale French Studies* 85 (1994): 98–106.

9. In conjunction with a 1996 photographic exhibit in Warsaw, "And I Still See Their Faces," one Zahava Bromberg writes: "I carried this photograph of my mama through two selections by Dr. Mengele at Auschwitz. Once I held it in

my mouth, the second time I had it taped with a bandage to the bottom of my foot. I was 14 years old." *New York Times* (May 19, 1996): 1.

10. I have deliberately quoted only that part of Adorno's sentence which has become so determinative and familiar. The actual sentence reads: "Perennial suffering has as much right to expression as a tortured man has to scream; hence it may have been wrong to say that after Auschwitz you could no longer write poems." *Negative Dialectics,* trans. E. B. Ashton (New York: Continuum, 1973), p. 362. In his later essay, "Commitment" (1962), Adorno elaborates: "I have no wish to soften the saying that to write lyric poetry after Auschwitz is barbaric; it expresses in negative form the impulse which inspires committed literature . . . Yet this suffering . . . also demands the continued existence of art while it prohibits it; it is now virtually in art alone that suffering can still find its own voice, consolation, without immediately being betrayed by it." Andrew Arato and Eike Gebhardt, eds., *The Essential Frankfurt School Reader* (New York: Urizen Books, 1978), p. 312. But this seeming reversal of his original injunction is subject to further rethinking in the essay: "The esthetic principle of stylization . . . makes an unthinkable fate appear to have some meaning; it is transfigured, something of its horror is removed . . . Even the sound of despair pays its tribute to a hideous affirmation" (313).

11. Peter Haidu, "The Dialectics of Unspeakability: Language, Silence, and The Narratives of Desubjectification," in Saul Friedlander, ed., *Probing the Limits of Representation: Nazism and the "Final Solution"* (Cambridge, Mass.: Harvard University Press, 1992), p. 294.

12. Julia Kristeva, "The Pain of Sorrow in the Modern World: The Works of Marguerite Duras," *PMLA* 102 (March 1987): 139. Clearly, this profusion of images must be seen in relation to their absence, as well. With their massive extermination program, Nazis systematically destroyed the very records of Jewish life, documents and photographs, that could attest to its history. Many survivor families, unlike the Spiegelmans and the Jakubowiczs, have no pictures of their prewar life. I am grateful to Lori Lefkowitz for pointing out this corrective to Kristeva's argument.

13. Cited in Andrea Liss, "Trespassing Through Shadows: History, Mourning, and Photography in Representations of Holocaust Memory," *Framework* 4, no. 1 (1991): 33.

14. Art Spiegelman, "Maus & Man," *Voice Literary Supplement* (June 6, 1989): 21. But the Pulitzer prize committee invented a special category for *Maus,* suggesting the impossibility of categorizing it as either fiction or nonfiction. As Lawrence Langer says in his review of *Maus II,* "It resists defining labels." "A Fable of the Holocaust," *New York Times Book Review* (Nov. 3, 1991): 1.

15. Christina Von Braun, *Die schamlose Schönheit des Vergangenen: Zum Verhältnis von Geschlecht und Geschichte* (Frankfurt: Neue Kritik, 1989), pp. 116, 118, 119 (my translation).

16. W. J. T. Mitchell points out that "*Maus* attenuates visual access to its narrative by thickening its frame story . . . and by veiling the human body at all levels of the visual narrative with the figures of animals" (*Picture Theory,* 93). We might add that the few photos that cut through that veil can thus acquire their particular force through contrast.

17. See Alice Yaeger Kaplan's comparison of *Maus* as the text of the child of survivors to Klaus Theweleit's *Male Fantasies* as the text of the child of the perpetrators, "Theweleit and Spiegelman: Of Men and Mice," in *Remaking History,* ed. Barbara Kruger and Phil Mariani (Seattle: Dia Art Foundation, Bay Press, 1989). See also Angelika Bammer, "Mother Tongues and Other Strangers: Writing 'Family' Across Cultural Divides," in *Displacements: Cultural Identities in Question,* ed. Angelika Bammer (Bloomington: Indiana University Press, 1994), p. 93: "The formal composition of *Maus* creates a structure that bridges, even though it cannot fill in, the spaces of silence created by the people whose stories had remained untold."

18. See Nancy K. Miller's account of the 1992 "Maus" exhibition at the Museum of Modern Art, where some of Vladek's tapes could be heard. "Cartoons of the Self: Portrait of the Artist as a Young Murderer, Art Spiegelman's *Maus.*" *M/E/A/N/I/N/G* 12 (1992): 43–54. Miller analyzes the levels of mediation and transformation that separate the father's voice from the son's text. In the CD-Rom *The Complete Maus* (New York: Voyager, 1994), we can hear the oral testimony and can compare the aural and visual texts; we can assess the transformations and revisions that the son performs on his father's words as he tries to fit them into preset cartoon bubbles.

19. Shoshana Felman and Dori Laub, *Testimony: Crises of Witnessing in Literature, Psychoanalysis and History* (New York: Routledge, 1992), p. 48.

20. The CD-Rom edition of *Maus* features a number of additional photographs in the appendix that outlines the Spiegelmans's and the Zylberbergs's family trees. We can click on some of the names to make the photographs appear. As in the book edition, the photographs function to reassemble what has been severed. Mostly the photographs feature pairs, Anja and Vladek, parents, siblings. They are formal pictures, such as wedding photos. Together, they help to rebuild the family tree of a fractured family. In this version, however, they do not intervene in the narrative, but stand apart. In addition, any of the pictures' ambiguity is removed since, in this medium, each image is clearly labeled.

21. I take this phrase from the title of Alvin K. Rosenfeld's book on the literature of the Holocaust, *A Double Dying: Reflections on Holocaust Literature* (Bloomington: Indiana University Press, 1980).

22. In "Mad Youth," *Life* (July 1992): 91, Spiegelman describes another snapshot in which the 11-year-old Art and his mother sit on their back porch looking at an issue of *Mad:* "You can't see my mother's left forearm behind the magazine. She usually wears a broad gold bracelet—Vladek gives them to her as birthday and

anniversary gifts—to cover the blue Auschwitz number tattooed above her wrist. On occasion my friends have noticed the number and have asked her about it. She explains it's a phone number she doesn't want to forget."

23. See also Miller's incisive analysis, in "Cartoons of the Self," of the missing mother's story as the basis for the father/son relationship in *Maus*, and more generally her discussion of the intergenerational and relational nature of the autobiographical project. In Miller's reading in "Representing Others: Gender and the Subjects of Autobiography," *Differences* 6, no. 1 (1994): 1–27, Anja Spiegelman duplicates the generative power of St. Augustine's Monica.

24. Klaus Theweleit, *Buch der Könige, 1: Orpheus und Euridike* (Frankfurt: Roter Stern, 1989).

25. Debórah Dwork, *Children with a Star: Jewish Youth in Nazi Europe* (New Haven: Yale University Press, 1991), p. xxxiii.

## 2. reframing the human family romance

1. George Vecxey, "Riddick Bowe Has Family in Scarsdale," *New York Times* (Feb. 3, 1993): B7.

2. Jo Spence and Patricia Holland, eds., *Family Snaps: The Meanings of Domestic Photography* (London: Virago, 1991), p. 4.

3. Pierre Bourdieu, *Photography: A Middle-Brow Art,* trans. Shaun Whiteside (Stanford: Stanford University Press, 1990), p. 19.

4. Laura Wexler's "Seeing Sentiment: Photography, Race, and the Innocent Eye," in Elizabeth Abel, Helene Moglen, and Barbara Smith, eds., *Female Subjects in Black and White: Race, Feminism, Psychoanalysis* (Berkeley: University of California Press, 1997), examines this issue in turn-of-the-century photography.

5. Edward Steichen, *The Family of Man* (New York: Museum of Modern Art, 1955), pp. 4, 5.

6. Edward Steichen, *A Life in Photography* (New York: Doubleday, 1966), ch. 13.

7. Rita Sylvan with Avis Berman, "Edward Steichen, A Memoir, the Making of *The Family of Man,*" *Connoisseur* 218 (Feb. 1988): 121.

8. Rpt. in Nathan Lyons, ed., *Photographers on Photography: A Critical Anthology* (Englewood Cliffs, N.J.: Prentice Hall, 1966), p. 107.

9. For an excellent discussion of the persistence of universalism see the special issue of *Differences* 7, no. 1 (Spring 1995), entitled "Universalism."

10. Kaja Silverman's distinction between ideopathic and heteropathic identification provides a useful model for this process, though the familial gaze adds another dimension to the notion of identification. To admit the other into one's familial image offers different and broader possibilities from admitting the other into one's image of self. The latter process, as Silverman shows, is most often incorporative and cannibalistic, ideopathic. But the former, especially if based on the connection between familiality and humanity, is no less problematic. The question of this chapter is whether the familial gaze can allow for a truly heteropathic

nonappropriative form of affiliation. See Kaja Silverman, *The Threshold of the Visible World* (New York, Routledge, 1996), esp. ch. 1.

11. Alan Sekula, "The Traffic in Photographs," in *Photography Against the Grain: Essays and Photo Works, 1973–1983* (Halifax: Press of Nova Scotia College of Art and Design, 1984), p. 89.

12. Sigmund Freud, "Family Romances" ("Der Familienroman der Neurotiker," 1908), in *The Standard Edition of the Complete Works of Sigmund Freud*, ed. James Strachey, 24 vols. (London: Hogarth, 1953–1974), vol. 9, pp. 237–241.

13. Victor Burgin, "Family Romance," in Lucien Taylor, ed., *Visualizing Theory: Selected Essays from V.A.R., 1990–1994* (New York: Routledge, 1994), pp. 452, 453.

14. In his "Looking at Photographs," Victor Burgin defines "four basic types of look in the photograph: the look of the camera as it photographs the 'pro-photo-graphic' event; the look of the viewer as he or she looks at the photograph; the 'intra-diegetic' looks exchanged between people (actors) depicted in the photograph (and/or looks from actors toward objects); and the look the actor may direct at the camera" Victor Burgin, "Looking at Photographs," in *Thinking Photography* (London: Macmillan, 1982), p. 148. See also Catherine Lutz and Jane Collins's "The Photograph as an Intersection of Gazes," in their *Reading National Geographic* (Chicago: University of Chicago Press, 1993), pp. 187–216.

15. Echoing Steichen's own motivations, Sandeen concludes his introduction thus: "As I sit before my computer screen in the summer of 1994, Yugoslavia is devouring itself in ethnic and religious warfare. To think of humankind as one, in these circumstances, may not be an unhealthy exercise." *Picturing an Exhibition: "The Family of Man" and 1950's America* (Albuquerque: University of New Mexico Press, 1995). Sandeen's reading, however, is closely contextualized and thus does distance itself from Steichen's easy universalism. Sandeen also points out the difficulty of reading Steichen's exhibit, which, in effect, has disappeared. Using, as I do, the book and installation phonographs as well as published contemporary accounts, is less than an ideal solution. Sandeen spent years trying to reconstruct the exhibit itself, through conversations with Steichen's assistant Wayne Miller. It is no wonder he feels as close to it as he does.

16. The spontaneity of this photograph is called into question by the recent suits brought against Doisneau which reveal that many of his kissing couples might have been actors hired by him to stage the street kissing scenes.

17. Roland Barthes, *Mythologies*, trans. Annette Lavers (New York: Hill and Wang, 1972), p. 101.

18. Etienne Balibar, "Racism and Nationalism," in Etienne Balibar and Immanuel Wallerstein, eds., *Race, Nation, Class: Ambiguous Identities* (London: Verso, 1991), pp. 63, 64.

19. Edmundo Desnoes, *Punto de Vista* (Havana: Instituto de Libro, 1967), pp. 82, 83 (my translation). See also Julia Lesage's trans., "The Photographic Image of Underdevelopment," *Jump Cut* 33 (Feb. 1988): 69–81.

20. See the article in the *Sioux City Journal* (Aug. 26, 1959) reporting on this controversy.
21. "Why I tore down America's pictures at Moscow Fair," *Washington, D.C., Afro-American* (Aug. 22, 1959).
22. Paula Rabinowitz, "Voyeurism and Class Consciousness: James Agee and Walker Evans, *Let Us Now Praise Famous Men*," *Cultural Critique* (Spring 1992): 166.
23. David Cohen, ed., *The Circle of Life: Rituals from the Human Family Album* (New York: HarperCollins, 1991); Peter Menzel, ed., *Material World: A Global Family Portrait* (San Francisco: Sierra Club, 1994).
24. Christian Boltanski, *Menschlich* (Köln: Thouet Verlag, 1994).
25. Tzvetan Todorov, *On Human Diversity: Nationalism, Racism, Exoticism,* trans. Catherine Porter (Cambridge, Mass.: Harvard University Press, 1993). See the "Universalism" issue of *Differences* for several provocative discussions of current debates on universalism and particularism.
26. Jamaica Kincaid, *Lucy* (New York: Farrar Straus Giroux, 1990).
27. Homi Bhabha, *The Location of Culture* (New York: Routledge, 1994); Françoise Lionnet, *Autobiographical Voices: Gender, Race and Self-Portraiture* (Ithaca: Cornell University Press, 1989); Edward Said, *Culture and Imperialism* (New York: Knopf, 1993).

### 3. masking the subject

1. Marianne Hirsch, *The Mother/Daughter Plot: Narrative, Psychoanalysis, Feminism* (Bloomington: Indiana University Press, 1989).
2. For an exploration of the relational construction of the autobiographical subject, see Nancy K. Miller, "Representing Others: Gender and the Subjects of Autobiography," *Differences* 6, no. 1 (1994): 1–27. For a review and articulation of theories of intersubjectivity, see Jessica Benjamin, *Like Subjects, Love Objects: Essays on Recognition and Sexual Difference* (New Haven: Yale University Press, 1995). See also Chapter 5 of this book for a discussion of Benjamin's argument.
3. See Timothy Dow Adams, "Life Writing and Light Writing: Autobiography and Photography," his introduction to the special issue of *Modern Fiction Studies* 40, 3 (Fall 1994) entitled "Autobiography, Photography and Narrative." For an analysis of the relationship of autobiography and reference, see Paul John Eakin, *Touching the World: Reference in Autobiography* (Princeton: Princeton University Press, 1992), esp. ch. 1.
4. Philippe Lacoue-Labarthe, *Portrait de l'artiste, en général* (Paris: Christian Bourgois, 1979), p. 91.
5. In her *The Photograph: A Strange Confined Space,* Mary Price usefully explores the multiple dimensions of masking in relation to photography (Stanford: Stanford University Press, 1994), esp. ch. 6.

6. Roland Barthes, *Camera Lucida: Reflections on Photography*, trans. Richard Howard (New York: Hill and Wang, 1981), p. 34.

7. Charles Baudelaire, "The Modern Public and Photography," Salon of 1959 in *Classic Essays on Photography*, ed. Alan Trachtenberg (New Haven: Leete's Island Books, 1980). Lacoue-Labarthe's title and his first epigram, "Portrait de l'artiste, en général," is also a quote from Baudelaire's autobiographical fragments "Mon coeur mis à nu."

8. Jacques Lacan, "The Mirror Stage as Formative of the Function of the I as Revealed in Psychoanalytic Experience," in *Ecrits: A Selection*, trans. Alan Sheridan (New York: Norton, 1977).

9. Roland Barthes, "The Photographic Message," *Image/Music/Text*, trans. Stephen Heath (New York: Hill and Wang, 1977), pp. 16, 17.

10. Marjorie Garber, *Vested Interests: Cross-Dressing and Cultural Anxiety* (New York: Routledge, 1992), p. 11.

11. Ralph Eugene Meatyard, *The Family Album of Lucybelle Crater* (The Jargon Society, distributed by Millerton; New York: The Book Organization, 1974).

12. In Flannery O'Connor, *The Complete Stories* (New York: Farrar, Strauss and Giroux, 1986).

13. Julia Hirsch, *Family Photographs: Content, Meaning and Effect* (New York: Oxford, 1981), p. 95.

14. See Richard Brilliant, *Portraiture* (Cambridge, Mass.: Harvard University Press, 1991), pp. 112–113, on the relationship between portraiture and masking.

15. David L. Jacobs, "Seeing the Unseen, Saying the Unsayable," in *Ralph Eugene Meatyard: An American Visionary*, ed. Barbara Tannenbaum (Akron, Ohio: Akron Art Museum, and New York: Rizzoli, 1991), p. 66.

16. Jo Spence, *Putting Myself in the Picture: A Political, Personal and Photographic Autobiography* (Seattle: Real Comet Press, 1988), p. 136.

17. See Kaja Silverman's interpretation of the mirror stage in *The Threshold of the Visible World* (New York, Routledge, 1996), ch. 1.

18. Jacques Lacan, *Four Fundamental Concepts of Psychoanalysis*, trans. Alan Sheridan (New York: Norton, 1978), p. 106.

19. See Kaja Silverman's reading of Lacan's *Four Fundamental Concepts of Psychoanalysis* in *The Acoustic Mirror: The Female Voice in Psychoanalysis and Cinema* (Bloomington: Indiana University Press, 1988), p. 161, where she usefully comments on the notion of the "photo-session" to be distinguished from the mirror stage: "There are thus two crucial ways of understanding the subject's relation to visual representation, both of which stress his or her captation—the mirror stage and the 'photo session.' In the former, he or she incorporates an image, and in the latter, he or she is appropriated as image."

20. For an excellent discussion of the political implications of Lacan's theories of vision, and of the interplay between visibility and invisibility, see Peggy Phelan, *Unmarked: The Politics of Performance* (London: Routledge, 1993), esp. ch. 1.

21. Kaja Silverman, "Fassbinder and Lacan: A Reconsideration of Gaze, Look, and Image," in *Male Subjectivity at the Margins* (New York: Routledge, 1992), pp. 149, 150. See also *The Threshold of the Visible World*, ch. 6.

22. As Silverman argues, still glossing Lacan, "Since the gaze always emerges for us within the field of vision, and since we ourselves are always being photographed by it even as we look, all binarizations of spectator and spectacle mystify the scopic relations in which we are held. The subject is generally both . . . if the viewer cannot see the object without the intervention of the image/screen, neither does he or she have a direct visual access to the gaze. In both cases the relationship is mediated by a 'mask, double [or] envelope,' and in both instances 'misrecognition' would seem to be the inevitable outcome" (*Male Subjectivity*, pp. 151–152). See also Kaja Silverman, "What Is a Camera? or: History in the Field of Vision," *Discourse* 15, no. 3 (Spring 1993): 12.

23. Victor Burgin, "Looking at Photographs," in *Thinking Photography* (London: Macmillan, 1982), p. 152.

24. *Putting Myself in the Picture*, p. 94.

25. Lisbet Nilson, "Q&A, Cindy Sherman: Interview with Lisbet Nilson," *American Photographer* (1983): 73.

26. Lisa Phillips, "Cindy Sherman's Cindy Shermans," in *Cindy Sherman* (New York: Whitney Museum, 1987), p. 87.

27. Henry Sayre, *The Object of Performance: The American Avant-Garde since 1970* (Chicago: University of Chicago Press, 1989), p. 57.

28. Paul de Man, "Autobiography as De-facement," in *The Rhetoric of Romanticism* (New York: Columbia University Press, 1984), p. 69.

29. See Stephen W. Melville, "The Time of Exposure: Allegorical Self-Portraiture in Cindy Sherman," *Arts Magazine* 60 (1986): 17–21, for a fascinating reading of Sherman's pictures as "allegorical self-portraits" and his connection between allegory and otherness, a connection which allows him also to bring in Lacoue-Labarthe's *Portrait*.

30. For an alternate reading of Sherman see Phelan, *Unmarked*, ch. 2: "Was there a way, Sherman wondered, to look under the surface of the photographic print? To reposition the negative, ontologically and psychologically? If so, perhaps 'feminine identity' might be seen as something-other-than a surface pose, an endlessly reproductive imitation of nothing but surface" (66). Also Kaja Silverman in *The Threshold of the Visible World*, ch. 6, where, through detailed readings of several of the *Untitled Film Stills*, she identifies elements in the pictures that seem to defy or exceed the camera gaze, to resist rather than confirm the cultural stereotypes in the images: "The tenderness with which Sherman details the protagonists' narcissistic ambitions, and the fact that she literally puts herself in their place . . . encourages us to identify with them" (224).

31. Rosalind Krauss, "A Note on Photography and the Simulacral," in *The Critical Image: Essays on Contemporary Photography*, ed. Carol Squiers (Seattle: Bay Press, 1990), p. 22.

32. Kaja Silverman's *Threshold* is an exception. For a review of critical discussions of Sherman's work and, in particular, of the critics who recast her images as representations of "our common humanity," see Abigail Solomon-Godeau, "Suitable for Framing: The Critical Recasting of Cindy Sherman," *Parkett,* no. 29 (1991): 112–115.

33. Cathy Davidson, "Photographs of the Dead: Sherman, Daguerre, Hawthorne," *South Atlantic Quarterly* 89, no. 4 (Fall 1990): 667–701.

### *4. unconscious optics*

1. Walter Benjamin, "The Work of Art in the Age of Mechanical Reproduction," in *Illuminations* (New York: Schocken, 1969), pp. 236–237.

2. Sigmund Freud, *The Interpretation of Dreams* (1900), in *The Standard Edition of the Complete Psychological Works of Sigmund Freud,* ed. James Strachey, 24 vols. (London: Hogarth Press, 1953–74), vol. 5, p. 611.

3. For an excellent discussion of Benjamin's critique of the mimetic function of photography and his critique of realism, see Eduardo Cadava, "Words of Light: Theses on the Photography of History," in *Fugitive Images: From Photography to Video,* ed. Patrice Petro (Bloomington: Indiana University Press, 1995).

4. In her recent book *The Optical Unconscious* (Cambridge, Mass.: MIT Press, 1993), Rosalind Krauss borrows Benjamin's term for a very different purpose. In her reading the "optical unconscious" is a particular counter-strand of modernism, including artists such as Ernst, Breton, Dalí, Giacometti, Man Ray, and so on, who acknowledge that "human vision can be thought to be less than a master of all it surveys" (179). The artists of the "optical unconscious" thus find an anti-vision, often in language, and explore the dimension of opacity, the irrational and uncanny that undermine the mastery of the eye. Krauss understands Benjamin to mean that the optical field has an unconscious, and she finds this suggestion to be contrary to Freud's notion of the unconscious. In contrast, I read Benjamin's allusive line as an extension of Freud's unconscious into the realm of optics, not different but differently accessible, rather than an addition of another unconscious in the field of vision. See Krauss, pp. 178 ff.

5. Sue Miller, *Family Pictures* (New York: Harper and Row, 1990).

6. Jo Spence, *Putting Myself in the Picture: A Political, Personal and Photographic Autobiography (*Seattle: Real Comet Press, 1988).

7. "Untitled (Kitchen Table Series)" is included in *Carrie Mae Weems,* ed. Andrea Kirsh and Susan Fisher Sterling (Washington: National Museum for Women and the Arts, 1993).

8. See the discussion of these gender divisions in Brenda O. Daley, "The Transformational Rhetoric of Photography in Sue Miller's *Family Pictures,*" *Willa* 1 (Fall 1990): 22.

9. My reading of Spence's work diverges significantly from that of James Guimond in "Auteurs as Autobiographers: Jo Spence and Cindy Sherman," in *Modern*

*Fiction Studies* 40, no. 3 (Fall 1994): 573–592, a special issue on "Autobiography, Photography, Narrative," ed. Timothy Dow Adams. Guimond sees Spence as a modernist to Sherman's postmodernism, whereas I highlight the subversive and postmodern strategies in Spence's work.

10. "Talking Art with Carrie Mae Weems," in bell hooks, *Art on My Mind: Visual Politics* (New York: New Press, 1995), p. 92.

11. This installation is excerpted in *Carrie Mae Weems*. It appears in its entirety in *Family Pictures and Stories: A Photographic Installation,* artist's book (San Diego: Alternative Space Gallery, 1984).

12. Elizabeth Abel elaborates on this argument in "Tables, Mirrors, Telephones: Family Borders in Carrie Mae Weems," paper delivered at the Family Pictures: Shapes of Memory conference, Dartmouth College, May 1996.

### 5. maternal exposures

1. Sally Mann, *Immediate Family* (New York: Aperture, 1992).

2. Marie Cardinal, *The Words to Say It: An Autobiographical Novel,* trans. Pat Goodheart (Cambridge, Mass.: Van Vactor and Goodheart, 1983).

3. Kathryn Harrison, *Exposure* (New York: Warner Books, 1993).

4. Joanne Leonard, "Photography, Feminism, and the Good Enough Mother (Or, the Good Enough Mother with a Camera)," paper delivered at the College Art Association Conference, New York, 1994.

5. Naomi Scheman, "Missing Mothers/Desiring Daughters: Framing the Sight of Women," *Critical Inquiry* 15, no. 1 (August 1988): 88.

6. "Shooting Back" is the name of a photographic project based in Washington, D.C., which teaches very young homeless children to use a camera so as to record their world and their experiences from their own perspectives. Seeing mothers as "shooting back" is seeing them as victims of familiality who want to record, as subjects, a system within which they have been constructed as objects.

7. Within these theoretical frameworks, mothers are still treated as the primary parental figures and are therefore subject to particular scrutiny. Laura Berry has aptly commented on the "endurance and the perverse insistence with which we have indulged the considerable pleasures of looking in on those moments at which the eyes of mother and child meet." Response to MLA conference session "The Other Mother," San Diego, December 1994.

8. Jacques Lacan, "The Mirror Stage as Formative of the Function of the I as Revealed in Psychoanalytic Experience," in *Ecrits: A Selection,* trans. Alan Sheridan (New York: Norton, 1977).

9. Laura Mulvey, "Visual Pleasure and Narrative Cinema," in *Visual and Other Pleasures* (Bloomington: Indiana University Press, 1989). Mulvey is writing about the film camera and not about still images, but it seems to me that in its reception, her argument has been and can be extended to the camera gaze more generally.

10. For critiques, elaborations, and reformulations of Mulvey's argument, see Teresa de Lauretis, *Alice Doesn't: Feminism, Semiotics, Cinema* (Bloomington: Indiana University Press, 1984), ch. 5; Gaylyn Studlar, "Masochism and the Perverse Pleasures of the Cinema," *Quarterly Review of Film Studies* 9, no. 4 (Fall 1984): 267–282; D. N. Rodowick, "The Difficulty of Difference," *Wide Angle* 5, no. 1: 4–15; Regina Schwartz, "Rethinking Voyeurism and Patriarchy: The Case of *Paradise Lost*," *Representations* 34 (Spring 1991): 85–103; Scheman, "Missing Mothers/Desiring Daughters."

11. Jacques Lacan, *Four Fundamental Concepts of Psychoanalysis,* trans. Alan Sheridan (New York: Norton, 1978), ch. 6, "The Split between the Eye and the Gaze."

12. On modern and postmodern conceptions of vision, see Jonathan Crary, *Techniques of the Observer: On Vision and Modernity in the Nineteenth Century* (Cambridge, Mass.: MIT Press, 1990); Martin Jay, *Downcast Eyes: The Denigration of Vision in Twentieth-Century French Thought* (Berkeley: University of California Press, 1993); and Paul Virilio, *The Vision Machine* (Bloomington: Indiana University Press and The British Film Institute, 1994).

13. Kaja Silverman, *The Threshold of the Visible World* (New York, Routledge, 1996), p. 134. See ch. 4 on the gaze.

14. D. W. Winnicott, "Mirror-Role of Mother and Family in Child Development," in *Playing and Reality* (New York: Basic Books, 1971), pp. 112, 113, 114.

15. Daniel N. Stern, *The Interpersonal World of the Infant: A View from Psychoanalysis and Developmental Psychology* (New York: Basic Books, 1985), p. 21.

16. Jessica Benjamin, "The Omnipotent Mother: A Psychoanalytic Study of Fantasy and Reality," in *Representations of Motherhood,* ed. Donna Bassin, Margaret Honey, and Meryle Kaplan (New Haven: Yale University Press, 1994), and Jessica Benjamin, *Like Subjects, Love Objects: Essays on Recognition and Sexual Difference* (New Haven: Yale University Press, 1995).

17. Alice Rose George, Abigail Heyman, and Ethan Hoffman, eds., *Flesh and Blood: Photographers' Images of Their Own Families* (New York: Picture Project, 1992), p. 156.

18. Steven Cantor and Peter Spirer, directors, *Blood Ties: The Life and Work of Sally Mann* (1993).

19. Richard B. Woodward, "The Disturbing Photography of Sally Mann," *New York Times Magazine* (Sept. 27, 1992): 52.

20. In *Blood Ties,* Mann calls these everyday moments simply "true."

21. Note that in *Blood Ties,* Jessie chooses this picture as "one of [her] favorites."

22. Originally published in *American Review* 18 (1973). Page numbers refer to *A Rosellen Brown Reader: Selected Poetry and Prose* (Hanover, N.H.: University Press of New England, 1992).

23. Brown's protagonist echoes here Sally Mann's comment about the ordinariness of such violent images in the space of domesticity. See also the title of the 1992 MOMA exhibit, "The Pleasures and Terrors of Domestic Comfort."

24. Brown refers to Gilman when she describes the "wallpaper they couldn't hide: symmetrical and graceless, cabbage roses with stars between" (152).
25. Susan Suleiman, *Risking Who One Is: Encounters with Contemporary Writers* (Cambridge, Mass.: Harvard University Press, 1993).
26. This heading is a quotation from Zoë Sofia, "Exterminating Fetuses: Abortion, Disarmament, and the Sexo-Semiotics of Extraterrestrialism," *Diacritics* 14, no. 2 (Summer 1984): 48.
27. Elissa Marder, "Flat Death: Photography, Allegory, History," paper delivered at the Twentieth-Century French Studies Conference, Philadelphia, 1993.
28. Vance Gellert, "CarlVision" (Portland, Ore.: Blue Sky Gallery, 1987).
29. When Jo Spence takes a picture of herself in the bathtub, she refuses this connection between birth and photography: set between thick black parentheses, Spence is lying in the bathtub on her belly, her back and buttocks facing up, her glasses lying on the rim. If she is the object of the gaze, she refocuses it by taking off her glasses and closing her eyes as she submerges her face in the water. With neither face nor front showing, her body is genderless, indeterminate, and defiant of the viewer's look. Jo Spence, *Putting Myself in the Picture: A Political, Personal and Photographic Autobiography* (Seattle: Real Comet Press, 1988), p. 133.
30. Rosalind Pollack Petcheski, "Fetal Images: The Power of Visual Culture in the Politics of Reproduction," *Feminist Studies* 13, no. 2 (Summer 1987): 263–292.
31. In an article that builds on Petcheski's argument, Carol Stabile focuses on the effect of fetal imagery, the historically unprecedented division between woman and fetus: "This process of disarticulation, which has been underway for at least two decades, can be alternately read as anti-essentialist (insofar as it denies the material specificity of women's bodies) or as a process of humanizing technology, which then figures as the sign of paternalistic intervention." "Shooting the Mother: Fetal Photography and the Politics of Disappearance," *Camera Obscura* 28, no. 1 (Fall 1992): 180.
32. See Evelyn Fox Keller and Christine R. Grontkowski, "The Mind's Eye," in *Discovering Reality: Feminist Perspectives on Epistemology, Metaphysics, Methodology and Philosophy of Science,* ed. Sandra Harding and Merrill B. Hintikka (Dordrecht: D. Reidel, 1983).
33. Sara Ruddick, *Maternal Thinking: Toward a Politics of Peace* (Boston: Beacon, 1989).
34. Cited in Keller and Grontkowski, p. 219.
35. Roland Barthes, *Camera Lucida: Reflections on Photography,* trans. Richard Howard (New York: Hill and Wang, 1981), p. 14.
36. Eric Santner, *Stranded Objects: Mourning, Memory and Film in Postwar Germany* (Ithaca: Cornell University Press, 1990).
37. Hatch-Billops Productions, 491 Broadway, 7th floor, New York, NY 10012.
38. Valerie Smith, *"Finding Christa," Black Film Review* 7, no. 2 (1993): 14.

39. Discussion following film showing of *Finding Christa*, Dartmouth College, May 1996.

40. Valerie Smith, "Telling Family Secrets: Narrative and Ideology in *Suzanne, Suzanne* by Camille Billops and James Hatch," in *Multiple Voices in Feminist Film Criticism*, ed. Diane Carson, Linda Dittmar, and Janice R. Welsch (Minneapolis: University of Minnesota Press, 1994), p. 386.


*6. resisting images*

1. Jamaica Kincaid, *Annie John* (New York: Penguin, 1984).

2. Teresa de Lauretis, *Technologies of Gender: Essays on Theory, Film and Fiction* (Bloomington: Indiana University Press, 1987), p. 26.

3. Carol Gilligan, "Women's Psychological Development: Implications for Psychotherapy," in Carol Gilligan, Annie G. Rogers, and Deborah L. Tolman, eds., *Women, Girls and Psychotherapy: Reframing Resistance* (Binghamton, N.Y.: Harrington Park Press, 1991), pp. 5–6. See also Carol Gilligan, Nona P. Lyons, and Rudy Hanmer, eds., *Making Connections: The Relational View of Adolescent Girls at Emma Willard School* (Troy, N.Y.: Emma Willard, 1989), and Carol Gilligan, Carol Janie Victoria Ward, and Jill McLean Taylor, *Mapping the Moral Domain: A Contribution of Women's Thinking to Psychological Theory and Education* (Cambridge, Mass.: Harvard University Press, 1988).

4. Marguerite Duras, *The Lover*, trans. Barbara Bray (New York: Pantheon, 1985).

5. On the novel's photographic origin, see the reviews by Marcine de Martinoir, *Nouvelle Revue Française* 383 (1984): 92–95, and Jean-Marc Turine, "Marguerite Duras fabriquant un livre," *La Nouvelle Revue* 80 (1984): 553–555. See also Madeleine Borgomano, "*L'Amant:* une hypertextualité illimitée," *Revue des sciences humaines* 73, no. 202 (April-June 1986): 67–77, for an analysis of the role of photographs as "hypotexts" structuring the narrative.

6. *Practicalities: Marguerite Duras Speaks to Michel Beaujour*, trans. Barbara Bray (New York: Grove Weidenfeld, 1990), p. 89.

7. For a fuller analysis of how this dichotomy structures Duras's text, see Nina S. Hellerstein, "'Image' and Absence in Marguerite Duras' *L'Amant*," *Modern Language Studies* 21, no. 2 (Spring 1991): 45–56.

8. Paul Smith, *Discerning the Subject* (Minneapolis: University of Minnesota Press, 1988), p. 156.

9. Liz Heron, ed., *Truth, Dare or Promise: Girls Growing Up in the Fifties* (London: Virago, 1985); Jo Spence and Patricia Holland, eds., *Family Snaps: The Meanings of Domestic Photography* (London: Virago, 1991). Both essays have also been included in Valerie Walkerdine, *Schoolgirl Fictions* (London: Verso, 1990).

10. Peter Galassi, ed., *Pleasures and Terrors of Domestic Comfort* (New York: Museum of Modern Art, 1991).

11. Rene Claude Barilleaux, "A Conversation with Lorie Novak," "Projections," Madison Art Center, 1990–1991.

12. This is Kaja Silverman's appeal at the end of *The Threshold of the Visible World* (New York, Routledge, 1996), p. 227: "The reader may have remarked that it was only with the greatest difficulty that I found some basis . . . for maintaining the possibility of productive vision—of an eye capable of seeing something other than what is given to be seen . . . I utter only one short but passionate appeal to those now working in such areas: help us to see differently."

## 7. pictures of a displaced girlhood

1. Eva Hoffman, *Lost in Translation: A Life in a New Language* (New York: Penguin, 1987).

2. Susan Suleiman has coined the useful notion of "autobiographical reading" to describe this response, in *Risking Who One Is: Encounters With Contemporary Writers* (Cambridge, Mass.: Harvard University Press, 1993).

3. Carol Gilligan, Nona P. Lyons, and Rudy Hanmer, eds., *Making Connections: The Relational View of Adolescent Girls at Emma Willard School* (Troy, N.Y.: Emma Willard, 1989); Carol Gilligan, Carol Janie Victoria Ward, and Jill McLean Taylor, *Mapping the Moral Domain: A Contribution of Women's Thinking to Psychological Theory and Education* (Cambridge, Mass.: Harvard University Press, 1988); and Carol Gilligan, Annie G. Rogers, and Deborah L. Tolman, eds., *Women, Girls and Psychotherapy: Reframing Resistance* (Binghamton, N.Y.: Harrington Park Press, 1991).

4. In his "Assimilation in Recent American Jewish Autobiographies," *Contemporary Literature* 34, no. 3 (Fall 1993), Mark Krupnick makes a similar point: "But her idea of the Fall as the loss of linguistic unselfconsciousness requires that there be a time before the Fall. So Poland, unlikely candidate though it may seem, becomes the name for the unalienated condition that Hoffman, in other moods, would probably acknowledge can never have existed" (458). Krupnick also notes Hoffman's "relative unconcern about her Jewishness" (460), and, in a letter to me about this chapter, he charges me with a similar unconcern. Although from the American Jewish perspective we may well seem equally distant, I believe I have processed the postmemory of the Holocaust differently from Hoffman.

5. Mark Krupnick, *Displacement: Derrida and After* (Bloomington: Indiana University Press, 1983), p. 5.

6. In *Risking Who One Is* and in her subsequent work Susan Suleiman maintains that autobiographical reading leads to autobiographical writing. For the term "autohistory" I am indebted to Mieke Bal and the other participants in a 1996 Humanities Institute on "Cultural Memory and the Present" at Dartmouth College.

7. Marianne Hirsch and Evelyn Fox Keller, eds., *Conflicts in Feminism* (New York: Routledge, 1991), p. 381.
8. See Frances Bartkowski's reading of how Hoffman translates this process of dislocation into life-writing in *Travelers, Immigrants, Inmates: Essays in Estrangement* (Minneapolis: University of Minnesota Press, 1995), pp. 109–177.

## 8. past lives

1. Yoram Kaniuk, "Dreienhalb Stunden und fünfzig Jahre mit Günter Grass in Berlin," *Die Zeit* (June 26–28, 1991): 17–18.
2. "Ich entscheide hiermit, daß wir hier in einem kleinen Berlin gewohnt haben, das wir Tel Aviv nannten und aus dem wir am liebsten wieder zurückkehren oder uns untermischen würden." Translations in the text are mine.
3. Nadine Fresco, "La Diaspora des cendres," *Nouvelle Revue de Psychoanalyse* (1981): 209.
4. For a discussion of Jewish identity as inherently diasporic see Daniel Boyarin and Jonathan Boyarin, "Diaspora: Generation and the Ground of Jewish Identity," *Critical Inquiry* 19 (Summer 1993): 693–725.
5. Henri Raczymow, "Memory Shot Through with Holes," trans. Alan Astro, *Yale French Studies* 85 (1994): 104.
6. Alain Finkielkraut, *The Imaginary Jew,* trans. Kevin O'Neill and David Suchoff (Lincoln: University of Nebraska Press, 1994), p. 114.
7. In a very touching response to a draft of this chapter, Lori Lefkowitz reminded me of the differences among European Jewish communities, and the different feelings of mourning and longing they elicit in those of us who were born after. As she pointed out, we have to remember, for example, the difference between the secular urban world of my family in Austria and Rumania, and the orthodox world of hers in the Polish shtetl where she would have grown up as a traditional Orthodox woman wearing a wig, raising many children, with much hard work and few opportunities for education.
8. Jonathan Boyarin and Jack Kugelmass, *From a Ruined Garden: The Memorial Books of Polish Jewry* (New York: Schocken, 1983), p. 6.
9. Henri Raczymow, *Contes d'exil et d'oubli* (Paris: Gallimard, 1979). Translations in the text are mine.
10. "Le nom des morts n'est-il pas disponible à nos fantaisies, Simon?"
11. Raczymow speaks of Roman Vishniac's photographs of the world of the shtetl: "How could they be nostalgic for the filth, the wretchedness, the poverty shown in those pictures?" ("Memory Shot Through," 101).
12. See Ernst van Alphen's provocative and to my mind problematic term "Holocaust effect" to characterize this mode of reenactment in the work of a number of contemporary artists: *Caught by History: Holocaust Effects in Contemporary Art and Theory* (Palo Alto: Stanford University Press, 1997).

13. I am grateful to Lori Lefkowitz for continuing to remind me of this sad fact.

14. Speech to visiting student group, November 1994.

15. See Kaja Silverman's useful notion of "heteropathic" memory and identification in *The Threshold of the Visible World* (New York, Routledge, 1996), ch. 5.

16. Kristine Stiles usefully defines this notion of rememoration in her "Remembering Invisibility: Photography and the Formation of Community in a Nuclear Age" (manuscript, Duke University).

17. Andrea Liss, "Contours of Naming: The Identity Card Project and the Tower of Faces at the United States Holocaust Memorial Museum," *Public* 8 (1993): 126.

18. Edward Linenthal gives the background to this installation in *Preserving Memory: The Struggle to Create America's Holocaust Museum* (New York: Viking, 1995), pp. 171–186.

19. Lynn Gumpert, *Christian Boltanski* (Paris: Flammarion, 1993), p. 59.

20. Georgia Marsh, "An Interview with Christian Boltanski," in Christian Boltanski, *Reconstitution,* Exhibit Catalogue (London: Whitechapel Art Gallery, 1990), p. 10.

21. In *Caught by History* Ernst van Alphen offers a reading of Boltanski's work not as a representation or an evocation of the Holocaust but as the creation of a "Holocaust effect" based on the reenactment of Nazi techniques of objectification, dehumanization, archivization, lying, and so on that led to and were part of the Holocaust. See chs. 4 and 6.

22. Talk at the Institute of Contemporary Art, Boston, January 25, 1995.

23. Shimon Attie, *The Writing on the Wall: Projections in Berlin's Jewish Quarter* (Heidelberg: Edition Braus, 1994), p. 9.

24. Dominick LaCapra, *Representing the Holocaust: History, Theory, Trauma* (Ithaca: Cornell University Press, 1994), p. 188.

25. Fran Bartkowski, *Travelers, Immigrants, Inmates: Essays in Estrangement* (Minneapolis: University of Minnesota Press, 1995), p. 3.

Earlier versions of some of the material in this book were published previously: part of Chapter 1 as "Family Pictures: *Maus,* Mourning, and Post-Memory," *Discourse* 15, no. 2 (winter 1992–93); part of Chapter 3 as "Masking the Subject," in *The Point of Theory,* ed. Mieke Bal and Inge Boer (Amsterdam: Amsterdam University Press, 1994); part of Chapter 4 as "Photos de famille," trans. Lori Saint-Martin, in Lori Saint-Martin, ed., special issue of *Tangence* (1995); Chapter 6 as "Resisting Images: Rereading Adolescence," in *Provoking Agents: Theorizing Gender and Agency,* ed. Judith Kegan Gardiner (Urbana: University of Illinois Press, 1994); part of Chapter 7 as "Pictures of a Displaced Girlhood," in *Displacements: Cultural Identities in Question,* ed. Angelika Bammer (Bloomington: Indiana University Press, 1994); and part of Chapter 8 as "Past Lives: Postmemories in Exile," in *Poetics Today* 17, no. 4 (winter 1996).

*Illustrations*

0.1 Daniel Boudinet, "Polaroïd" (1976)
    Courtesy of Association française pour la diffusion du patrimoine photographique
1.1 Maus I, 1st ed., author portrait
1.2 Maus II, author portrait
1.3 Maus II, p. 115
1.4 Maus II, p. 116
1.5 Maus I, p. 100
1.6 Maus II, dedication page
1.7 Maus II, p. 134
    1.1–1.7 *Maus I: A Survivor's Tale: My Father Bleeds History,* by Art Spiegelman, copyright © 1973, 1980, 1981, 1982, 1983, 1984, 1985, 1986 by Art Spiegelman, reprinted by permission of Pantheon Books, a division of Random House, Inc. *Maus II: A Survivor's Tale: And Here My Troubles Began,* by Art Spiegelman, copyright © 1986, 1989, 1990, 1991 by Art Spiegelman, reprinted by permission of Pantheon Books, a division of Random House, Inc.
2.1–2.4 From the Goldstein family album
    Courtesy of Robert A. Goldstein family

2.5   *The Family of Man,* p. 10
2.6   *The Family of Man,* p. 56
2.7   *The Family of Man,* p. 57
2.8   *The Family of Man,* p. 58
2.9   *The Family of Man,* p. 59
2.10  *The Family of Man,* p. 33
2.11  *The Family of Man,* p. 32
      2.5–2.11 From *The Family of Man,* by Edward Steichen; The Museum of Modern Art, New York, 1955
3.1   Omama and Tante Fritzi (ca. 1908)
3.2   ID picture (1959)
      3.1–3.2 From the Hirsch family album
3.3   Urs Lüthi, "Just Another Story about Leaving" #1 (1974)
3.4   Urs Lüthi, "Just Another Story about Leaving" #9 (1974)
      3.3–3.4 Courtesy Galerie Stadler
3.5   Ralph Eugene Meatyard, "Lucybelle Crater and her 46-year-old husband Lucybelle Crater" (1971)
3.6   Ralph Eugene Meatyard, "Lucybelle Crater and close friend Lucybelle Crater in the grape arbor" (1971)
3.7   Ralph Eugene Meatyard, "Lucybelle Crater and 20yr old son's 3yr old son, also her 3 yr old grandson—Lucybelle Crater" (1971)
      3.5–3.7 Courtesy Christopher Meatyard
3.9   Jon Gilbert Fox, "Marianne and Lotte Hirsch" (1990). Courtesy of the photographer
3.10  Cindy Sherman, "Untitled Film Still" #14 (1978) Courtesy of the artist and Metro Pictures
4.1   Jo Spence, "Revisualization" (1981)
4.2   Jo Spence, "Shame-work" (1988)
4.3   Jo Spence, "The Picture of Health?" (1982)
      4.1–4.3 Courtesy of Jo Spence Memorial Archive
4.4   Carrie Mae Weems, "Untitled (Man and mirror)" (1990)
4.5   Carrie Mae Weems, "Untitled (Man smoking)" (1990)
4.6   Carrie Mae Weems, "Untitled (Woman and daughter with makeup)" (1990)
      4.4–4.6 Courtesy PPOW Gallery, New York
5.1   Sally Mann, "Emmett, Jessie & Virginia" (1989)
5.2   Sally Mann, "Emmett, Jessie & Virginia" (1990)
5.3   Sally Mann, "The Terrible Picture" (1989)
5.4   Sally Mann, "Hayhook" (1989)
      5.1–5.4 Copyright © Sally Mann, courtesy Houk Friedman Gallery, New York
5.5   Vance Gellert, Untitled, from the series CARLVISION (1983) Courtesy of the artist

5.6    Patrick Zachmann, "Florence and Theo in the Bath" (1986)
Courtesy Magnum Photos Inc., New York

5.7    Camille Billops and James Hatch, "Finding Christa," Film Still (1991)
Courtesy Hatch-Billops Collection, Inc.

5.8    Marianne and Oliver (1977)

6.1–6.2    Hiking in the Carpathians and in the White Mountains (1959, 1964)

6.3–6.4    Carl with Marianne, Oliver and Gabriel (1953, 1978, 1983)
5.8–6.4 From the Hirsch family album

6.5    Valerie Walkerdine, "The bluebell fairy," from the *Derby Evening Telegraph* (1953)

6.6–6.8    Valerie Walkerdine, "Behind the Painted Smile" (1980s)
6.5–6.8 Courtesy Valerie Walkerdine

6.9    Lorie Novak, "Fragments" (1987)
Color photograph, courtesy of the artist

7.1    Marianne and Klementine (1962)

7.2    Angelika and Vladimir (1962)

7.3    Nathan Bishop Junior High School graduation (1963)

7.4    Marianne and Mona (1963–64)

7.5    Marianne and Marta (1966)
7.1–7.5 From the Hirsch family album

7.6    Nancy Wasserman, "The Dartmouth Collective" (1981)
Courtesy of the photographer

8.1    Lorie Novak, "Past Lives" (1987)
Color photograph, courtesy of the artist

8.2    Yaffa Eliach Collection; photo by Alan Gilbert
Courtesy of the United States Holocaust Memorial Museum

8.3–8.4    The Tower of Faces
Courtesy of The Yaffa Eliach Shtetl Collection©

8.5    Christian Boltanski, "Monument" (1987)
Courtesy of Marian Goodman Gallery

8.6    "Das Chajesgymnasium"
From *Die Mazzesinsel*

8.7    Christian Boltanski, "Autel Chases" (1987)

8.8    Christian Boltanski, "Jewish School of Grosse Hamburgerstrasse in 1938" (1994)
8.7–8.8 Courtesy of Marian Goodman Gallery

8.9    Shimon Attie, "Mulackstrasse 32, Berlin, Diaprojektionen jüdischer Anwohner und eines hebräischen Leesesaals, 1931" (1991)

8.10    Shimon Attie, "Linienstr. 137, Berlin, Diaprojektionen einer Polizeirazzia bei jüdischen Anwohnern, 1920" (1991)
8.9–8.10 Color photographs, courtesy of the artist